Governing the Global Polity

Governing the Global Polity
Practice, Mentality, Rationality

Iver B. Neumann and Ole Jacob Sending

The University of Michigan Press | *Ann Arbor*

Copyright © by the University of Michigan 2010
All rights reserved
Published in the United States of America by
The University of Michigan Press
Manufactured in the United States of America
⊚ Printed on acid-free paper

2013   2012   2011   2010   4   3   2   1

No part of this publication may be reproduced,
stored in a retrieval system, or transmitted in any form
or by any means, electronic, mechanical, or otherwise,
without the written permission of the publisher.

A CIP catalog record for this book is available from the British Library.

Library of Congress Cataloging-in-Publication Data

Neumann, Iver B.
   Governing the global polity : practice, mentality, rationality /
Iver B. Neumann and Ole Jacob Sending.
     p.   cm.
   Includes bibliographical references and index.
   ISBN 978-0-472-07093-0 (cloth : alk. paper) —
   ISBN 978-0-472-05093-2 (pbk. : alk. paper) —
   ISBN 978-0-472-02245-8 (ebook)
   1. Geopolitics.   2. Globalization.   3. Non-governmental
organizations.   4. International agencies.   5. Political science.
I. Sending, Ole Jacob.   II. Title.

JC319.N44   2010
341.2—dc22   2009050398

Contents

Preface and Acknowledgments vii

Introduction ... 1

1 | Foucault's Concept of Governmentality: Emergence, Purchase, Promise ... 18

2 | Global Politics as Governmentality ... 46

3 | Governing a Great Power: Russia's Oddness Reconsidered ... 70

4 | Nongovernmental Organizations: From Sovereignty to Liberal Governmentality ... 110

5 | International Organizations: Liberalism, Sovereignty, and Police ... 132

Conclusion: Liberal Sovereignty in the Global Polity ... 157

References 183
Index 201

Preface and Acknowledgments

This book is about how states govern at a distance, through other types of agents. One such agent is the academic community. The book has its origins in academic resistance to governmentality in Norway. There exists a peculiar Scandinavian institution whereby the state pays a clutch of establishment researchers to write R&D-style analyses of how power works in the Scandinavian states. By writing the mandate for the research, funding it, and orchestrating the ensuing political debate about power differentials in "their" states, Scandinavian politicians effectively co-opt and neutralize a key part of the national conversation about power: that of the research community. As these are efforts at the national level, little or nothing of this material finds its way into the global scholarly debate about the phenomena that are supposed to be studied. A further characteristic of this institution, then, is what has been called "methodological nationalism": it is taken for granted that power resides in national processes and is properly studied within the locus of the state.

When, in 1998, politicians in our native Norway once again decided to activate this institution, a group of young scholars reacted. Finding such an institution problematic in terms of its ethics, its scholarship, as well as its political implications if allowed to parade as "the" academic Scandinavian approach to power, they took the initiative to a book series to match what the state intended to spawn. By marginalizing the state-sponsored production of production, this course of action proved effective on the national level—but having to work in the Norwegian language entailed distinct limitations as far as our international scholarly ambitions were concerned. One possible course of action was to apply what theoretical headway we had made not only to the national level, but to the global one as well. This book is the result of that effort.

Our first debt of gratitude is to the group of people with whom we worked on our previous project, on governmentality in Norway: anthropologists Runar Døving, Thomas Hylland Eriksen, Ida Hydle, Knut Nustad, and Tian Sørhaug; literary historians Christian Refsum, Eivind Røssaak, and Knut Stene-Johansen; historian of religion Torkel Brekke; historian of ideas Ketil Jakobsen; and legal scholar Inger-Johanne Sand. Thanks to Jens Bartelson for additional comments on chapter 1, and to Morten Andersen for research assistance. Benjamin de Carvalho, Nina Græger, and Halvard Leira have been our interlocutors throughout the process. Thanks to Patrick Jackson, Fritz Kratochwil, and Stefano Guzzini, as well as to Fredrik Engelstad, Cecilie Basberg Neumann, Arild Underdal, and Mike Williams, for written comments on chapter 2, and to Hiski Haukkala, Ted Hopf, Pål Kolstø, Alexander Sergunin, Jennifer Sterling-Folker, Shogo Suzuki, William Wolforth, and Stefano Guzzini again for comments on what is now chapter 3. Thanks to Tore Fougner and Dan Nexon for written comments on chapter 4. We should also like to express our gratitude to Tanja Aalberts, Jacqueline Best, Sara Kalm, and Andrea Paras, who commented on the entire draft, and to Melody Herr for ongoing support and encouragement.

While the book has been a joint undertaking from the very start, chapters 1, 2, and 3 were drafted by Neumann, whereas chapters 4 and 5 were drafted by Sending. Chapter 2 appeared as Iver B. Neumann and Ole Jacob Sending, "'The International' as Governmentality," *Millennium: Journal of International Relations* 35 (3): 677–701 (2007), reproduced with permission from Sage Publications. A distant forerunner of chapter 3 is Iver B. Neumann, "Russia as a Great Power, 1815–2007," *Journal of International Relations and Development* 11 (2): 128–51 (2008), reproduced with permission from Palgrave Macmillan. Chapter 4 consists of the last three-fourths of Ole Jacob Sending and Iver B. Neumann, "Governance to Governmentality: Analysing States, NGOs, and Power," *International Studies Quarterly* 50 (3): 651–72 (2006), reproduced with the permission of Wiley-Blackwell.

Introduction

Globalization changes what the state does, and how the state does it. Those who hold that the state remains the same—realists being prominent among them—overlook the kind of empirical evidence that we present below. Even more important, they overlook the fact that something does exist "above" the state: a liberal rationality of government. Those who hold that the state is being marginalized by other kinds of agents—constructivists and others—overlook the way in which states are working through these other agents. The changes wrought by globalization have become so massive that we need a new framework for studying global politics. This book is our response to that challenge.

More specifically, we wish to make three contributions to international relations (IR) scholarship. First, while we celebrate the growth in scholarship on the political character and impact of globalization on global politics, we are critical of the prevailing approach to studying it within IR. This approach, which we may broadly label *global governance,* tends to treat the process of globalization as one of how norms spread and how ever-new institutions and groups of people are socialized into following them. The effects of these transformative processes are held to result in the emergence of a more "network-like" system for governing at the global stage where states share much of their power with nongovernmental organizations (NGOs), corporations, and international organizations (Rosenau 2002; Held and McGrew 2002). While recent scholarship on the subject presents a more nuanced view of the processes and effects of "globalization"—including analyses of how the state is reconfigured in terms of, for example, the relationship between territory, authority, and rights (Sassen 2006)—we propose a focus on governmentality in order to fuse the analytics of power with the analytics of the various processes through which governing operates at the transnational level. We aim to show that the transformations entailed by globalization do not result in states losing their power, but that the rationality of governing shifts—resulting, for example, in the emergence of a global-level governmental rationality that reconstitutes the meaning and significance of sovereignty.

More specifically, we argue in chapter 3 that great power status and hierarchy in global politics must be understood—at least as far as Russia is concerned—as emanating largely through the governmentalization of the state that took place in Europe from the eighteenth century onward. It was the governmental rationality prevailing in Europe that constituted the framework within which the status of Russia was determined. As explained in chapter 2, we detect a governmentalization of global politics in the twentieth century. On this reading, the domestic governmentalization of the state described by Foucault oscillates with a global-level governmentalization of international politics—global governance. On this basis we offer, in chapter 4, a new interpretation of the relation between state and nonstate actors, arguing that what sets up civil society as a key vehicle for governing is not, as claimed in the largely constructivist literature on global governance, a transfer of power from the state to nonstate actors, but the emergence of a new governmental rationality. In chapter 5, we show that the meaning and significance of sovereignty are increasingly determined within and through such a global-level governmental rationality, as evidenced by how international organizations (IOs) define and act on fragile states.

The identification of this shift in rationality of governing is closely linked to a second aim: to transcend the divide between realist and constructivist interpretations of global politics by introducing a focus on power in the dynamics by which liberal norms and principles shape global politics. For realism, world politics (realists do not use the concept "global politics") is constituted by the distribution and relations of power. The diffusion and institutionalization of liberal norms and institutions as documented by constructivist scholarship does not, in their view, change this fundamental fact. So defined, realist analysis is poorly suited to account for systemic changes in the contents and logic of politics that may develop over time.

For constructivists, global politics is increasingly defined and driven by the actors' internalization of liberally oriented norms, leading to a veritable shift toward a more Lockean or even Kantian world order (cf. Wendt 1999). Examination of the role of power involved in these transformations, however, is conspicuously absent in these analyses (Risse 2000; Checkel and Zürn 2005). This leads to an unsatisfactory view of politics at the transnational level. By contrast, a focus on governmentality decenters the analysis of power from any particular actor and looks instead at the different processes and techniques of the "conduct of conduct," thereby enabling a focus on the power relations implied in the global spread of liberally oriented norms and institutions (cf. Simmons et al. 2008). Importantly, a focus on governmental rationalities allows us to retain key insights from realism about the centrality of power to understand global politics. As we discuss in chapter 2, situating Morgenthau's concept of politics within a framework where sovereignty is no longer the unmoved mover of things international makes it possible to bring together key constructivist and realist insights.

Our third aim is a corollary of the first two. It is the highly traditional one of seeking to bring together conceptual and empirical material in a theory-led empirical enquiry, aiming to show the emergence of a global governmentality that generates a new and different form and logic of politics. This new form of politics is arrived at through an extension of Morgenthau's formulation of politics as a question of intensity. We specify the contents and workings of two interrelated modes of governing that are pervasive in global politics. One is that of liberal or neoliberal governmentality whereby more and more areas are subjected to modes of governing modeled on the market and operating "through freedom." This mode of governing is about governing less—seeking instead to set up registers of meaning, evaluation, and justification that can guide, induce, and enable actors to act in certain ways.

The other is that of police. The police mode seeks to govern more: increasingly detailed knowledge and direct forms of governing are employed to regulate, control, and police various phenomena and actors. A key example of this form of government can be found in the case of "failed" or "fragile" states. Here it is evident how the institution of sovereignty is an *object* of government by a transnationally constituted network of states, IOs, and NGOs. Global politics is, in our view, increasingly characterized by debates over and the establishment of these two forms of governing. The trick is to identify when, how, and with what effects certain objects and phenomena are identified as needing which forms of governing. Global politics is increasingly characterized by debates and struggles over what *type of governing* is seen as appropriate for different groups and phenomena. The institution of sovereignty assumes, in this view, a position that is more variable and shaped by its position within governmental rationalities. It has become a liberal-practice selector. It constitutes objects of governing within global politics. This also makes it a key focus for resisting the universalizing drive of liberal forms of governing.

Governance, Liberalism, and Power

During the course of the 1990s, global governance emerged as a new and powerful research agenda. It quickly merged with burgeoning constructivist scholarship. This literature produced a wealth of insights about the changing roles and significance of sovereign states in the governing of global or transnational affairs. Here we review and criticize three key claims in this literature, before presenting our alternative reading. We also review central findings from the constructivist literature on the diffusion and institutionalization of liberal norms. Together, these two strands of literature provide a launching pad for our formulation of a governmental reading of global politics.

We pursue the underlying, constructivist claims of the global governance literature at length in chapter 2. By way of introduction, we should like to highlight three specific, interrelated claims made by that literature. The first is that government must be studied as a process, not as an institution. This analytical move is said to make it possible to analyze changes from hierarchical and sovereignty-based modes of governing to more horizontal, network-based modes of governing (Held and McGrew 2002; Rosenau 1999; Rosenau and Czempiel 1992). The second is that various nonstate actors have become much more powerful in global politics, with the state less powerful than before (Keck and Sikkink 1998; Rosenau 2002).[1] The third is that political authority is increasingly becoming dislodged from the sovereign state and is drifting in the direction of transnational policy networks and functionally specific "spheres of authority," where the state plays a strategic but not necessarily dominant role (Rosenau 1999, 2002). The analytical power of studies of global governance is thus said to lie in their ability to move beyond state-centric analyses to include a focus on the processes of governance, to highlight the power of nonstate actors, and to identify and theorize about the changing forms and institutionalization of political authority (Held and McGrew 2002).

We argue, first, that while the literature on global governance high-

---

1. An important source of inspiration for the perspective advanced in these studies is the work on transgovernmentalism first formulated by Keohane and Nye (e.g., 1972) in the 1970s. For a good overview of the literature on the role of nonstate actors, see Risse 2002.

lights governance as a set of interrelated processes, it does not provide the analytical tools for studying these processes. Second, studies of global governance operate with a zero-sum conception of power where an increase in the power and influence of nonstate actors is ipso facto defined as a simultaneous reduction in state power and authority. Third, studies of global governance perpetuate the very same analytical framework that they purport to transcend, as their key findings—about the power of nonstate actors and the diffusion of political authority from the state to other actors—are dependent on an analytical framework tied to the triad involving sovereignty, authority, and legitimacy.

Grasping the role of NGOs and IOs requires an approach that can theorize about the specific relations between state and other types of actors within the processes of governance. For example, various types of nonstate actors are often funded, actively encouraged, and supported by states—to mobilize political constituencies, to confer legitimacy to policy processes, to implement policies, and to monitor and evaluate them. Similarly, IOs are arenas for states to negotiate and establish governmental efforts at the global level, as well as being actors in their own right that can and often do shape how states act. The literature on global governance mentions these dimensions but fails to theorize them with a view to understanding the implicit mechanisms of power.

In a governmentality perspective, the role of IOs or NGOs in shaping and carrying out global governance functions is not an instance of transfer of power from the state to nonstate actors (Foucault [1982] 2000, 341). Rather, it is an expression of a changing logic or rationality of government (defined as a type of power) by which civil society is redefined from a passive object of government to be acted upon and into an entity that is both an object *and* a subject of government. Similarly, this rationality of government accords to IOs a central position not only because of the liberal goals they typically advance but also because of the global scale of their mode of governing. The self-association and political will-formation characteristic of civil society and nonstate actors are thus coupled with the global reach and standardizing ability of IOs. These do not stand in opposition to the political power of the state but are a central feature of how power operates in late modern society. We argue that new insights can be generated from studying the sociopolitical functions of governance in their own right, seeking to identify their *rationality as governmental practices*.[2] This perspective on power enables us to identify dimensions of

---

2. Following Gordon (1991) we employ the terms *governmentality* and *governmental rationality* interchangeably.

global governance missing in much of the literature, and makes it possible to challenge some core claims in this literature about the autonomy and power of civil society actors, on the one hand, and the role of IOs, on the other. In both cases, the status and role of sovereignty are central. As we show in subsequent chapters, while sovereignty has been universalized as the central *form* of institutionalized political authority, it does not determine the *contents* of political rule at the national or global level. In this view, the meaning and role of sovereignty are largely defined by governmental rationalities that now increasingly operate on the global level. The liberal rationality of government exerts structural pressure on states to open more and more interfaces with other agents, preferably on a global scale.

Certainly, a key claim in much contemporary theory is that the "social" must be included in analyses of global politics (see Ruggie 1998, 856). The social world is a world of "our making" (Onuf 1989), and it is thus important to explore the production, content, and effects of "constituted social facts" and of the "constitutive role of ideational factors" (Wendt 1999). One particular kind of theory, constructivism, which has become dominant in this regard (Fearon and Wendt 2002), has focused primarily on norms as a specification of intersubjectively shared ideational factors that other theories seem to have overlooked. To them, norms are the key "independent variable" used to study changes in states' interests and identities and changes in international policies and institutions (Finnemore 1996; Gurowitz 1999; Katzenstein 1996). Moreover, analysts have provided detailed accounts of how states are socialized into a political community, such as the EU, by adopting new norms that govern their behavior (Finnemore and Sikkink 1998; Rieker 2006; Zürn and Checkel 2005). As Adler (2002, 103) sums it up, "Norms constitute social identities and give national interests their content and meaning." These theorists paint a picture of the international as a realm that is becoming increasingly liberal and socially embedded: (liberal) norms powerfully shape actors' identities and interests, and the anarchy of the international is thereby transcended. States' identities and their interests are increasingly shaped by shared international norms that define a liberal political space comprising norms about democracy, human rights, the rule of law, and the market economy (Checkel 2001; Gurowitz 1999; Risse 2000; Risse et al. 1999b; Zürn and Checkel 2005).[3] To these "thin" constructivists, the international is be-

---

3. As demonstrated by Wendt (1999) such views may account for the content of, and changes in, different world orders. Wendt summarizes these ideal-typical world orders, or different conceptions of "the international," as Hobbesian, Lockean, or Kantian.

coming progressively "thicker," as the identities, interests, and actions of states are increasingly shaped by internationally established liberal norms.[4]

While we concur with this interpretation of the international becoming both thicker and more liberal in orientation—a process in which advocacy networks and international organizations play a key role in formulating and advancing liberally oriented norms and best practices (Barnett and Finnemore 2004; Park 2006)—these studies can be criticized for employing a strikingly thin concept of politics and of power. By ignoring or downplaying issues of power, these analyses say little about politics. As Stefano Guzzini has noted, "Connected as it is to the idea of the 'art of the possible,' attributing 'power' to an issue immediately implies that 'we could have done things otherwise.' . . . attributing power to an issue immediately raises the stakes for political justification and action or nonaction" (2005, 497). To talk about the "power" of norms in producing a convergence of interests and identities in the international realm is to think of power solely in terms of the alleged causal efficacy of norms in transforming the interests and behavior of states in a process of "social learning," "deliberation," "persuasion," or the like.

Privileging change understood as change in norms brackets the importance of power. A central goal of this book is to introduce power, and thus also politics, into the account of the role of liberally oriented norms in the international realm. For the traditional power analyst, politics in the international space is about conflict and tensions lodged at the level of the state, driven by material interests and resources. For the norms-oriented analyst, global politics is emptied of tension and conflict as it highlights learning, deliberation, and persuasion as the central mechanisms through which norm-driven change is brought about. We submit that if we are to get a grip on the changing content of the international, we have to establish a historically sensitive concept of politics—one able to capture how politics remains a power struggle, while at the same time recognizing that it assumes different forms and expressions in different historical periods. We need a concept of politics that retains realism's focus on power and

---

4. In this view, the international realm is defined in much the same way as did the founders of international law. Under the heading "The Flight from Politics" Koskenniemi (1990, 1) argues that "since the publication of Emmeric de Vattel's *Droit des gens* . . . (1758), jurists have written about international matters by assuming that the liberal principles of the Enlightenment and their logical corollary, the Rule of Law, could be extended to apply in the organization of international society just as they had been used in the domestic one." Constructivist theory—at least in its (American) moderate version—brings to bear a similar view of the international realm.

politics yet recognizes the centrality of ideational factors such as norms in the transformation of global politics. Morgenthau's realism is grounded in a particular view of human nature, derived from Freud, that gives rise to a view of politics defined in terms of intensity (cf. Koskenniemi 2004). It was eminently clear to Morgenthau, however, that the expression or logic of politics is highly contextual—that it may assume many *different forms*, depending on institutional, cultural, and economic structures.

Morgenthau's identification of the political as an ideal-typical sphere where ideational factors seem to have little place *should not* lead to the conclusion that this view of politics, and of power, has no room for social theoretical insights as found in constructivist theory. By placing Morgenthau's concept of the political within the contemporary setting, we will suggest that his concept of politics as intensity is both transferable to and supportive of Foucault's concept of power as government. In fact, we show that Foucault, in his lectures on the "Birth of Biopolitics," came to define politics in terms of intensity.

Governmentality: A Different Take on Governance and Liberalism

In their recent volume *Power in Global Governance,* Barnett and Duvall (2005b) argue that studies of global governance have been inattentive to power. We concur with this interpretation and advance an argument to the effect that the research agenda on global governance can be enriched by analyzing not only power generally but one of its modes—governmentality—specifically.[5] Governmentality analysis is well suited to provide a better account of the diffusion of liberal norms as a process that does not "displace" or reduce the relevance of power politics. Liberalism, however, recasts and defines new modes of governing at the global level, in the process producing new points of contention and contestation in global politics. Governmentality analysis is also better placed to make sense of the relation between states and other actors in global governance. Far from reducing the power of the states, as global governance theories typically argue, we show that it reconfigures the governmental rationality within which states operate: the relationship between actors follows

---

5. Our argument is somewhat parallel to that of Rose and Miller 1992; for related views, see Lipschutz 2005a, b; Dillon and Reid 2001; Merlingen 2003; Rose 2000; Debrix 1999.

largely from the rationality of governing within which they are situated and operate.

To grasp the meaning and import of "government" as a form of power it is useful to contrast it with that of sovereignty. Foucault identifies a historically significant transformation occurring from the sixteenth century onward in which what he terms the "art of government" emerged to form a distinct set of thinking and associated practices of political rule that was separate and partly autonomous from the principle and practice of sovereignty ([1978] 1991). "In contrast to sovereignty," Foucault ([1978] 2000a, 216–17) notes, "government has as its purpose not the act of government itself, but the welfare of the population, the improvement of its conditions, the increase of its wealth, longevity, health, and so on." Government is for Foucault thus defined in terms of the "conduct of conducts," involving a range of techniques and practices, performed by different actors, aimed to shape, guide, and direct the behavior and actions of individuals and groups in particular directions (2000c, 341; 2000a). The central elements of government as a form of power are captured in the following distinction made between the workings of sovereignty and the workings of government.

> With sovereignty, the instrument that allowed it to achieve its aim—that is, obedience to the laws—was the law itself: law and sovereignty were absolutely inseparable. . . . With government it is a question not of imposing law on men but of disposing things: that is, of employing tactics rather than laws, and even of using laws themselves as tactics—to arrange things in such a way that, through a certain number of means, such-and-such ends may be achieved. ([1978] 2000a, 211)

The concepts of "disposing things" and "employing tactics" are essential features of government as a form of power. In contrast to both sovereignty and discipline, which are the two other modes of power theorized by Foucault, government takes the freedom and agency of those that are governed as both an end and a means for governing (see Dean 1999).[6]

A focus on governmentality implies at least three things. First, there is a focus on investigating the specific practices and techniques of governing

---

6. Note Foucault's use of *sovereignty* both for a mode of power (where it contrasts with domination and, once he had developed it, governmentality) and for a historical phenomenon, namely, the relationship between sovereigns (particularly in early modern Europe). For the relationship between them, see the conclusion to this book. For a good analysis of some of Foucault's key terms and a discussion of the theme of resistance, see Hoy 2004.

as an empirical phenomenon, thus seeking to replace a focus on institutions (e.g., most IR studies of sovereignty) with a focus on practices. Second is a focus on identifying the "mentality" or rationality that characterizes the systematic thinking and knowledge that is integral to and renders possible different modes of governing. Third, a focus on the mode of power called governmentality does not replace sovereignty or discipline—each of which represents distinct forms of power (Gordon 1991, 7). As Mitchell Dean (1999, 20) argues, "rather than displacing discipline or sovereignty, the modern art of government recasts them within this concern for the population and its optimization (in terms of wealth, health, happiness, prosperity, efficiency), and the forms of knowledge and technical means appropriate to it." Sovereignty and discipline are reconfigured in that, as Foucault (2000a) puts it, the essential aspect of government is the introduction of economy into political practice.

The key point to recognize is that this analytical perspective focuses on how certain identities and action-orientations are defined as appropriate and normal and how relations of power are implicated in these processes. A focus on governmentality, therefore, seeks to analyze the "relation between individuals and the political order from the perspective of the *different processes whereby the former are objectified as certain kinds of subjects through the ways they are targeted by political power*" (Burchell 1991, 119; emphasis added). The perspective of governmentality offers a good optic for analyses. First, it explicitly builds on, and was originally developed as a tool for, studying the *processes* of governing. Second, it delivers a conception of the relation between the state and other actors, such as NGOs and IOs, that places the focus of sovereignty within a more general concern for changes in the rationality of governing. Taken together, this allows us to unpack central features of liberalism and global governance and to present a different reading of global politics.

Considered as a governmental rationality, liberalism is about ways of governing and disposing things, about the conduct of conduct. This immediately brings into view the role of liberal norms in transforming the international sphere: if constructivists are right in their documentation of the "thickening" of the international realm by virtue of liberally oriented norms, such as human rights, democracy, market economy, then a key question is how these norms represent a form of power that works, through more or less consciously established governing practices, to redefine and reconstitute the identity and subjectivity of groups and individuals. Liberalism, we argue, shapes global governance both in terms of its scale and its mode of operation. First, with respect to scale, states and other actors become involved in efforts to govern ever more phenomena through some form of coordinated effort. Liberal goals and norms (Barnett and Finnemore 2004) provide the impetus for the extension of governing from the national to the global, be it in the form of humanitarian intervention, more detailed global regulation of financial markets, or establishing "global best practices" for how to organize the economy, combat corruption, improve educational standards, combat global terrorism, or address the threats of "failed states." Second, and at the same time, these liberal norms define a new standard, a test, according to which some phenomena and groups are most appropriately governed "through freedom" whereas others are judged to be in need of direct regulation, surveillance, and control, sometimes with brute force.

For Foucault, the market and the ideal of competition perform under liberalism the role of a "test" for whether one governs appropriately. As Barry Hindess has observed, however, this is a test that "surely cuts both ways, suggesting not only that some people and some fields of activity can best be governed through the promotion of suitable forms of free behavior, but also that there are other cases for which alternative forms of rule will be required" (2005, 28). There are, in other words, some phenomena—terrorism, fragile states, recalcitrant states, corruption, say—that are judged to be in need not of less but of more governing. They are judged to be unsuited—either because of how the problem or threat is defined or because of the conditions under which such governing will have to operate—for governing through freedom, at which point variants of police governing kick in. The politics of global governance, we argue, is increasingly organized around debates and struggles over what should be governed through liberal forms of government and what should be governed through police forms of government.

The International as Governmentality

At a sociopolitical level, the identification of power as government is predicated upon how political economy, as expressed in the works of Adam Smith, dissolves the unity of knowledge and political thinking and acting that had characterized the police as a form of thinking and acting associated when the frame of reference for politics and governing was the territory as an extension of the king's household. Political economy introduced a new reality in which the ruler had to operate, and this new reality was society. This new rationality of political rule—in essence a new realm of politics—is predicated upon how "society" emerges in the late eighteenth century as an entity *external to and qualitatively different from* the territory and the inventory of the state. Hence is introduced, Foucault argues, a new modality of power defined as "government."

> What was discovered at that time—and this was one of the great discoveries of political thought at the end of the eighteenth century—was the idea of society. That is to say, that government not only has to deal with a territory, with a domain, and with its subjects, but that it also has its own laws and mechanisms of disturbance. This new reality is society. ([1982] 1989, 261)

The identification of what we may call a "governmental" conception of politics is thus inspired by the identification of an important rupture in political thinking and action occurring, first, by a discourse on the "art of government" starting in the sixteenth century and later by its institutionalization in the postrevolutionary environment of the late eighteenth century. It concerns that specifically modern dimension of politics that arises when the "society" over which the sovereign rules emerges as a distinct entity, as something qualitatively different from the state, as containing individuals whose rights and autonomy must be respected and whose behavioral patterns must be known in order to be governed effectively. As a distinct logic of power, liberalism is about "governing through freedom" (Hindess 2005, 403). Methodologically, this means that we must pay particular heed to Foucault's dictum to study power by looking at "the formation of a whole series of specific governmental apparatuses" that are aimed at fostering, guiding, and shaping the action of free and autonomous individuals (Gordon 1991, 12–13). For Foucault, liberalism is a particular logic of governing—a form of power that is characteristic of modern society that operates indirectly by shaping and fostering autonomous and responsible individuals through the "conduct of conduct" and the ensemble of "governmental techniques" (Dean 1999; Rose 1999b). This "productive power" operates through distant social relations to set up standards for what is appropriate, effective, and legitimate for groups or individuals to do. It is a power that works to "structure the possible field of action of others" (Foucault [1982] 2000, 341; Barnett and Duvall 2005a). It is precisely here that the governmental concept of power is useful for an analysis of the reconfiguration of the international. That is, norms of intervention and of sovereignty have changed, and practices of the market and of democracy do define models for how to govern. Moreover, registers of evaluation and justification are increasingly global, and liberal, in orientation, subjecting states to a set of global best practices that they ignore at their political, economic, and diplomatic peril.

Foucauldian approaches to this *problématique* do not hold the field alone. We note, specifically, the importance of the Stanford school of sociology and their concept of "world society" (for an introduction, see Meyer 2009). This perspective treats the series of nation-states as the mainstay of world society and concentrates on cultural isomorphism. The Stanford school derives the concept of the world polity from a macrosociological account where the cultural constitution of modern actors and agency takes center stage. As noted by Meyer and Jepperson (2000, 102), one key difference between such a macrosociological account and our governmentality perspective is that we attend more to what the Stanford school thinks of as "meso-institutional structures." These are the specific locales (states, NGOs, IOs, etc.) within which modern agencies emerge. Since we focus on how changing practices change states and state sovereignty, we stick to the governmentality perspective, which evolved exactly for this kind of analysis. Within sociology, there are also the studies inspired by German sociologist Niklas Luhmann's work (for an IR application, see Albert and Hilkermeier 2004). Within the discipline of IR, there is the work of the English school (see, particularly, Linklater and Suganami 2006 for an update of the Kantian project of studying the forging of a cosmopolitanism world society). We differ from all these in foregrounding power and the importance of a specific, historic rationality of government—liberalism—for the ongoing transformation of global politics. Admittedly, since the Stanford school does indeed concern itself with questions of power, the added value of Foucault's work on governmentality is in part specific to the discipline of IR. As detailed in chapter 2, the governmentality approach may be made into a theoretically and historically informed cousin perspective to the authoritative realist perspective of IR theory's perhaps biggest name, Hans Morgenthau. Due to its much broader concept of power, governmentality analysis may also augment realist perspectives by actually accounting for the important transformations taking place in world politics. Our claim, then, is that the governmentality perspective retains the many valid insights of realism, while at the same time accounting for new dynamics in global politics. It provides a view of power, a factor neglected by constructivists, while at the same time accounting for the role of ideational factors, which has been the value-added of constructivism. A final value-added is that the governmentality approach offers a new perspective on global governance as a set of interrelated practices with a distinct logic or rationality, a dimension lacking in the largely constructivist-inspired extant accounts of global governance.

Moving a perspective from one area of application to another always involves changes in the perspective. In our case, these changes are rather extensive. As noted by Dillon and Reid (2000, 136; also 2009; Hindess 2002; Kalm 2008), if we look at governmentality on the global level, Foucault's focus on a fairly sedentary population that is the object of governance needs revision. We would add that the trajectory of governing at the national level, as described by Foucault, was one that evolved *from* police and *to* liberal governmentality, with the latter emerging when "society" and autonomous individuals become the parameter for effective governing. At the international level, the trajectory is different, with liberal norms becoming more powerful in determining how to govern at home and abroad. Caution is in order, therefore, when one attempts to transport Foucault's reading of the emergence of liberal forms of governing from the level of the state to a global one. On the level of the state, the rationality of government that preceded liberalism, as laid out by Foucault, was *raison d'état*, where government was directed inward, toward itself, and where government assumed a total character, with sovereignty enabling coercion, surveillance, discipline, and punishment as central governing tools. With the introduction of "political economy" into the calculus and the emergence of "society" as a semiautonomous, separate sphere, power assumed new forms, hence the birth of biopower.

At the transnational or international level, we can detect a similar trend, but it is one that points in two different directions, one toward liberalism, the other toward police. It is also a trajectory that starts from a very different origin. That is, what *preceded* the contemporary era's tightening of global governing mechanisms and the diffusion of liberally oriented norms and principles was, if anything, the *opposite* of the total control and surveillance and sovereignty that characterized *raison d'état*. Hence, while the trajectory of government at the *national* level is one from sovereignty and direct control to biopower and liberalism, the trajectory of government at the global level is one from interstate cooperation, diplomacy, and balancing, one could say, and toward a postsovereign mode of governing called "global governance" where liberal forms of governing are superimposed on the preexisting framework of the sovereignty-based competition, cooperation, and conflict between states. In this context, the contemporary era's thickening of governing mechanisms is in part driven by the establishment of governing modes modeled on the liberal governing already established in Western liberal democracies.

Here, government clearly operates "through freedom," as when global best practices are established for virtually every sector of society, and where global ratings and evaluations put all actors on notice in terms of how they perform vis-à-vis others. It is also, however, driven by the establishment of police forms of governing, where a discourse of global threats and risks has been defined as requiring surveillance, control, and direct regulation, including such phenomena as migration, global pandemics, climate change, nonproliferation, and—more generally—"failed" or "fragile" states.

Organization of the Book

The plan of the book is straightforward: A presentation of the chosen perspective, a series of analytical applications of that perspective on critical cases, a discussion of the perspective's claim to being a new framework for studying global politics. Chapter 1 introduces the concept of governmentality. The historical emergence of governmentality, understood as an indirect way of governing, followed the demise of attempts to rule directly. Historically, the emergence of governmentality was and remains greatly helped by the subjects themselves, who in a number of ways welcomed governmentality and willingly engaged in the self- and other-monitoring on which it depends (installing fire protection, throwing away rubbish at allotted places, showing up for vaccinations, etc.). Addressing the phenomenon of globalization head on, we asked in conclusion whether we are now witnessing the coming of governmentality on the global level, as a coda of its emergence on the national level during the eighteenth century.

In chapter 2 we clear away some hindrances to applying the analytics of governmentality to the international level. These hindrances have to do with the way IR scholars have traditionally conceptualized the nature of international relations, understood as a realm that is not only politically but also ontologically different from domestic politics. If this remains so, then applying the concept of governmentality to transnational analysis would be a case of unwarranted domestic analogy. We demonstrate, however, that in the thinking of Hans Morgenthau, a scholar who remains a linchpin to arguments against the domestic analogy, historical circumstances change in all possible kinds of ways. The status that Morgenthau gave to his own conceptualization of international politics was that of a Weberian ideal type. Ideal types are in need of frequent updating—and this book may be read as such an update. This we demonstrate by connecting the works of Weber, Morgenthau, and Foucault, showing that Morgenthau and Foucault shared the same concept of the political, and recognizing that Morgenthau's definition of politics among nations was ideal-typical and hence in need of revision and updating from its historical context. We argue that most conceptualizations of the international hail from Weber via Morgenthau, for whom international politics was an ideal type applied to the realm between states. Morgenthau's identification of the political as an ideal-typical sphere where ideational factors seem to have little place *should not* lead to the conclusion that this view of politics, and of power, has no room for social theoretical insights as found in constructivist theory. Building on Foucault, we define the international as a socially embedded realm of governmentality. It is a structure (defined by relations of power) that generates different and changing practices of political rule (defined as governmental rationality).

Chapter 3 details the type of actor that has traditionally been seen as the key agent of IR—the state. We seek to show that the states system itself is a site of governmentality, inasmuch as full recognition as a first-class member (a "great power") seems to rest on the precondition that the state in question be governed according to broad principles that dominate in the core members of the system at any given time. Applied to the case of Russia, we account for how and why Russia has always been considered "different." Specifically, we argue that what has mattered for the (lack of) recognition of Russia as a great power has not been its civilizational standard, understood as something abstract that has to do with social life in general, but rather the standard of civilization understood specifically as a mode of governing that is in effect at home and abroad. Whereas other great powers at the time were transitioning toward an institutionalization of liberal forms of government, Russia was still seen as operating according to a police logic.

We then turn to how a liberal form of governing is becoming detectable at the global level and how the emergence of this liberal governmentality reconfigures the relations between states and other actors. In chapter 4 we examine the claim that the state has lost power to nonstate actors and that political authority is increasingly institutionalized in spheres not controlled by states. Rather than focusing on the relative power of states and nonstate actors, we concentrate on the sociopolitical functions and processes of governance in their own right, seeking to identify their rationality as practices of political rule. In this perspective, the role of nonstate actors in shaping and carrying out global governance functions is not an instance of transfer of power from the state to nonstate actors, but rather an expression of a changing logic or rationality of government (defined as a type of power) by which civil society is redefined from a passive object of government to be acted on into an entity that is both an object *and* a subject of government. The argument will be illustrated by two case studies: the international campaign to ban land mines, and international population policy.

In chapter 5, we show how international organizations (IOs) are central sites for the formulation and execution of truly global governmental efforts, where global best practices, performance evaluations, and ratings make up a global grid for states and other actors alike to navigate and identify "good" policies. We show that the current framing of whether IOs are "arenas" or "actors" is misplaced, and that the key to understanding IOs—in this case the World Bank—is to look at the governing practices that they set up and apply to states.

In the conclusion, we draw together the central claims of each chapter in an attempt to fashion a new framework for studying global politics. Following Morgenthau, we define politics as a question of intensity. We proceed to update Morgenthau's description of the international context and to show how a definition of politics as intensity is eminently applicable to a concept of power as government as found in Foucault. Contemporary global politics is, in this interpretation, about the drawing and redrawing of the boundaries to determine which phenomena and which actors require either liberal or police forms of governing. A governmentalization of sovereignty is under way at the global level, where liberalism and police are the central governmental rationalities within which the institution of sovereignty assumes its meaning.

1 | Foucault's Concept of Governmentality: Emergence, Purchase, Promise

The concept of *gouvernementalité* was first introduced by Michel Foucault on February 1, 1978, in a lecture at the Collège de France (2000a). In the quarter of a century that has passed since then, the concept has been further developed in several different directions, first by researchers who in their time collaborated with Foucault (see, e.g., Gordon 1991), later particularly by English-writing researchers, including Australians such as Toby Miller (1993) and Mitchell Dean (1999, 2007) and Britons such as Nikolas Rose (1990, 1999).[1] The concept has furthermore been utilized in a number of empirical works.

Foucault developed the concept of governmentality in order to grasp exactly what characterizes the exercise of power in modern societies. In his 1975–76 lectures to the Collège de France ([1976] 2003, esp. 34ff.), he laid out this field as consisting of sovereignty and dominance. Taking stock in order to find new ground was one of Foucault's habits. In this case, it led him to formulate the concept of governmentality. Foucault's work on power placed him in apparent opposition to half a millennium of political theoretical tradition, where the key point had been to seek to understand power as something universal and eternally present—as a constant for human nature. Foucault's core argument, in contrast, is that speculative statements about the nature of man, as well as universally valid as-

---

1. Already in the description of his annual course of lectures at the Collège de France, Foucault (1989) refers to works by Pasquino, Moulin, Delaporte, and Ewald on equal terms with his own. Hence, the government literature must from the beginning be seen as a collective project, but with Foucault as the primus inter pares. Bourdieu (2004) overstates his case when he insists that his own work was part of a collective effort, whereas Foucault's was not.

sumptions about political life as we know them from the entire range of political theorists from Hobbes and Kant onward, block empirical research on how power is in fact exerted. If humans are shaped by their social environment, and if this social environment takes on radically different forms, such assumptions are not only a hindrance to understanding, but they can be directly misleading.

Foucault invites a move whereby theoretical assumptions are replaced by empirical research, and universal suppositions are replaced by specific analyses. The exercise of power in terms of "how A gets B to do something against B's own will" has been analyzed over and over again, and thus seems ready for complementation. The center of attention in studies of power needs to be shifted away from "force," on which traditional understanding focuses, to the logically prior question of the origin of this "will" that B is said to possess. Hobbes's thoughts on this matter, in the first twelve chapters of his principal work *Leviathan*, have later become a gateway to a great deal of the research on power. The question is to what extent these considerations, which derived from and were directed toward specific social circumstances, remain valid today. "Will" is a phenomenon that in its concrete appearance rests on a number of historical preconditions. An adequate study of power must therefore focus on the historical preconditions that society consists of, including a set of subject positions, a set of relations between the subjects, a set of institutions supporting the society, and finally a set of strategies safeguarding it. The overarching aim of the governmentality concept lies exactly here.

Foucault seeks to demonstrate that governmentality is the response to a challenge that gradually arose in early modern time (around 1500 to 1700): the establishment of a civil society. Governmentality is a new type of power technology, which comes in addition to and modifies already existing power technologies, which Foucault labeled "sovereignty" and "discipline." The fact that we have not chosen to focus on these other types of technologies in this volume does not by any means imply that they are unimportant. It is, however, always more necessary, challenging, and satisfying to theorize the new and untheorized, rather than to carry out yet another analysis of phenomena that are well-known and have already been thoroughly discussed. This is particularly the case when it comes to studies of power, which often rest upon their ability to establish new concepts of power, and by way of empirical analyses demonstrate that they are fruitful.

Given that governmentality as a power technology is so central to the exercise of power in modern societies in general, a study of its historical origins as well as its current application also becomes a way of understanding power as a phenomenon today. Such a Foucauldian perspective has the advantage of placing the empirical focus on what is de facto going on in society, rather than speculating about general political institutions. Hence, this perspective is arguably much closer to the actual exercise of power than that of traditional political analysis. Foucault asks the same questions as the people who consider themselves executors of power: What needs to be done? How should it be done? His point of departure is ongoing social life, actual practices, the writing of manuals that instruct such practices, the preconditions for such practices to evolve—as opposed to speculative reasoning about human nature and the natural state.

A Foucauldian perspective thus begins with the historical preconditions for action. This way of thinking may also be applied to the political action of constructing the concept of governmentality. Foucault had, for several decades, been concentrating on what he called "discipline," in which a key point was to analyze power in a way different from the definition where power is understood as what A gets B to do against B's own will.[2] Foucault's point of departure remained that power must be understood as a relation—a strategic and productive relation—and the challenge is therefore to understand the potential forms of these relations (what Foucault calls its "modalities")—in particular those forms that appear in the Western tradition. In every one of Foucault's annual courses about his ongoing research at the Collège de France from 1971 until 1984, he touched on this issue. In his works on discipline, Foucault solved the problem by analyzing power as a relation between A and B, but without seeing A and B as independent actors. A is decentered—Foucault was particularly critical toward the idea of the state as a big A that can exert power over its subjects—and B is often given the kind of status that Foucault describes as "docile bodies."

Foucault was not the only one who put the concept of acting subjects (A, B) into parentheses. In a French intellectual context, this can be seen as an early example of confrontation with deterministic structuralism. However, immediately after the incidents in Paris and other places in 1968,

---

2. While Foucault's revision is aimed at the entire political tradition, the definition of power that he particularly challenges is that of Weber. Hence, it should be noted that Weber (1968, I, 53) himself took a keen interest in discipline, and that he used a definition that does not, in essence, block Foucault's project: "Discipline is the probability that by virtue of habituation a command will receive prompt and automatic obedience in stereotyped forms, on the part of a given group of persons." For a methodical comparison of Foucault's and Weber's intellectual development, where the point is that these key figures in the social philosophy of the twentieth century are closely related, see Szakolczai 1998.

where students and others on strike emerged as surprisingly successful in challenging the state *without* getting any type of "revolutionary" consequences, everyone who wished to analyze political life needed to take into consideration that the state had to be something else and more than simply a bureaucratic power center. The students were largely successful in beheading the French state. Nevertheless, the state remained functioning. On the one hand, this shows that one could in fact put parentheses around the state as an acting subject. More important, however, it showed that a new understanding was needed of what the state is—since something that could be labeled "state" remained functioning even after the fall of the head of state. Hence, defining the concept of state remained difficult for theorists, and even a leading structuralist like Foucault's old teacher, Louis Althusser, concluded that the state was bound to rest on a broader foundation. In a renowned essay, he specifies this foundation as a series of "ideological state apparatuses"—schools, prisons, hospitals, and so forth ([1970] 1971).[3] Thus, we observe that even this prominent structuralist to some extent followed Foucault's movement away from the centralized state concept.

Another important precondition for constructing the concept of governmentality can be found in Foucault's intellectual biography. As with any other perspective, Foucault's early focus on discipline involved some costs. His critics highlighted two in particular. First, given his emphasis on discipline in specific institutions such as prisons, schools, and hospitals, Foucault refrained from saying anything explicit about the state as such. This was problematic, as it is evident that the state is important in modern society in a range of situations (regardless of whether it is seen as decentered or not). Second, it was problematic that acting subjects were not only implicitly bracketed as a consequence of the focus on institutions but were in fact explicitly seen as docile and compliant bodies (esp. [1975] 1977, 135–69). Critics claimed that statements to this effect deprived humans of their status as acting subjects and hence also removed the potential for power resistance, and perhaps even for political participation altogether. For the late Foucault, who acknowledged this criticism as both relevant and challenging, it became a principal concern to respond to it by complementing the earlier analyses of power as discipline. In one way or another, A and B had to be brought back into the analysis. Foucault's response to this is the concept of governmentality, which is an attempt to

---

3. This tendency is, however, most central in Niklas Luhmann's project, where such systems are seen as self-governing.

theorize the modern state and its power technologies, and what he calls "ethics": how individuals seek to establish and govern themselves within the power field in which they are situated.[4]

A leading expert on Foucault, Colin Gordon (1991), who is particularly famous for emphasizing the cohesion of Foucault's works, claims that Foucault's lectures between 1978 and 1979 about governmentality constitute the core of his authorship. In any case, the development of the concept of governmentality can be seen as a direct prolongation of Foucault's project. The development of a concept about *gouvernementalité* can also be seen as a response to the criticism that he had ignored acting subjects, and by that particularly the state and the individual. Furthermore, this is largely about confronting and dissociating oneself from the dominant contractarian tradition in modern political thinking, where the ruler and his subjects are assumed to agree on the terms of a social contract, and in so doing abolish the "state of nature" that supposedly precedes such a contract. This starting point produces a series of questions, such as who can come to power under such circumstances, what type of exercise of power is normatively optimal, and so on. This has been the broad tradition in political philosophy since Hobbes, and much of the significance of Foucault thus lies in the fact that, to a large extent, he succeeds in complementing these issues, and raising new and alternative ones.[5]

However, Foucault does consider this broad tradition of knowledge production to be of key interest for historical reasons (as can be seen for instance in his lecture on governmentality from February 1, 1978). He characterizes the issues raised in connection with sovereignty as essential, and he uses the struggle between sovereign wills as an example of one of the three key types of power relations in Europe over the last five centuries. The point is rather that, because this type of relation has been discussed both in the broad and sometimes also in the deep sense of tradition, it is more important to look at the third cardinal type of relations that has been added to sovereignty and discipline in the last two hundred years or so: this is *gouvernementalité*, or governmentality.

---

4. In an English contribution, Foucault (1984, 212) writes, "There are two meanings of the word *subject:* subject to someone else by control and dependence, and tied to his own identity by a conscience or self-knowledge. Both meanings suggest a form of power which subjugates and makes subject to." In light of this, it appears as if the early Foucault in his works on discipline starts from the former definition, whereas the late Foucault in his works on government and ethics starts from the latter.

5. On several occasions, Foucault emphasized that it was not primarily the research on power that he wished to renew but rather its area of impact. For a reading of Foucault as a renewer of the main tradition from Hobbes and Locke, see Hindess 1997.

Foucault's development of a concept of *gouvernementalité* can also be read as his response to the claim that social factors have become so diverse and diffuse that power relations no longer play a central role—that politics has ceased to exist. While this is above all a postmodern principal criticism of everyone who has a political point of departure in their study of society, this approach does have its forerunners. In Foucault's case, the central criticism of this kind was Jean Baudrillard's *Oublier Foucault* (*Forget Foucault*). According to Baudrillard, Foucault is ignorant of the fact that the disciplining discourses he writes genealogies for and complains about have disappeared, and been replaced by endless floating simulacra. Such a reading strikes one as superficial. In a famous interview from 1980, Foucault was asked precisely if the problem of our times rests on a lack of creativity and relevant philosophizing.

> No, I do not believe the old saw about decadence, the lack of authors, the sterility of thought, our bleak and foreboding horizon. I believe the opposite, that it [i.e., the problem] is plenty. We do not suffer from emptiness, but from an inability to think about all that is happening. ([1980] 1994b, 108)

We may triangulate Foucault within his contemporary French political landscape as marginal to and as a dissident toward all the three major positions—Marxism, mainstream, and radical postmodernism.[6]

---

6. Foucault's further development of the concept as well as its relations with ethics in the years from 1978 to 1984 is worth an excursion. It can mainly be read from the courses at the Collège de France: "The first course of 1980 started in a theatrical manner, by a description of the rituals of power practiced by the Roman emperor Septimus Severus. For anybody who was expecting the continuation of the [previous year's] lectures on bio-power or liberalism, it took a while to understand what was going on. He then explicitly spelled out the break, stating that from now on, he would abandon the methodology of power/knowledge and would instead focus on the question of 'government by truth.'" In his last lecture in 1979, he had actually claimed that this was simply a tactic that could be observed in early stages of governance; however, he had now distanced himself from this thought. In 1982 he formulated the idea of the technologies of the self, defined as technologies that permit individuals to effect by their own means or with the help of others a certain number of operations on their own bodies and souls, thoughts, conduct, and way of being, so as to transform themselves in order to attain a certain state of happiness, purity, wisdom, perfection, or immortality (Foucault 1988b). The 1982 Collège de France course was about the subject's hermeneutics, and during this period, Foucault planned a book with the working title "Governing the Self and the Others" (Szakolczai 1998, 251). In the 1984 course about the technologies of the self, the essential point is that the care of the self is not only a concern for oneself. But it also raises the question of master and supervisor. During ancient times, the relationship between student and supervisor was rather random. However, with Christian confession this role was institutionalized. Consequently, Foucault now claimed that parrhesis also in the deepest sense was a po-

Governmentality between Sovereignty and Dominance

The late Foucault operates with three principal forms of power relations: dominance, sovereignty, and governmentality (see particularly [1978] 2000a, 219; 1994a, 728).[7] Dominance is a direct type of power relation where there is no question who is the master (Lat: *dominus*, which also was the name of a subgroup of the king's men in the Middle Ages [Olesen 2000, 9]). In a close reading of Foucault's discipline concept, Ransom (1997, 57) concludes by defining this as "those micromechanisms of power whereby individuals are molded to serve the needs of power." These practices are specific: Ransom's examples are a worker on the production line, a soldier in the army, a student in the classroom. The result of discipline is thus that the individual develops a new ability, making him or her capable of fulfilling a new role.

The subjects are, as objects under dominance, "free" in a much more limited sense. They can, however, offer resistance, because according to Foucault, there cannot be any power relation without resistance; where there is only one will that frictionlessly writes its truth into another, there are no relations, and thus no power. The subjects, says Foucault (1994a,

---

litical, and not a spiritual, way of existing in the world. As far as we can see, one may therefore talk about a similarity in form between self-care at the individual level and parrhesis at the societal level—a further development of the two topics that ties them together and defines a whole way of being in the world in late modernity. Yet, Szakolczai's reading of Foucault is to a large extent about showing that power is subordinate to truth: "He could only solve the difficulties of his work once he succeeded in removing the concern with 'power' from its centre" (cf. Foucault 1983, 208: "the goal of my work during the last twenty years . . . has not been to analyse the phenomena of power . . . it is not power, but the subject, which is the general theme of my research"). For Szakolczai, Foucault's entire work is a movement toward one single issue, namely, the relationship between the individual who seeks to express a truth, and the truth itself. According to Szakolczai, he discovered by the end of 1980 "that the most important specificity of modern society, defining its heart, but also its most dangerous and questionable element, is the deployment of techniques for the formation of identity; the way in which individuals construct themselves, by their own activity and by incorporating the recognition of others, and then recognise the product of their own construction as their 'truth.'" However, as Szakolczai himself writes, he simultaneously realizes that what he together with the ancient Greeks call parrhesis—to seek to tell the truth as straightforwardly as possible, directly to the power in such a way that it is dangerous to oneself—is originally a political rather than a spiritual activity. To disclose the foundation of human nature is a social practice that appeared in ancient philosophy and has been maintained by some philosophers at the border of academia the last couple of centuries (he mentions Stirner, Schopenhauer, and Nietzsche), but in this period first and foremost by artists (the examples here are the author Baudelaire and the painters Manet and Francis Bacon).

7. Sovereignty is but one historical instantiation of strategy. Each form may have subforms; Foucault offers an analysis of biopower as a particular form of governmentality.

720), are always "free" in the sense that they can commit suicide or murder their masters. The key point is that regardless of what they do, this will not be sufficient for asking the question of who is the master—because it will always be the other person. If we are dealing with a relationship characterized by dominance, the actions of the weaker part can never be anything but resistance—resistance toward an order that the subject cannot change by the power of his actions alone. This is the type of power relations in institutions (in prisons, schools, hospitals) that the early Foucault studied, but the late Foucault offers the marriages of the eighteenth and nineteenth centuries as an example.

> We cannot say that there is nothing but man's power: The woman could do a number of things: cheat on him, take his money, turn him down sexually. She still remained in a state of domination, to the extent that all this was in the last instance a set of tricks that could never turn the situation around. (1994a, 720–21)

Sovereignty is a game between different wills. As opposed to dominance, where it is always clear who is the master, strategic relations are often characterized by the fact that this is not always evident. It is this type of power relations—understood as an ongoing negotiation between subjects regarding who is right and who can dictate the other person's actions, where it is constantly open who is the superior part—that according to Foucault is ever-present in relations between human beings. Strategic action is central in most analyses of power but will not be discussed in any detail here.

Three points should nevertheless be mentioned. First, Foucault emphasizes that even though power relations permeate society, society cannot be reduced simply to power relations. He exemplifies this by noting that negotiations about truth with regard to psychiatric medication and mathematics have a value of their own, regardless of the power relations they are incorporated into. However, if one were to analyze these practices as *social* practices, one would not be able to identify these power relations. Second, Foucault mentions explicitly that this type of strategic game could very well be present in, for instance, a study situation. Hence, institutionalization of one field does *not* necessarily imply that subjects are reduced to docile bodies. In light of the analyses that follow, this is a central point. Here it should be noted that subjects are not considered "free" outside the discourse—they are only as free as Foucauldian subjects can be, meaning free to act within the discourses that constitute the subject.

Third, the strategic game between different sovereigns (first the king himself, then the states understood as collective sovereign subjects) has been the typical form of power in the European state system. The establishment of the state system from the late thirteenth century onward is inextricably linked to the increase in relations between sovereigns, built on what has later been called "sovereignty." Sovereignty can be understood exactly as a strategic game, but one where there are no built-in restrictions hindering dominance to be utilized as a complementary power strategy. Poggi (1978, 48) introduces the shift from *Ständestaat* to autocracy in the following way.

> The strengthening of territorial rule and the absorption of smaller and weaker territories into larger and stronger ones—processes that had gone on throughout the historical career of the Ständestaat—led to the formation of a relatively small number of mutually independent states, each defining itself as sovereign and engaged with the others in an inherently open-ended, competitive, and risk-laden power struggle.

As part of this shift in form from state of estates to autocracy, a set of consolidated borders emerges, constituting relations across borders as relations between sovereigns. Note that the historical situation where sovereignty, and also governmentality, arose bears a key structural similarity to our own. "Globalization" is a concept that attempts to capture the breakdown of these borders, as well as the new preconditions for social life that has surfaced for these reasons, such as with regard to what types of power relations are the most dominant. A main problem for present-day theorizing of the state is that the monism characterizing the nation-state (all decisions are claimed to be taken at *one* level—that of the nation-state) is abandoned in favor of a situation where it becomes a question of negotiation whether issues are to be decided upon at the global level, the regional level, the national level, or the local level. An example of such a built-in bargaining process may, however, be seen in the embryonic European state: "The Ständestaat differed from the feudal system in being more institutionalized in its operations, in having an explicit territorial reference, and in being dualistic, since it confronted the ruler with the Stände and associated the two elements in rule as distinct power centers" (Poggi 1978, 48). Governmentality has proven an effective theoretical tool for analyzing the shift in polities during the early modern period. It thereby becomes a promising contender for analyses of present-day shifts as well.

Governmentality is a type of power relation that comes between dominance and sovereignty, and that is connected to the reflexive—how the self governs itself. The degree of freedom the self possesses to do this lies between, on the one hand, acting strategically, and, on the other, being dominated, because whenever you attempt to govern yourself, you will seek to draw on a set of technologies taken from various fields: from your own experience with institutions such as the school system, from the attempts of others to govern you, from technologies such as meditation and prayer. This is a power form that Foucault traced from freemen's *arche* in ancient Greece, such as technologies to govern one's own sexual life (see table 1).

Hence, the reason Foucault formulates and emphasizes the type of power relation that he calls "governmentality" is its central and understudied role in contemporary postindustrial societies. This is particularly connected with the fact that these human collectives are characterized by firm institutionalization, where what we call "society" places itself in between the subjects and the sovereign (in ancient Greece and in the Roman Empire, this institutionalization was less firm, and other technologies for controlling the self became even more important). The institutionalization thus has a decisive impact on the formation of the subjects, and these processes will be the focus of the following chapters. The rest of this chapter will discuss how societies like ours have become what they are today.

The Rise of Governmentality

In light of Foucault's radical historicism, it is hardly productive to discuss to what degree some forms of power are more fundamental than others. Time and space need specifying. In the lecture on governmentality men-

TABLE 1. Modes of Power in the Late Foucault

	Relation	*Institutionalized as part of*	*Type of practice*
Dominance	Directly, between master and servant	Settlement, hierarchical differentiation	Discipline
Governmentality	Indirectly, even subject internal	The 1700s, social differentiation	Staging
Sovereignty	Directly, between equals	Always between individuals, 1500s territorial differentiation	Game

Note: The order is not chronological, but functional, since Foucault (1994a, 728) sees governmentality as an in-between when he insists that "between the games of power and the states of domination, you have the governmental technologies."

tioned earlier Foucault ([1978] 2000) talked about dominance, sovereignty, and governmentality as a triangle that writes power into a given discourse (in his case, [post-] modern Europe). Hence, the idea is that these different forms together constitute a specific type of power constellation. This would seem to offer a more productive point of departure. It must, of course, be emphasized that these constellations are historically specific, so that certain forms in a given discourse may be more or less evident in a given period. William Connolly (1985, 366) summarizes Foucault's critical project as follows: "The claim, in short, is that the will to truth that governs modernity is the will to extend discipline, to impose form over that which was not designed to receive it." In this context, the whole idea is that discipline played a main role in modernity, and that such a statement is comparative by nature: There must be other social constellations where discipline is less apparent. The main focus for Foucault is precisely the relationship between different forms of power: how governmentality emerges as a complementary power form in relation to dominance and sovereignty. For Foucault, it appears as if these power forms are premises for each other—for example, when he writes about biopower as a component of governmentality.

As for the broad political tradition, sovereignty for Foucault is a phenomenon that emerged in the transition from the Middle Ages to early modernity, from the late 1400s to the mid-1600s.[8] The sovereign (the prince or the king) is a concrete person with the right to maintain law and order and to enforce discipline upon his subjects. The sovereign king is exemplary for the sovereign individual. With the introduction of autocracy, the sovereign's right to reign is transcendentally based on a mandate from God himself. The exercise of power took shape especially as two types of practice: first as *raison d'état* (or *prudencia mixta;* see Oestreich 1982, 48; Leira 2008), and second as what in French and English was actually called *police*, in German *Policey* (later *Polizei*), in Danish *polliti, politi*, and so forth.[9] The *raison d'état* (reason of state) is simply the doctrine about the state's position in the world, as well as its lawful position. The main point of introducing the reason of state can be seen in the title of a book by Albert Hirschman (1977), *The Passion and the Interests*. While the ruling

---

8. The Italian cities preceded this development; cf. Ferguson and Mansbach 1996.

9. These two concepts were actually used rather interchangeably at that time. Giovanni Botero's *Della ragion di stato* from 1589 was, for example, translated into German seven years later as *Johannis Boteri Gründlicher Berich von Anordnung gutter Polizeien und Regiments: auch Fürsten und Herren standes;* cf. Oestreich 1982.

class of the Middle Ages considered their own existence to be a matter of defending their honor—a question of passion accompanied by spectacular rituals such as knight tournaments and duels—there now came a shift toward the ideal that the sovereign should defend his position by using rational deliberations. Defense of honor and the passions that came with it were put aside, replaced by defense of rationally calculated interests aimed at keeping one's possessions. A central theorist like Machiavelli writes precisely within this tension field.

The late Foucault's overarching project is to understand how knowledge and power are interconnected. He searches for the characteristics of a period by looking at the changes in the ways in which the two are bound together. Hence, Foucault introduces a nuance that often disappears in the work of other theorists, between on the one hand Machiavelli and others who focus on offering advice to a prince (the person in charge of any polity, be it a chiefdom, a state, an empire) and on the other hand those who write about the state per se, about its actions and the logic these actions should follow. For someone like Machiavelli, the prince's object of governance is his territory. For the others, who came later, this object of governance is the population. These latter, who write about *raison d'etat*, are also the ones who formulate detailed handbooks about operative and practical knowledge. This knowledge, which in other respects can be read as important contributions to the emergence of social sciences, also addresses power explicitly and directly, with references to what was at the time known as suggestions about improving the police, understood as ways of controlling the population. The knowledge regarding how this was to be carried out assumed two competing forms, police and rule (or governmentality), where the latter gradually gained momentum at the cost of the former.

Police—Early Illiberal Governmentality

Police was a concept that was commonly used when referring to different types of statutory provisions that various power centers produced in early modern times.

> *Police* had the connotation of administration in the broadest sense, that is, institutional means and procedures necessary to secure peaceful and orderly existence for the population of the land (that is, territory). Police

in this sense, obviously a sense derived directly from *polis,* was apparently first used in Burgundy (hence the original German spelling *policie* and *policey*) in the late 15th century, from where it passed to the Hapsburg chanceries. (Raeff 1983, 5)

The first known use in German is from Würzburg in 1476, but the most frequent use was made of it during the sixteenth- and seventeenth-century wars of religion (Oestreich 1982, 155–65). One reason the sovereign became sovereign was because he gradually succeeded in obtaining exclusive rights to produce such statutory provisions. The meaning of the police concept thus changed and became a general and contemporary description of the sovereign's ideal order based on the reason of state. "The concept of 'police' covered the authority which the ruler arrogated to himself to issue commands and prohibitions. The new structure of command and obedience contributed to a further break-up of feudal society," writes the early modern historian Oestreich (1982, 157). The consequence was that police pervaded almost all conceivable aspects of human life, in what was called *der wohlgeordnete Polizeistaat*—the well-ordered police state.

The late Foucault seems to lean on the works of Oestreich. There are also striking similarities between Oestreich's assumption that the main historic trend in early modern times is what he calls "discipline" and the early Foucault's works on exactly what he too calls "discipline."[10] Oestreich's main hypothesis is that the neostoicism developed by fourteenth-century intellectuals such as Justus Lipsius and his successors, as a response to the religious, political, and social conflicts of that time, was constitutive for a thorough disciplining of almost all aspects of social life. It is a well-established fact that there in early modern times was a broad reception (rebirth or renaissance) of ancient thought, especially that of Romans such as Tacitus, and that there for that reason was a growth in knowledge in such varied areas as law, medicine, warfare, mining, and agriculture. All of this had a concrete impact by means of a power technology that first Oestreich and later Foucault call "discipline," and this was possible not least because the increasing rush of people to the cities led to demands from the citizens themselves for new methods for sustaining the social order.[11] This need appeared even more urgent since the Church, which tra-

---

10. Foucault used specific historians as empirical stepping-stones in his work on clinics and Greek sexuality as well.

11. Oestreich (1982, 37) particularly emphasizes that the thinking of that time, or the dimension of opinion, must be seen as constitutive for political order, and not be reduced to a reflection of the material: "The elaboration of army organization and state finance, two of the

ditionally had played a central part in regulating daily life, now had become both divided and weakened. Hence, the emission and enforcement of secular statutory instruments, what contemporary society called "police," were intensified.

> In the late Middle Ages almost every town in the [Holy Roman] Empire issued edicts concerning blasphemy, adultery, seduction, gambling, excessive drinking, ostentatious expenditure, and so forth. The new problems posed by crowded living and the increased possibilities of friction, together with the alarming migrations due to plagues, led to wide-ranging "police" activity in the towns before it was taken up in the rural areas. Now it was necessary to achieve the acculturation of the immigrants by issuing further rules of hygiene, social ethics, and conduct in the economic sphere. The authorities were reacting to a challenge; the town councils, often in response to pressure from the citizens, acted at first by issuing separate decrees, and subsequently by publishing comprehensive "police ordinances." (Oestreich 1982, 156–57)

Policing is a response to demographic and social changes, but according to Oestreich, neostoicism plays a central role when it comes to defining the challenges of governance, and formulating detailed answers to them. The Roman models for neostoicism can be read directly from central concepts in this thinking such as *auctoritas* (authority), *prudentia* (reason of state), and *disciplina*. All were taken from the Roman literature and maintained, at least at first, their Latin form. Moreover, as in Rome, there were two parallel processes on the state and household/individual levels respectively.

> Neo-stoicism was an important and constructive element in the political thought at the turn of the sixteenth century. Its aim was to increase the power and efficiency of the state by an acceptance of the central role of force and of the army. At the same time, Neo-stoicism also demanded self-discipline and the extension of the duties of the ruler and the moral education of the army, the officials, and indeed the whole people, to a life of work, frugality, dutifulness, and obedience. The result was a general enhancement of social discipline in all spheres of life, and this en-

---

most important instruments at the state's disposal in the sixteenth and seventeenth centuries, are held to have resulted from military and political necessity and to have evolved by themselves in response to the requirements of the real world: that, we are told, is where we should look for the motive forces behind such developments. [However,] political humanism, as it originated in and spread from the Netherlands, addressed itself to precisely such practical tasks—the government of a community, the political education of the rulers, the structure of the army and the administration." For a discussion of the importance to IR, cf. Leira 2008.

hancement produced, in its turn, a change in the ethos of the individual and his self-perception. This change was to play a crucial role in the later development of both modern individualism and democracy, both of which presupposed a work ethic and the willingness of the individual to take responsibility. (Oestreich 1982, 7; see also page 88, where he claims there is a historic military line from Lipsius via Clausewitz to our times)

Discipline is for Justus Lipsius and other neostoics an overarching power technique resting on four components: systematic training (*exercitium*); order (*ordo*), understood as hierarchy and standardized sequences of conduct (cf. the expression *order of battle*); self-discipline (*coercio*), understood as moderation in conduct of life and restraint with regard to temptations; and finally example (*exempla*), that is, evaluation of conduct by way of reward or punishment (Oestreich 1982, 52–54). Discipline is a fully developed way of existing in the world, for collectives and individuals alike.

While neostoicism on the one hand gave direction to the individual way of living by emphasizing each individual's disciplined existence in the world, it was also highly suitable as self-insight for the autocracies that emerged in the 1600s. Neostoicism dealt largely with how, through discipline, one could build a state as strong as possible, and this doctrine was effectuated by the absolute kings and their trusted men (Oestreich 1982, 131). In the first phase of Swedish political science in the early seventeenth century, for instance, King Gustav Adolph's mentor Johann Skytte remained loyal to Lipsius and neostoicism, whereas Axel Oxenstierna, who wanted to defend the traditionally strong position of the aristocracy, looked instead to a federative thinker like Althusius. In absolutist Denmark, where the state did not receive the necessary capacity to orchestrate discipline as rapidly as in military Sweden, and the king did not defeat the aristocracy until 1660, neostoicism did not gain momentum until later. When Denmark's Christian IV founded the Academy at Sorø in 1623, and thereby took an important step toward administrative professionalization by institutionalizing the training of the absolute state's servants, the position in history and rhetoric was given to one of Lipsius's students, who brought with him neostoicism and its doctrine of discipline (Oestreich 1982, 109–13).

Oestreich also emphasizes that discipline and the need to have a "good police" was a central theme in the division of Europe's states into *amts* (counties, from German *Ämter:* offices; Oestreich 1982, 225). For illustration, let us turn to the Danish composite state where the feudal term *lendsmand* (sheriff) disappeared only the year after autocracy was exerted (1662), and was replaced by *amtmand* (county governor). Simultaneously, the service was demilitarized, the market towns—the domain of the citizens—were excluded from their jurisdiction, and their numbers went down from forty-seven when autocracy was introduced to twenty-five in 1730. Administrative historian Lind (2000, 171) mentions three headings for the domestic activity of the autocracy: "Church, Justice, and Police." As an example of the latter, which he describes as "one of the fashion-words of the time," he mentions the chief constable in Copenhagen's introduction of a unitary system for weight and measures, an examination for compass makers, the introduction of the Gregorian calendar (in 1700), and surveillance of roads (172). However, the establishment of an independent Police and Commerce Collegium on the state level in 1704 was no success and was shut down in 1731 (Feldbæk 2000, 247). The fact that police thus proved more manageable in local and limited fields of administration than at the top dovetails nicely with the transformation Foucault points at from direct to indirect governance, from police as illiberal governmentality to a liberal variant where the object of governance is not behavior, but people, and increasingly people's souls (Rose 1999a).[12]

In retrospect, the concept of an increasingly better police was accentuated by its own success, because the decrease in infant mortality combined with the economic boom led to rapid population growth throughout the 1700s. As a consequence, there was a relative increase in the number of small farmers and farmhands, which in turn increased the rush of new people to the market towns and thus also the need for justice and order. The strategic situation in early modern times, which Oestreich and Foucault analyze by using concepts such as discipline, police, and order, is absolutely central here, because liberal governmentality, as indicated previously, is about a *further developing* of these power techniques.

> Police in its archaic sense is absolutely vital to a genealogy of present forms of governmentality.... In Germany, after the seventeenth century, it gave rise to a distinct *science* of police, *Polizeiwissenschaft*.... According to Knemeyer, police was both the condition of order in the community and the ordinances that sought the institution and maintenance of that order in the fifteenth- to seventeenth-century German statute law.

---

12. Foucault draws on Bentham's suggestion of how direct legislation should be supplemented with a new instrument of governance, namely, what Bentham himself calls "indirect legislation." He calls for what he describes as a new subject: a new "art of government," which is to deliver proposals on how this can be done; see Ransom 1997.

Later, he continues, it begins to accept a further set of meanings, embracing the concept of commonality itself in humanistic and theological literature. Nevertheless, order remained the paramount focus. When, in the seventeenth and eighteenth centuries, a science of police was formed, it was concerned with the content of that order, and so theorized the specific conditions of its institution and maintenance. This science of police was thus led to an evaluation of the objectives of the *state* and the proper form of the *state* itself. (Dean 1999, 89–90)

In 1747 it was decided at Sorø Academy, in accordance with the development of a *Polizeiwissenschaft* in Germany, that one should teach the economic, commercial, and commersal sciences (see Schytte 1773–76). A central book at Sorø was Montesquieu's *L'esprit de lois,* which Foucault mentions as a good example of the type of knowledge production about people and country that was meant to give the state an opportunity to keep better police (Dreyfus and Rabinow 1984, 137–38). Ludvig Holberg's *Dannemark og Norriges Beskrivelse* (Description of Denmark and Norway) from 1979 and *Det Kongerige Norge* (The Kingdom of Norway) from 1793 are local examples of similar texts (they were obviously seen as useful—Holberg was ennobled for the first title; see Neumann 2003, 46). However, the limitation and the change in the meaning of the concept meant that later knowledge production happened in such a way that the old, wider meaning was overshadowed by the newer. In *Dansk politihistorisk bibliografi 1632–1938* [Danish police-historical bibliography, 1632–1938], for instance, the selection criteria with regard to entries are described in the following way.

> The actual content of the word police was among other things determined by means of the Dictionary of the Danish language. Hence, we became aware of, that there was no uniform definition of the concept police, and that the police institution itself had taken on a wide range of tasks over the years which one would not today associate with the police role. In order not to enter into too many difficulties . . . we decided to leave out this material. (Dilling and Mikkelsen 1983, IV)

The definition offered in the dictionary in question is as follows.

> A state's, a local government's (or a smaller society's, and institution's) entire organisation, arrangement, condition, administration (cf. meaning 2 [which is the principal meaning today]) in particular with regard

to the maintenance of peace and order, legal affairs (often in connection with keeping good police, good order). (Dilling and Mikkelsen 1983, IV)

As an example, a part of Christian III's Kolding Recess from 1558 is given—one out of many decisions made by assemblies (*herredager*)—where mayors and councils in each of the country's market towns are instructed to maintain good customs and police (compare with Petersen 2000, 58). As late as in the 1600s, there were, however, relatively few people involved in this work, which means that they could not have succeeded without the cooperation of the burghers themselves (Jespersen 2000, 117). The latter observation is largely in accordance with Oestreich's point that the initiative to more police often came from citizens, which suggests the internalization of power relations that succeeds the shift from police to governmentality.

The historian Marc Raeff has made an important contribution when it comes to the transition from a social order based on direct and specific discipline from above to one resting on a more indirect and general approach. In an impressive study of "the well-ordered police-state," he uses Oestreich's concept of discipline as his point of departure but emphasizes that Oestreich's focus is too narrow. In looking only at how the state disciplined the aristocracy and other contenders to power by assessing them and mobilizing them for war, he ignores the existence of parallel and complementary processes on the cultural arena. As an example, Raeff cites the ordinances directed at limiting each individual's luxury consumption. He concludes that this is about discipline in a

> much broader context—that is, the aim of adapting the population to the performance and attainment of the new economic and productive goals set by the state. In a sense, this disciplining aimed at installing a new attitude, Gesinnung, toward the vita activa, to dethrone the respect paid formerly to the vita contemplativa as man's highest achievement on this earth. This new attitude was to be fostered, in the opinion of the legislators, by establishing a closer connection between the moral realm and the lifestyle of the population. The moral notions to be inculcated by the religious, political, as well as pedagogic establishments were those of sobriety and purposefulness, the voluntary and stoic acceptance of the duties of earthly existence for its own sake. It was imperative that the same norms and values inform every activity of the individual and the group. (1983, 87)

This is certainly a reading along the same lines as those of Foucault. Raeff underlines that the phenomenon Foucault calls "governmentality" is an *intended* project; that it emerges in prolongation of the police state, first by supplying the political disciplining, later by gradually becoming comprehended by subject and society; that this is about a neostoicism and about sedimentation of what Raeff calls "lifestyle" and Foucault calls "technologies of the self."

In our context, the 1700s and their social order are relevant first and foremost because it is in liberalism's critique of the nature of this police order as a too *direct* power technique that a foundation for governmentality is formed. In the absolute state, for instance, one had already experienced the state's limited ability to directly govern economic life: "Around 1615, the state sought, through a number of mercantile experiments with whaling, silk production, soap, trading companies etc. to breathe some life into production. To a large extent, the experiments failed, and in the 1620s the state withdrew from such working life activities" (Jespersen 2000, 125). Interestingly, it was an *indirect* part of the mercantile program, the foundation of Sorø Academy—whose purpose was to prevent many of the autocracy's young men from traveling the Continent on so-called peregrinations where they, inter alia, might make contact with Catholics and other false teachers—that proved the most enduring. In the absolute state—Denmark had been Protestant since the inauguration of Christian III (Brekke 2002)—there was little or no tension between church and state. Hence, the state could not only make direct use of what is referred to below as the priests' pastoral power to get people to talk: it could also draw on the Church's institutional resources to collect taxes. The introduction of the system of church registers in 1645 was for instance directly related to getting a means of introducing taxation (Jespersen 2000, 145). Christian IV's motto was in fact "Fear of God strengthens the Kingdom" (Langslet 1997, 117).

Governmentality as a Liberal Form of Power

Governmentality is indelibly marked by the emergence of a European bourgeoisie and this social group's understanding of itself, liberalism. Liberals, from Scottish Enlightenment thinkers such as Adam Smith and beyond, criticize reason of state and police for resting on shaky ground. For them, it is simply *not possible* to have full information about society. The famous "invisible hand" is invisible because one can observe, in retrospect, that it has been there, but not in the present; it can be known only indirectly by its effects, not directly by its operations. If it is so that a dense web of social reality has come between the sovereign and each individual that one can call "society," and moreover that this society operates in the way that Smith and later liberals assume, this has three completely central implications. First, planning direct intervention in society becomes impossible. Second, it becomes undesirable, because if one is unaware of that in which one intervenes, the effects of one's actions are likely to be destructive. It becomes imperative that the tasks of the state are limited to upholding the framework around the scope of society, so that society can function by its own laws, and function well. Third, it becomes a precondition that society is to function in such a way that subjects are individualized, meaning that they obtain a certain liberty to act so that they can fulfill the societal function that liberalism has attributed to them (Hindess 1996, 127). With such a philosophy police becomes a form of knowledge that is not sufficient for ruling society, and the consequence of putting an alternative, liberal form of governance into effect thus becomes creating individuals who in turn serve a social order: "Considered a political philosophy, liberalism is usually held to favor limited governmentality because of its prior commitment to individual liberty; considered as a rationality of governmentality, it views the operation of individual liberty as necessary to the practical ends of government" (Dean and Hindess 1998, 17). It becomes an aim to go from police to liberal governmentality. Liberal governmentality thus emerges in the *prolongation* of pastoral power and police (see next section). It would seem, however, that when governmentality does not lead to what, at any given time and in any given field, is seen as a normal degree of order, dominance will emerge. Any subject incapable of governing itself could still be locked up in hospital or prison when necessary.

Jacques Donzelot (1993) follows up Foucault's observation about liberalism as a reflexive approach to societal problems by studying when the concepts "society" and "economy" part company. He concludes that this is the republic's way of addressing a key challenge. The challenge was that one had proclaimed *both* the right to work *and* a reserved approach regarding intervention in questions such as personal liberty or private property. The solution, Donzelot claims, was found in the web of insurance arrangements that were emerging by the end of the 1800s and that had the development of statistics as a condition for action. With the introduction of insurance arrangements (e.g., national health insurance), the employee was no longer directly dependent on the employer, and the conflict between work and capital was transferred to a more general societal level.

The welfare state emerges in an extension of this development, which, with its pronounced (however impracticable) ambition of taking responsibility to lead society, assumed responsibility for the individual from the cradle to the grave. This is an impracticable aim because it opens the door to an indefinite elasticity in the demands voiced by subjects—there will never be a "maximum limit" in questions of old-age pension, health care, and so on. The demand is, in principle, endless, while the economy can provide only a finite offer. Hence, the state's task and responsibility become to get the two to overlap to the largest extent possible—but never with ultimate success. Besides, there are other types of expenses.

> It is that, having eliminated responsibility for the sphere of social relations, the disposition of the State and individuals is such that the former has to make allocations to everyone as the price of the promised progress for which it is responsible, while individuals settle for being permanent claimants from the State as compensation for the grip on their evolution of which it has dispossessed them. And it is that between State and individual, so it comes to be said, there is no longer a society. (Donzelot 1993, 136)

Liberalism's diagnosis of society thus leads to a fundamental criticism of contemporary practices. Where police instructed directly, by way of more or less general orders concerning behavior, liberals argued that the state as a generalized sovereign now had constantly to ask itself whether it should do *less*, in order to further stimulate society's capacity for self-organization. Consequently, economic life underwent a radical change, as is thoroughly discussed in the literature.[13] If society is an independent unit, then its economic life can no longer be seen as an extension of the king's household. This observation has several implications as regards the possibility and the desirability of intervening.

Such a liberal situation gives birth to two key tensions. For the subject, individualization becomes vital to the cause of freedom: without freedom, it cannot fulfill its societal task. The introduction of freedom, then, is systemically requisite, or compulsory. Liberalism thus gives rise to a major question for the state. How should it respond to those subjects who can-

---

13. The Scottish Enlightenment's attack on mercantilism is here exemplary. "In its internal aspect, mercantilism, the distinctive economic policy of the absolutist regimes, was largely a matter of diminishing the autonomy of locally based organs of economic regulation either by suppressing them or, more often, by integrating them into a uniform, statewide system that was more technically sophisticated, less tradition-bound, and more effectively policed than such local organs had been" (Poggi 1978, 64).

not or will not be individualized? Should they be killed? Castrated? Sterilized? Should their offspring be placed in foster care? Should they be institutionalized in specially designed schools? and so on. The state also faces another vital tension. On the one hand, the state is dependent upon the ability of society to produce an optimum amount of resources. If keeping one's hands off the goods leads to increased production, this can be seen as an argument to do exactly that. On the other hand, if it favors indirect rather than direct power execution (as before), the state must abandon a central technique connected to the form of power that it has employed both to govern and to maximize production.

Governmentality as Pastoral Power Plus Public Spirit

The form of governance that the liberal state produces as a solution to these two key tensions is liberal *gouvernementalité* or governmentality. Governmentality is directed at the newly emergent layers of societal relations between subjects (society). These were relations that were not easy to handle by the king's extant arsenal of strategic actions. In Foucault's words, the state accepts "a theory of right to be superimposed upon the mechanisms of discipline in such a way as to conceal its actual procedures, the element of domination in its techniques, and to guarantee to everyone, by virtue of the sovereignty of the State, the exercise of his proper sovereign rights" ([1980] 1994b, 105).

This rights-based thinking is now rapidly changing. As it grows more costly to govern directly, the statesmanlike thing to do is to find new ways of governing indirectly.[14] In such a historical context, considerable energy will be expended on discussing and activating historical traditions that delegate responsibility to the individual. Foucault mentions two such traditions: first of all, and in accordance with tradition, public spirit or citizenship-mindedness, and second, innovatively, what he calls "pastoral power." For Foucault, the new power form *governmentality* emerges as a hybrid between these two traditions, as a power form specifically tied to the new reality that has intervened between the sovereign and his subjects: society. In the best genealogical traditions, he is careful to stress that in order to understand the modern state one must study the history of Western culture as a whole. Therefore, he approaches these traditions by way of

---

14. Where intentionality is concerned, this is probably an example of what Hume had in mind when he wrote about phenomena that were the result of "human action" but not of "human design."

ancient Greece, Egypt, Assyria, the Jews, and the Fathers of the Church. Neither is it a coincidence that the traditions he mentions are a prolongation of the two perhaps most important breaks with feudalism in early modern time: the Renaissance and the Reformation. On the one hand, it is about the republican tradition, where public spirit (*eunoi*) is central. Here, the focus is precisely on the idea that certain subjects have internalized the interests of the *polis* to such an extent that the life of the city becomes their own. This is well known, not least because the main tradition in political theory focuses on exactly these questions and thus is a central legitimating force for the self-understanding of these societies (who is to govern, on what grounds, what are the citizens' duties and responsibilities, etc.). Foucault's central and innovative move is to show that this tradition is followed by what he calls "pastoral power." Considering that the nature of this pastoral power is radically different from that of republicanism, the claim that pastoral power has played a central role in the emergence of the modern state automatically becomes a fundamental critique of the main tradition in political theory in the form in which it has emerged over the last half millennium or so. Here, the impact of pastoral power has systematically been ignored.

Foucault ([1980] 2002) mentions four central areas in which earlier representations of "pastor" suggest an approach to the political that is different from that of republicanism. First, it is the group (meaning the citizens of modern society, what came to be known as the population) that is the object of the exercise of power (not territoriality, as in republicanism). Second, this group is always in need of their pastor, otherwise they will get lost (while republicanism argues that legislation is a constitutive phenomenon that needs follow-up but that nonetheless is seen as exogenously given; cf. Onuf 1998). Third, it is the pastor's mission to lead his group to salvation, each and every member, in all aspects of life, unceasingly (whereas republicanism emphasized the specifically political aspect, especially in times of crisis). Fourth, the pastor has a *duty* to continuously lead and rescue (while republicanism emphasizes specific action in specific and necessary situations, such as war). Foucault then shows how the Fathers of the Church intensified this manner of conceptualizing the political, by insisting that the pastor is responsible for all members of the group and thus is required to know their thoughts and actions in detail; that obedience is a central virtue; and that obedience is, inter alia, about incorporating the pastor's manner of living in this world (and on the way to the next) in toto. While the ancient republican ideal is a *philopatris*—one who loves his city—the ideal here is *philoptochos*—one who loves the underprivileged (see Dean 1999, 79). It seems obvious where this is heading. Foucault claims that from the end of the 1700s, pastoral power has served as a point of departure for a new mode of power: governmentality.

The pastoral power perspective is not territorial but focuses on the pastor and his group—on subjects. They are the focus of attention, not the ground on which they walk. This is particularly interesting because the power technology sovereignty in the European state system is directly and territorially framed (the idea being to define and defend in the clearest and most spectacular manner). The state system's sovereignty and pastoral power thus complement one another, in the sense that one focuses on the territory and the other on the citizens. Pastoral power is also central because it demonstrates the close connections between governance of the self and the governance of the emergent society. The technologies for taking care of the self and for governing society have shared origins in the Judeo-Christian tradition, especially in the concept of the shepherd who cares for his flock. The sheep's salvation must be guaranteed—for instance, through practices such as confession. Here, the line goes further to the welfare state's ideal of responsibility for subjects from cradle to grave, institutionalizing *care* as a state responsibility. It should be noted that, whereas Foucault castigates the confluence of public spirit and pastoral power as lending a demonlike aspect to the state, he also explicitly (1994a, 728) celebrates a shift of emphasis from dominance to governmentality, complete with statutory provisions (*règles de droit*), as a desirable instrument.

Liberalism's program for indirect governance lies in the extension of a republican tradition. When it takes over, a power vacuum emerges, which is in turn filled when the Christian tradition of persistent and detailed control is introduced by way of the disaggregated state. Foucault's statement that political theory needs "to cut off the King's head" is frequently quoted—in other words: the main tradition has been blinded by the direct exercise of power that the sovereign or the sovereign state possesses, and it has ignored the type of phenomena that Foucault seeks to capture with his concept of pastoral power.

Taking this into consideration, the government's main responsibility was, from the beginning, its citizens and the very preconditions for their existence and being. It is in fact when such a need was revealed that the concept of "population" emerged. While sovereignty was characterized by being based on the king's entitlement to *take* lives, governmentality is characterized by its seeking to, if not give life, then at least to *regulate* it by means of what Foucault calls "biopolitics." This population, understood as a living and productive unity, is intended to bring about things that in turn could serve as resources for the state. Foucault employs standard concepts when he refers to this as economic policy. He emphasizes that the productive unity is the *entire* community, not only specific families or households (Gr. *oeikos*) as before. A central concern in this context is then to ensure that this society may function.

Conclusion

Liberalism's demand that one must always govern less should thus be seen historically in relation to the increasing demands for governance of the self. One is expected to take responsibility for one's own life, and the lives of others, by taking out insurance, practicing safe sex, looking after one's health by eating a balanced diet and exercising, taking responsibility for one's own working situation by submitting to appraisal interviews, being an active job applicant, and so on—these demands are constantly rising. However, there will, at all times, be some people who are not capable of fulfilling all these demands. As Barry Hindess (2000) has pointed out, it is a historical fact that most people who have lived under liberal regimes have not been defined as fully capable of taking the responsibility for their own lives in the way called for by liberalism. Consequently, they have been put under various forms of administration. The independence of the individual is a historically created phenomenon.

Based on Foucault's point that liberalism operates with an ambiguous concept of the subject, Barry Hindess (1996) has also put forward an interesting historical thesis. On the one hand, liberalism claims that the individual is already independent, that people can take on responsibility for their own lives. Sometimes other people's lives are also included (and here, there is a tension not least when it comes to the individual's role in the family). On the other hand, independence or autonomy is seen as an ideal to strive for. The liberal subject is, on the one hand, actually present in the world; and on the other hand, it is an ideal demand. This tension is characteristic, not only of liberalism, but of much political thinking in general. For nationalism, the nation and the people are surrounded by a similar tension; for Marxism, the working class is an existing critical subject, but at the same time an ideal quantity that can be realized only in a brighter future. Hindess holds that the differences between classical liberalism as known from the 1800s and the neoliberalism of the postwar period are rooted in different historical preconditions concerning the independence of individuals.

The neo-liberal insistence on market mechanisms entails a repudiation of social programmes that many liberals of an earlier generation—along with social democrats and others—worked to promote. . . . Against the background of conditions in which the great nineteenth- and twentieth century social policy regimes were set in place, many governmental programmes now repudiated by neo-liberalism could plausibly be represented as promoting autonomy. Against a very different contemporary background in which, at least in the more advanced Western societies, the existence of a suitably calculable population is easily taken for granted, these same programmes can be seen as undermining autonomy. Neo-liberalism is a liberal response to the achievements of the liberal mode of government. (1996, 77–78)

Foucault, as well as later writers on governmentality, thus puts forward a fundamental critique of liberalism and the increase in the power relation of governmentality so characteristic of liberal forms of the exercise of power. Foucault is undoubtedly critical toward this, and for that matter toward any other forms of power, when he looks ahead: We need a new constellation of power relations that can keep the excessive power of political rationality at a distance (1984, 210). The literature provides little reason for celebrating governmentality as a form of power. However, at the same time it is a vital argument that power is productive and therefore not merely an inevitable but indeed a creative social phenomenon. There would appear to be three reasons why the greater governmentality that liberalism brings about can lead to a social life with more tolerable power constellations than known competitors.

First, a central characteristic of the shift from a constellation with strong elements of dominance to a constellation with increasingly strong elements of governmentality is that more and more exercise of power and normalization take place from a distance and are dependent upon internalization. Foucault points out that, as a consequence, an increasing number of subjects will not be able to meet the demands of normalization. Governmentality produces losers. At the same time, it seems clear that the potential for shaping *one's own* subject position increases. Foucault is not rejecting the impulse to govern less. On the contrary, he seems to see a potential here. All constellations of society have their costs, and it is for critical social researchers to bring them to light. If one at the same time rejects utopian ideas, like Foucault, this emphasis on costs does not in itself imply that the constellation is condemned. On the contrary, Foucault concerns himself with the fact that it is a legitimate and central task to criticize various forms of social life, *without* having to put up with accusations of nihilism, *without* having to come up with an alternative. In other words, writing a status quo report is different from writing an indictment.

Second, and by extension, we should recall that another of Foucault's later thrusts involved work on the care of the self, and the development of different techniques for producing a self can be seen as part of the literature on governmentality. In this ethical work, Foucault distances himself from his previous perspective where he viewed subjects as compliant bodies and instead celebrates the subject's ability to create itself. There exist various historical examples of such techniques: meditation, fasting, and prayer are classics, to which one could add recent examples from so-called alternative lifestyles. When in his work on governmentality Foucault works on the inside of the state's perspective, employing a state angle, the main emphasis is on how the subject is formed and on how this fits with many of the general shifts in the nature of politics. When he starts with the subject, however, the main emphasis is on self-creation. These two perspectives are mutually complementary.

Third, the international nature of governmentality means that the number of prototypes for self-creation and the many variations such self-creation can undertake are increasing rapidly. When the limits are seen as relative, hybrid forms emerge, and life takes on infinite diversity in infinite combinations. This has particularly been the focal area for Gilles Deleuze; characteristically, in his book on Foucault he celebrates the potential that surfaces once the chapter of modernity is concluded (1999). Such a celebration of globalization must of course be accompanied by criticism as well. For Foucault, governmentality surfaced as a reaction to the dense web of social relations—civil society—between the sovereign and the paterfamilias. In the tension between the sovereign's need to govern and need to extract a maximum of resources from this civil society, governmentality emerges as *indirect* governance. The political framework in which this took place was the early modern European state. The current situation may, by extension, be understood as follows. In the same way as there emerged in the 1600s and 1700s a set of social relations that political theorists labeled "society," we now see a concentration of global flows of people, information, technology, and so on, leading to the establishment of what social philosophers increasingly refer to as a "global society." But—and this is a key challenge—it is not given that there is any functional equivalent to the early modern state that can deliver a political framework within which this drama can take place.

On the one hand, globalization represents a challenge to the governmentality perspective, because globalization is a reminder that the unit with which the concept of governmentality begins—society—cannot be treated as a closed unit (either around itself or by the state). Historically, it was a precondition for the emergence of government that the political Europe already had discovered a form based on sovereignty—a form that divided territory into units clearly separated from each other in the political sense. On the other hand, globalization invites application of a governmentality perspective to the emerging social realities, where these borders are once again about to cease. That is exactly why we draw on it in the following chapters.

While governmentality as a liberal form of power chose the collectivity of citizens as its object of governance, with neoliberalism it has extended its repertoire to include also the individual as its object of governance. There also seems to be another, less clear and less studied trend. We begin to glimpse humankind as a whole as a tentative object of governance. We have stressed how governmentality pushed its way as a new form of power, in a situation where society emerged as a governance challenge. With the emergence of global society, governmentality increasingly plays its part on this level of social and political life as well.

At the heart of the governmentality that emerged in the sixteenth and seventeen centuries there lay a self-reflecting will to take the state as an object of governance. This will was, by necessity, directed toward each specific emerging state. That which did not offer itself as a possible object of governance became "foreign" (cf. Walker 1993). In principle, however, the will to govern did not stop at state borders; only other wills could stop it. This made for a certain tension where the status of "the foreign" was concerned. It was beyond government by necessity, but nonetheless a *potential* object of governance. In subsequent chapters, we argue that recent decades have seen a marked increase in global governance. The will to impose standards of governance from one state to another has been joined by an emergent set of practices on the global level itself that has now reached a degree of density that warrants talk about a rationality of governance on the global level itself (as distinct from on the level of each particular state). But first, in order to link these discussions to dominant IR discussions about the nature of global politics, the next chapter examines how the governmentality perspective presented here relates to those debates.

2 | Global Politics as Governmentality

When applied to contemporary global politics, the governmentality perspective poses a challenge not only to the literature on global governance but to conceptualizations of global politics overall. In this chapter, we place the concept of governmentality in relation to dominant strands of thought within the discipline of international relations. Most conceptualizations of the international as a political realm privilege either power or norms. The question of conceptualization is of direct practical interest. One issue is how to study whether or not we are in the midst of a change in the structure of global politics, away from a system of states in the direction of hegemony, empire, or something else. To answer this, empirical studies of specific social practices are needed. We will judge the usefulness of conceptualizations of the international by whether they are fruitful for such an undertaking.

Weber's Ideal Type

The key conceptualization of politics, definitely in international relations but arguably also in social theory generally, is that propounded by Max Weber (cf. Schmidt 1998). Weber placed the power struggle over norms at the center of his understanding of politics. His stress is on the formal quality of politics. As a consistently historical thinker, he refused to universalize questions of substance. Yet Weber's aim was maximalist; he wanted to account for the differing configurations of social life in different societies at different times, and that called for generalization. Weber was able to generalize without universalizing by introducing the methodological innovation of the *ideal type*. Politics, for example, could be thought of in terms of different ideal types of rule (traditional, charismatic, legal). Weber concentrated on politics in the literal sense, as the ordering of the relationship between the one and the many within a bounded polity in terms of norm allocation. However, his methodological innovation of the ideal type was applicable to all social phenomena—including relations between polities. As we will detail later, one of his students went on to conceptualize the international in terms of the ideal type, with far-reaching consequences. Since we will argue that today's IR realists seem to use Weber's methodological device of the "ideal type" in an unwarranted fashion, we first need to elucidate what Weber actually meant by the term.

Weber fashioned the ideal type in a series of methodological articles written at the very beginning of the twentieth century, concurrently with his writing of *The Protestant Ethic* ([1904–5] 1976; see esp. his own reference to former work on p. 200, n. 28). He summarized the key idea in his posthumously published *Economy and Society*.

> For the purposes of a typological scientific analysis it is convenient to treat all irrational, affectually determined elements of behavior as factors of deviation from a conceptually pure type of rational action.... in analyzing a political or military campaign it is convenient to determine in the first place what would have been a rational course, given the ends of the participants and adequate knowledge of all the circumstances. Only in this way is it possible to assess the causal significance of irrational factors as accounting for the deviations from this type. The construction of a purely rational course of action in such cases serves the sociologist as a type (ideal type) which has the merit of clear understandability and lack of ambiguity. By comparison with this it is possible to understand the ways in which actual action is influenced by irrational factors of all sorts, such as affects and errors, in that they account for deviation from the line of conduct which would be expected on the hypothesis that the action were purely rational. ([1922] 1968, I, 6)

Weber immediately goes on to specify that rationality is a question of what we may call analytical models—models fashioned after the fact, for a scientific purpose—and not what we may call folk models, which are the models or categorizations used as running guides for action by those who participate in society. The question of scientific rationality is a question that arises after the fact and only for those who use scientific, analytical models. It is not necessarily relevant on the level of social facts. According to Weber, ascribing rationalism to actors is a "danger" close at hand when one uses ideal-type analysis.

> Only in this respect and for these reasons of methodological convenience is the method of sociology "rationalistic." It is naturally not legitimate to interpret this procedure as involving a rationalistic bias of sociology, but only as a methodological device. It certainly does not involve a belief in the actual predominance of rational elements in human life, for on the question of how far this predominance does or does not exist, nothing whatever has been said. That there is, however, a danger of rationalistic interpretations where they are out of place cannot be denied. All experience unfortunately confirms the existence of this danger. ([1922] 1968, I, 6–7)

Weber had been clear on this problem throughout the hatching process of the concept. In his seminal article from 1904, for example, he writes, "A 'definition' of such synthetic historical terms according to the scheme of genus proximum and differentia specifica is naturally nonsense" ([1904] 1949, 93). We note, furthermore, that Weber used the ideal type in combination with other methodological approaches. First, we must acknowledge our own value commitments. Then we can try to understand the lifeworld of the people who are to be studied. Thus, Weber described the *Protestant Ethic* as "a contribution to the understanding of the manner in which ideas become effective forces in history" ([1904–5] 1976, 90). In *Economy and Society,* the thrust remains the same: "every artifact, such as for example a machine, can be understood only in terms of the meaning which its production and use have had or were intended to have, a meaning which may derive from a relation to exceedingly various purposes" (1968, I, 7).

The next task is, from an outsider's analytical standpoint, to identify ideal types. Weber grounds the possibility of doing this in phenomenology: Given the analyst's human capacity for empathy, interpretations tend to appear self-evident. This goes for interpretations of both rational and irrational courses of action. When the analyst is at all capable of transcending the folk models of the people he studies, Weber argues with the phenomenologists, that is because "the interpretive understanding of *rational* action has an additional feature: *Eindeutigkeit,* which could be translated as either 'unequivocality' or 'unambiguity'" (Muse [1981] 1991, 259). Weber took pains to underline the necessary gap between ideal type and actual historical occurrence. For example, he stressed how ideal types of authority will not usually "be found in historical cases in 'pure' form. . . . But even so it may be said of every historical phenomenon of authority that it is not likely to be 'as an open book.' Analysis in terms of sociological types has, after all, as compared with purely empirical historical investigation, certain advantages which should not be minimized" (1968, I, 216).

The ideal type was not, then, a substitute for studying meaning and action. No, it was a way of ordering the field, of drawing a baseline in relation to which actually occurring action could be analyzed. Neither was identifying the ideal type the end of the analysis. The final step should produce facts by using the ideal type as a basis for observation and as a baseline for comparison with what was being observed, in turn producing facts.

Although the epistemological emphasis on understanding and the methodological emphasis on the ideal type clearly take precedence in Weber's work (Jackson 2010b), Weber has invited a twofold reception (cf. Ringer 1997, 92–121).[1] The main problem here is that Weber's firm emphasis on the historically specific character of any ideal-type analysis has sometimes been overshadowed by the hankering of certain Weberians toward establishing universally valid findings. To receive such a reading has often been the lot of his students as well. The reception of the Weberian Hans Morgenthau is a case in point.

Morgenthau's Weberian Conceptualization of the International as an Ideal Type

In the modern academic political realist tradition, no light—with the possible exception of E. H. Carr—shines brighter than Hans Morgenthau's. In the United States after World War II, Morgenthau was pivotal in forging an understanding of world politics that went on to become orthodoxy for both academics and foreign policy intellectuals alike. This is borne out not only positively, but also negatively; every new heterodoxy attacked Morgenthau's conception, thereby underwriting and further contributing to its pivotal status.[2] He was also, as Guzzini (1998, 26) points out, "one of

---

1. Such a duality is probably a prerequisite for a thinker to become a classic, for without it, there will not be that contradictory reception that guarantees the texts their status as present. There are direct parallels to be drawn here to other founders of sociological thought: causal versus functional explanations in Durkheim, voluntaristic versus materialistic explanations in Marx, etc.

2. Conceptual contenders included sundry peace researchers, budding poststructuralists (Ashley 1981), and of course constructivists.

the few writers who rooted and defined the concept of power and of politics." In terms of knowledge production at least, Morgenthau's conceptualization of politics and world politics therefore remains central.

Writing in the contexts first of interwar Germany and then of exile in Cold War America, Morgenthau saw as his main priority to offer an account that could salvage the specificity of politics as something more than and different from the use of force. The opponents of liberal democracy at the time, German Nazism and Soviet communism, subscribed to an understanding of politics that focused on the ethnic or class purity of the collective. Such an understanding stressed how politics was not a sphere of its own in the Weberian sense, but an aspect of all different kinds of life in society. In such a scheme, as set out most succinctly by Carl Schmitt ([1932] 1995), the specificity of international politics is to be found in the importance of maintaining a distinction between *us* and *them*.

Morgenthau's response to this all-encompassing view of politics as substance (friend/foe) was, as Mike Williams (2004) has shown, to insist on the specificity of politics as the sphere of struggle over the determination of values and wills, on the importance of keeping spheres separate, and on the relevance of each and every sphere of social life. For Morgenthau, what defines the political is a question of intensity, not substance (cf. Koskenniemi 2004). Politics, then, becomes a general feature of social life that can be found in *all spheres.* On the other hand, Morgenthau was uneasy with this Schmittian understanding, for it was exactly this way of defining politics that was also key to all the totalitarian ideologies of the day (communism, fascism, Nazism). Morgenthau's overall project, before as well as after World War II, was to offer an understanding of politics that left parts of the social relatively untouched by it and that left room for deliberation. In formulating his *Politics Among Nations,* therefore, Morgenthau restricted the concept of the political to an ideal-typical and semiautonomous sphere. As a result, there is a tension in Morgenthau between thinking of power as intensity that pertains to the social overall, on the one hand, and thinking of power as a quality pertaining to a specific social sphere—that of the political—on the other. Morgenthau gave priority to the latter over the former.

The crucial point here is that Morgenthau explicitly privileged the conceptualization of power as pertaining to a specific sphere and focused on one particular part of that sphere—the international—for *analytical* purposes. Mike Williams (2004) has explained convincingly how Morgenthau drew on Weber's concept of the ideal type in order to give an account of the specificity not only of politics but of politics among what he referred to as "nations" and that we now call "nation-states," that is, international or world politics. Moreover, methodologically, following Weber, Morgenthau insisted on identifying ideal-typical spheres: "Each sphere is necessary for a fully human life, and it would be inappropriate to universalize the standards of one sphere to all others" (Williams 2004, 643). The whole point of Weber's ideal type was that it should account for a specific historical situation. Morgenthau, too, is quite specific regarding the area of validity of his analysis: it is the world of the period in which he writes. Other periods will have a different international politics.

> The kind of interest determining political action in a particular period of history *depends upon the political and cultural context within which foreign policy is formulated.* The goals that might be pursued by nations [i.e., states] in their foreign policy can run the whole gamut of objectives any nation has ever pursued or might possibly pursue. (1967, 9; emphasis added; see also Williams 2004, 638)

While Weber has conventionally been labeled a "political realist," his writings espouse a much broader, more socially embedded concept of power than what we usually associate with realism. As argued by Hobson and Seabrooke, Weber noted that states "which are wholly autonomous from society are weak and ineffectual—not strong—and above all, that they are dangerous for the reproduction of international society" (2001, 259). For both Weber and Morgenthau, then, power is not solely a matter of brute force or material resources. For both scholars, the source and the functioning of power alike are intimately linked to the sociocultural context (Hobson and Seabrook 2001; Owen 1997; Williams 2004).

Morgenthau is thoroughly rooted in the broad historical and legal sociological tradition, and his use of the Weberian ideal type is exemplary. Morgenthau's treatment of the international is no exception here. He consistently used Weber's concept of ideal type in order to delimit international politics as a field of study. We note, however, how Morgenthau increasingly ruled out the hermeneutic aspect of *Verstehen* from his approach. Guzzini (1998, 29–30) convincingly explains this slide in the direction of attempts to establish universal laws as a reaction to the intensification of the Cold War.[3]

As one of the watersheds in current IR debates is whether or not norms

---

3. Clearly, the influence of the Chicago school on Morgenthau was an additional factor.

are to be seen as causal social forces, it is small wonder to find that Weber's work is claimed not only by today's power-oriented IR scholars, but also by those working within the broad hermeneutically inspired tradition.[4]

Power and Norm: Two Competing Conceptualizations of the International

The tension in Weber may be rediscovered, mutatis mutandis, in present-day IR theory. T. S. Eliot once noted that people often ask why we should read the old masters, when we know so much more than they did. His answer was that we know what we know because of them, and that reading them therefore involves understanding not only where we have come from, but also who we are. We concur. It is not a question of whether or not IR is part of general social science—it is—but of the degree to which we are aware of this fact. To some, the international remains the system of states—an anarchic realm, qualitatively different from the domestic. To others, the international is increasingly a realm of shared norms, of a kind with other political realms.

Power, Not Change

To traditional power analysts, politics in the international space is about conflict and tensions lodged at the level of the state. Power struggles are seen as emanating either from the *animus dominandi* of human nature, or from fear, or from a mix of the two. The state may contain such struggles domestically, but, in the absence of a world ruler, relations between states must be based on self-help. Indeed, the question of how to implement rule is a moot one, for in the final instance, there exists no common denominator for measuring what is right and what is wrong between states, and so it remains undecided what kind of order should be implemented. Right stands against right. The result is a perennial fight about who gets what,

---

4. Note, for example, how this is a key theme in two authors who have inspired much recent work on norms: Habermas and Giddens. With a view to our Foucauldian critique of Weber's concept of the ideal type, it is worth noting that Giddens celebrates Weber's historical scholarship, but that he, too, is dismissive of its methodological reach. In introducing the *Protestant Ethic,* for example, he writes that this work and the other studies of world religions "were intended as analyses of divergent modes of the rationalization of culture, and as attempts to trace out the significance of such divergences for socio-economic development." Giddens states, "On the level of abstract method, Weber was not able to work out a satisfactory reconciliation of the diverse threads that he tried to knit together; but his effort at synthesis produced a distinctive style of historical study" (1976, 5, 2).

when, how—where the possibility of an escalating use of military force is never far away. For example, Stefano Guzzini has generalized about a group of traditional power theorists as follows.

> Realists define the political sphere by power and authority relations. Individuals, groups, and nations struggle for power, understood both as the effective control of means of coercion and authority relations based on legitimacy. History follows in eternal cycles, and no catharsis can put an end to these permanent struggles. (1998, 24)

We may disentangle various factors that may seem to reshape and even mitigate the power struggle. One such possible factor is a concert of great powers, another is a looser form of consensus about procedural rules for how to interact (mutual recognition of sovereignty, specific practices such as diplomacy or international law), yet another is a regime that regulates a particular issue-area (Bull 1977; Kissinger 1957; Krasner 1982). In the final analysis, however, these arrangements are no more stable than the cobwebs that grow on a cannon mouth in peacetime. Once the cannon is fired, they are gone. For our analysis, we need not catalog power theorists much further; the point is that power is privileged over change, and that variations in norms are consequently bracketed.

When viewed cross-culturally and across time, the observation that intense power struggles are at the heart of politics may hold up quite well. It is also, however, an empirical fact that the polities who struggle vary in type (Ferguson and Mansbach 1996). Polities also vary in how tightly they are knitted (even where states are concerned, state–society relations vary considerably), and the degree to which they are socially discrete units.[5] Realizing this, we aim in this book to offer an alternative structural perspective on how global politics may generate agencies. First, let us focus on realism and its dissuasive effect on empirical research. Realism's assumption of a continuous and basically homogeneous political struggle has come to serve as a barrier against inquiry into the actual practices of which specific struggles on specific levels of life (e.g., the international level) actually consist.

We would argue that this malaise may be explained in terms of how present-day power theorists pay little heed to Weber's warning against conflating the ideal type with an actually existing historical constellation,

---

5. A well-known critique of the so-called neorealists, for example, concerns how the structure (the state system) is seen as generating agencies (or "units," ipso facto, states); see Ruggie 1983.

and of analyzing the levels pertinent to that constellation. These levels will vary with constellations, with politics on a global level, world politics being only one possibility. Projecting the levels that exist and the relations between those levels back, forward, or cross-culturally on the premise that there exists a timeless international realm defined in terms of power struggle has no precedent in either Weber or Morgenthau, who both stressed the historically contingent character of the international. It is, nonetheless, easy to see how this error may materialize, for once Morgenthau in his later writings started to bracket understanding and increasingly played up how an ideal-typical understanding of international politics could be used as a springboard for isolating universal laws, he opened the door to the forgetting of meaning as an aspect of life and the ensuing importance of history-sensitive analysis—precisely, that is, the kind of error that Weber explicitly and repeatedly warned against.[6]

This means that there is no ready perspective within traditional power analysis from which to discuss systemic change. We need a conceptualization of the international that retains the sophisticated realist conception of the formal hallmark of politics as power struggle, but one that is at the same time *socially* embedded. Social embeddedness, in the form of norms, has been a key theme for various IR scholars in recent decades (Sterling-Folker 2000). We now ask whether a norms-based approach to the study of the present-day transformation of global politics has the necessary purchase.

Change, Not Power

Certainly, a key claim in much contemporary theory is that the "social" must be included in analyses of global politics (see Ruggie 1998, 856). The social world is a world of "our making" (Onuf 1989), and it is thus important to explore the production, content, and effects of "constituted social facts" and of the "constitutive role of ideational factors" (Wendt 1999). One particular kind of theory that has gained prominence has focused primarily on norms as a specification of intersubjectively shared ideational factors—"social facts"—that other theories have ostensibly overlooked (Fearon and Wendt 2002). Norms are seen as the key "independent variable" used to study changes in states' interests and identities, and changes in international policies and institutions (Finnemore 1996; Gurowitz 1999; Katzenstein 1996). Moreover, analysts have provided detailed accounts of how states are socialized into a political community,

---

6. Of course, a contemporary realist may hold the idea of a "timeless realm" regardless of any appeal to Weberian or Morgenthauian authority; the primary topic under discussion so far has been genealogy, not truth.

such as the European Union, by adopting new norms that govern their behavior (Finnemore and Sikkink 1998; Rieker 2006; Zürn and Checkel 2005).

These theorists paint a picture of the international as a realm that is becoming more and more liberal and socially embedded: (liberal) norms powerfully shape actors' identities and interests, and the anarchy of the international is thereby transcended. States' identities and their interests are increasingly shaped by shared international norms that define a liberal political space made up of norms about democracy, human rights, the rule of law, and the market economy (Checkel 2001; Gurowitz 1999; Risse 2000; Risse et al. 1999b; Zürn and Checkel 2005).[7] To these "thin" constructivists, the international is becoming progressively "thicker," as the identities, interests, and actions of states are increasingly shaped by liberal norms.[8]

While we concur with this interpretation of the international as becoming both thicker and more liberal in orientation—a process in which advocacy networks and international organizations play a key role in formulating and advancing liberally oriented norms and best practices (Barnett and Finnemore 2004; Park 2006)—these studies must be criticized for employing a strikingly thin concept of politics and of power. By ignoring or downplaying issues of power, these analyses say little about politics. As Stefano Guzzini has noted, "Connected as it is to the idea of the 'art of the possible,' attributing 'power' to an issue immediately implies that 'we could have done things otherwise.' . . . [This] immediately raises the stakes for political justification and action or non-action" (2005, 497). Talking about the "power" of norms in producing a convergence of interests and identities in the international realm is to think of power in a purely rationalistic way, as the causal efficacy of norms in transforming the interests and behavior of states in a process of "social learning," "deliberation," "persuasion," or the like.

---

7. As demonstrated by Wendt (1999) such views may account for the content of, and changes in, different world orders. Wendt summarizes these ideal-typical world orders, or different conceptions of "the international," as Hobbesian, Lockean, or Kantian.

8. In this view, the international realm is defined in much the same way as it is by the founders of international law. Under the heading "The Flight from Politics," Koskenniemi (1990, 1) argues that "since the publication of Emmeric de Vattel's *Droit des gens* . . . (1758), jurists have written about international matters by assuming that the liberal principles of the Enlightenment and their logical corollary, the Rule of Law, could be extended to apply in the organization of international society just as they had been used in the domestic one." Constructivist theory—at least in its (American) moderate version—brings to bear a similar view of the international realm.

To sum up, privileging power leads to an inability to study change, whereas privileging change understood as change in norms brackets the importance of power. At the heart of the matter lies the concept of politics embedded in these two theoretical approaches. For the traditional power analyst, politics in the international space is about conflict and tensions lodged at the level of the state, driven by material interests and resources. For the norms-oriented analyst, global politics is emptied of tension and conflict as it highlights learning, deliberation, and persuasion as the central mechanisms for bringing about norm-driven change.

To get a grip on the changing content of the international, we will have to establish a historically sensitive concept of politics—one that can capture how politics remains a power struggle, while also recognizing that it assumes different forms and expressions in different historical periods. We need a concept of politics that retains realism's focus on power and politics, yet recognizes the centrality of ideational factors such as norms in the transformation of global politics. As discussed earlier, Morgenthau's realism is grounded in a particular view of human nature, derived from Freud, that gives rise to a view of politics defined in terms of intensity. At the time of Morgenthau's writings the concept of politics as intensity was applied to make sense of the politics of the Weimar Republic, the fate of international law in the interwar years, and the state system after World War II (see also Koskenniemi 2004; Morgenthau 1940, 1948). It was eminently clear to Morgenthau, however, that the expression or logic of politics is highly contextual—that it may assume many *different forms,* depending on institutional, cultural, and economic structures. Morgenthau's identification of the political as an ideal-typical sphere where ideational factors seem to have little place *should not* lead to the conclusion that this view of politics, and of power, has no room for social theoretical insights as found in constructivist theory. Let us now proceeed to indicate one way in which Morgenthau's understanding of politics can be used as an intake to global politics today.

An Alternative Conceptualization: The International as Governmentality

When read against the backdrop of contemporary global politics, it is possible to claim that the "political and cultural context" of foreign policy of which Morgenthau speaks is thoroughly different today from when he himself was active. Indeed, the constructivist research reviewed here has helped to show this. Despite repeated attempts at re-creating the Cold War discourse of deadly ideological struggle, and the importance of what the United States has referred to as its "war on terror," what characterizes the present period is not primarily ideological struggle, but what John Ruggie (2004) refers to as the ever-increasing density of transnational relations. The social density of the international sphere puts more and more pressure on a concept of the international that emphasizes the isolated character of the political sphere relative to other spheres. But that would *not* imply that state politics—or perhaps even politics as such—has vanished from the scene, as norms-based theory often seems to imply. It may be useful to reflect more systematically on the interpenetration between politics and other spheres (the social, the economy, the legal), and to think systematically about how the logic of politics and the functioning of power may be transformed by the thickening of the international realm. What are the implications to the form and logic of politics of the intermeshing of international law and international politics? Does the tendency toward "legalization" of more and more global issues (e.g., food and pollution standards) reduce the level or significance of politics as defined by Morgenthau? Or does such an interpenetration of spheres merely shift where politics takes place, in the form, for example, of a "politicization" of international law (Goldstein and Martin 2000; Koskenniemi 2004; Reus-Smit 2004)?

To attempt a view of the international as thicker than presented by traditional power analysis and yet retain elements of the view of politics and the role of power in the analysis of the international, we now turn to a thoroughly social view of power that also bears a strong affinity to Morgenthau's: that of Michel Foucault.

> Morgenthau's understanding of power and interest has its closest analogues in social theories more commonly associated with the work of Pierre Bourdieu and Michel Foucault, with their *very broad understanding of power and the political field,* rather than the narrow understanding of politics that realism stands accused of adopting. (Williams 2004, 639; emphasis added)

While Williams convincingly identifies an intellectual affinity between Morgenthau and Foucault's concepts of power, it is an open question how elements of their respective theoretical concepts can be used together. How may Morgenthau's parsimonious concept of politics as the intensity of power struggle be linked to Foucault's broad concept of power? One clue can be found in Morgenthau's reflection on state–society relations. While realism is often defined in terms of the logic of diplomacy and great power politics as autonomous spheres, Morgenthau offers a highly instructive reflection on how the functioning of power and politics is transformed by changed state–society relations. For Morgenthau, mass nationalism implies a shift in the locus of power, from the elite to mass society. The defining feature of modernity—the "death of God"—implies a neo-Kantian grounding for the organizing principles of society, but for Weber as well as for Morgenthau, these organizing principles or ultimate values cannot be grounded in transcendental values. They are socially produced and thus subject to change and contestation.

This development has one significant effect for the "logic" of international politics: it leads to the demise of the hitherto shared international code among the aristocracy engaged in diplomatic practice, since legitimacy and authority must be grounded in the rights and preferences of individuals in society. Under conditions of mass democracy, governments must find ways to govern the people *and* to govern relations with other governments on behalf of the people and the "masses." The basis of sovereignty thus shifts from territory to society. For Morgenthau, this signals the emergence of potentially dangerous aspects of politics, hence his recourse to Weber's "ethic of responsibility" and to the prudence of statesmanship as ways to limit the potentially destructive elements of nationalism.

It is here—as Morgenthau reflects on changes in power and politics and their implications for relations between state and society—that we find a point of connection to Foucault. By revisiting Foucault's take on the shift from "territory" to "society" as the reference point for the functioning of power, we may also see how their respective modes of analysis may be brought together. What distinguishes Foucault from Morgenthau is not so much his different philosophical position (after all, they were both heavily influenced by Nietzsche; cf. Hennis 1988, 146–62), but Foucault's different take on the state. Foucault, very much like Morgenthau, bases his thinking on how there is a choice to be made about defining politics, and stakes a course between the two in such a way as to end up with an understanding of politics much like Morgenthau's understanding of politics as intensity.

> In short, two formulations: everything is political by the nature of things; everything is political by the existence of adversaries. It is a question of saying rather: nothing is political, everything can be politicized, everything may become political. Politics is no more or less than that

which is born with resistance to governmentality, the first uprising, the first confrontation. (Foucault, quoted in Senellart 2007, 390)

Politics is process; politics may take anything as its subject matter—it may intensify anything social. As Colin Gordon has observed, Foucault is highly skeptical of attempts to "deduce the modern activities of government from essential properties and propensities of the state" (Gordon 1991, 4). Instead, he holds that the nature of the institution of the state is a function of changes in practices of government (Foucault 2000a). Practices, not institutions, are Foucault's point of entry for the analysis of the functioning of power. For him, the "art of government" is about the "introduction of economy into political practice."

> To govern a state will mean, therefore, to apply economy, to set up an economy at the level of the entire state, which means exercising toward its inhabitants, and the wealth and behavior of each and all, a form of surveillance and control as attentive as that of a head of a family over his household and his goods. (2000a, 207)

Power is here defined in terms of the conduct of oneself and others, of the "action upon action," as David Owen notes.

> For Foucault, it is through relations of power and of ethics that the will ... is constituted, that is, that we are constituted as agents with certain capacities; consequently, any further conducting of our conduct by others or by ourselves can only be exercised in relation to those capacities for action we have. (1997, 154)

It is in this sense that Foucault writes of how "power is only exercised over free subjects, and only in so far as they are free." Power, then, operates through the modality of freedom. At the sociopolitical level, the identification of this modality of power—in the form of "government"—is predicated upon how political economy, as expressed in the works of Adam Smith, dissolves the previous unity of knowledge and political thinking and acting. That unity had been central to the cameral and police sciences that accompanied political reason when politics was conceptualized in terms of territory, and territory was conceptualized as an extension of the king's household. Political economy introduced a new reality toward which the ruler had to operate, and that new reality was society. Colin Gordon has elegantly described what this implies in terms of the inauguration of a new mode of objectification of governed reality, whose effect is to resituate governmental reason within a complicated, open, and "unstable politico-epistemic configuration" (1991). It is this unstable politico-epistemic configuration that unites Foucault and Morgenthau, as both are concerned with the lack of a stable source of authority under conditions of modernity.

In its most general form, this new rationality of political rule is identified by Foucault as "liberalism"—understood as an ethos and rationality of government rather than as a historical period or a philosophical doctrine. This new rationality of political rule—in essence a new realm of politics—is predicated upon how "society" has emerged since the late eighteenth century as an entity external to and qualitatively different from the territory and the inventory of the state. Hence is introduced, Foucault argues, a new modality of power defined as "government."

> What was discovered at that time—and this was one of the great discoveries of political thought at the end of the eighteenth century—was the idea of society. That is to say, that government not only has to deal with a territory, with a domain, and with its subjects, but that it also has its own laws and mechanisms of disturbance. This new reality is society. ([1982] 1989, 261)

The identification of a "governmental" conception of politics is thus inspired by the identification of an important rupture in political thinking and action that occurred, first, by a discourse on the "art of government" starting in the sixteenth century, followed by its institutionalization in the postrevolutionary environment of the late eighteenth century. It concerns that specifically modern dimension of politics that arises when the "society" over which the sovereign rules emerges as a distinct entity, qualitatively different from the state, containing individuals whose rights and autonomy must be respected, and whose behavioral patterns must be known if they are to be governed effectively. As a distinct logic of power, liberalism is about "governing through freedom" (Hindess 2005, 403).

Essentially, Foucault proposes that there has been a steady trend ever since the mid-sixteenth century by which "government," as a form of power, has been *replacing and reconfiguring other modes of power* (sovereignty, discipline). For Foucault, this implies a need for studying the functioning of power, and the rationality and content of politics, within the framework not of "norms" but of "the formation of a whole series of specific governmental apparatuses" aimed at fostering, guiding, and shaping the action of free and autonomous individuals (Gordon 1991, 12–13).

It is against this backdrop that we can understand Foucault's emphasis on studying changes in state institutions as a function of changes in practices of governing, rather than vice versa.

Foucault sees liberalism as a particular logic of governing—a form of power characteristic of modern society that operates indirectly by shaping and fostering autonomous and responsible individuals through the "conduct of conduct" and the ensemble of "governmental techniques" (Dean 1999; Rose 1999b). This is what Barnett and Duvall in a different context have referred to as a "productive power" that operates through distant social relations to set up standards for what is appropriate, effective, and legitimate for groups or individuals to do—a power that works to "structure the possible field of action of others" (Foucault [1982] 2000, 341). It is precisely here that the governmental concept of power is useful for an analysis of the international. If the international realm is thickening due to the institutionalization of liberal norms about human rights norms, market economy, democracy, and the rule of law, then there seems to be a good case for subjecting the preconditions for the emergence of these norms to a governmental reading. But how should global politics be approached within such an analytical framework? That leads us to some methodological issues.

Methodology: From Ideal Type to Discourse and Programs of Governing

Whereas Morgenthau emphasized the specificity of the political sphere by relying on Weber's ideal type, Foucault was at pains to trace the political in all spheres of social life by investigating the practices of governing. We note that Foucault actually saw himself as being engaged in an intellectual undertaking akin to Weber's.

> We should aim for a critical [form of] thinking that takes the form of an ontology of ourselves, an ontology of actuality; from Hegel to the Frankfurt School by way of Nietzsche and Max Weber it is this form of philosophy that has grounded a form of reflexion within which I myself am trying to work. (Foucault 1994c, 687–88)

Foucault nonetheless rejected the label "Weberian," pointing out that what interested him was the production of truth as a historically specific undertaking rather than rationality understood as a general category of the human mind (1980, 26). Whereas Weber (and through him, Morgenthau) saw ideal types as analytically formulated concepts aimed at distilling the "logic" or "essence" of a particular social phenomenon, Foucault distanced himself from the suggestion that he himself was dealing in ideal types, as he pointed out in an interview.

> I do not think that your comparison with Max Weber is exact. Schematically, you may say that "the ideal type" is a category of historic interpretation; it is a structure of understanding for the historian who wants to tie together a certain number of givens after the fact. It makes possible a reassessment of an "essence" (of Calvinism, or the state, or the capitalist undertaking) while beginning from general principles that were not at all there in the thoughts of the individuals whose concrete comportment we are supposed to understand. (1994e, 27)

Foucault notes three differences: Methodologically, his approach is not a retrospective understanding, but a reading of the programs that were actually used to govern. In terms of area of validity, his is not a universalizing anthropology but an analysis of how humans themselves participate in their own specific disciplining. Finally, far from conforming seamlessly to a preordained model, the discourses he studies typically expose gaps between the programs and the practices, and these gaps should be studied for their own sake. This is a key issue, for we do not think that a reconceptualization of the international should simply be a question of updating an ideal type, as allowed for and indeed suggested by Morgenthau. We think that it should also involve a shift from understanding the international as a rationalized concept to understanding it as a discursive one. This is the point at which our mode of analysis specifically breaks with Morgenthau's, for Morgenthau wanted to identify highly stylized (ideal-typical) models of the logic of the political, the economic, and the legal. A discursive approach has to be more tentative.

To Morgenthau, the political realist "thinks in terms of interests defined as power, as the economist thinks in terms of interests defined as wealth; the lawyer, of conformity of action with legal rules" (1948, 13). The approach advanced in this book would rather study the countless practices and programs of governing and seek to identify the *rationality of governing* rather than *the rationality of a particular sphere* (economic, legal, political). This rationality of government, inclusive of its constitutive practices, is what we refer to as "the international as governmentality." Methodologically, the study of it should also include the kinds of effects a particular rationality may have; our examples concern mainly how a specific rationality may engender specific kinds of actors. A focus on governmentality does not pretend to explain particular outcomes, and thus it restricts the idea of constitution to that which makes certain things possible. It has the added value, however, of introducing an explicit focus on power in these analyses, linking political logic and rationality to concrete practices as expressions of a particular form of power.

There already exist implicit traces of such a conceptualization in IR literature. For example, Laffey and Weldes describe how practices of "policing" (in the present-day sense) are central to liberal (or neoliberal) forms of governing in contemporary global politics (Laffey and Weldes 2005, 77; cf. Bigo 2006; Huysmans 2006; Prozorov 2006). They argue that "contrary to myths of progressive enlightenment in liberal democracies, the savage policing of political protest . . . has long been a defining feature of public life in the North Atlantic region." With reference to recent protests against the WTO and G7, they argue that "democratic protest becomes 'criminal activity'" (Laffey and Weldes 2005, 77). Furthermore, a governmentality perspective renders the analysis of how new norms shape global politics more systemic, in that it explores the system within which these norms are formulated and gain acceptance in terms of the underlying political rationality. Himadeep Muppidi provides a telling analysis of the answer given by Madeleine Albright to the question asked by a CBS reporter of whether the sanctions against Iraq were worth it, considering that they had resulted in the death of a half million children. Rather than analyzing the answer (whether it was "worth it"), Muppidi asks about the conditions that make it possible for the reporter to pose such a question to Albright in the first place.

> The question is what produces her as a capable of offering an acceptable answer; what produces her as acceptable to civilized society in the first place. . . . That such a choice is not ruled out as morally unimaginable or as fundamentally detestable—so reprehensible that that question cannot even be asked—speaks to the power of a colonial order that constantly empowers some actors, such as the United States, as subjects of this colonial order. (2005, 281)

We can locate the source of how liberal modes of governing give rise to such mechanisms—by dint of which some actors are accorded a position from which they may assert authoritatively what is appropriate, legitimate, effective, and so forth—within the liberal project itself (Mattern

2005). The world-society approach developed by John Meyer and colleagues is instructive here, as it asks why states are organized in (increasingly) similar ways and how such taken-for-granted terms as *actors* and *agency* are socioculturally constituted (Meyer and Jepperson 2000; Thomas 1987). Meyer and Jepperson argue, for example, that the modern, liberal ontology emptying the other-worldly of agency and setting up "Man" as the sole actor has spread rapidly since World War II, so that now "the nation-state form, with individuals as citizens, and organizations as components, is found worldwide" (2000, 106). They go on to note that "a surprising feature of the modern system is how completely the Western models dominate world discourse about the rights of individuals, the responsibilities and sovereignty of the state, and the nature of preferred organizational forms" (106).

The reading of the "international" found in this approach is strikingly similar to that provided by a governmentality reading of the spread of liberal norms and institutions at the global level—with the important difference that the latter offers a better handle on the relational aspects of power at the global level (a point to which we return later). Thus, governmentality analysis adds an explicit focus on relations of power to the norm literature by inquiring into the types of (governmental) practices and techniques that produce certain types of identities and behavior as appropriate, legitimate, effective, and so on. This in turn is in keeping with Foucault's scholarly project (Debrix 1999; Dillon and Reid 2001; Ferguson and Gupta 2002; Lipschutz 2005a, 2005b).

Governmentality in the International Sphere: Between Liberalism and Sovereignty

While Foucault was concerned with politics understood in terms of the content of and tensions between different governmental rationalities, he did not reflect systematically upon international politics, nor did he provide a concept of "politics" as traditionally understood in terms of conflicts and tensions between specific actors over the organization and governing of a particular society. Foucault circumvented the flexible view of politics as intensity that we find in the works of Hans Morgenthau. While both drew on Nietzsche for inspiration for their theoretical work, Foucault transformed the Nietzschean idea of will to power into a program for broad, historical analysis focused on the content and effects of different types of power found in practices of governing. Morgenthau, by contrast, took the same idea and instilled it with agency and parsimony by drawing on Weber's ideal types.

To put the point in a different way, the international is a political sphere increasingly defined by a liberal governmental rationality. While this transformation is arguably fundamental, it does not transform politics as formally defined by Morgenthau. Rather, new forms of politics are becoming more important, among them the "politics of categorizations." The source of the centrality of categorizations—as a precondition for programs of governing—can be found in the ambiguity surrounding the "essence" of man within the episteme where liberal governmental reason operates. Helliwell and Hindess elucidate it this way.

> Considered as a subject that knows, man is constituted by the faculties of reason and perception and is therefore capable of autonomous action, at least in principle, while considered as an object of knowledge, man appears as the effect of external forces and stimuli. Thus the qualities of rationality and moral autonomy invoked by the rhetoric of liberal constitutionalism are seen on the one hand as representing the *essence* of man and on the other as the *product of very particular conditions*. (2002, 2; emphasis added)

Inside liberalism, then, there is contingency and indeterminism with respect to how to categorize and thus also how to govern different types of populations and individuals in time and space. Political agency is thus involved in formulating and choosing who are regarded as capable of governing themselves and who are not. Helliwell and Hindess (2002, 2) argue, for example, that "modern political thought has normally taken the view that while there may be contexts in which suitable habits of self-government are able to take root, there are many more in which they are unable to do so." In a more recent article, Barry Hindess explores how such categorization has changed over time, precisely by reference to the strengthening of liberal norms internationally.

> Where liberalism could once rely on the decentralized despotism of indirect rule over colonial subjects, it now has to treat most of those who it sees as being in need of considerable improvement as if they, too, like the citizens of Western states, were endowed with "the capacity to exercise rights with some moderation." The old imperial divisions between citizens, colonial subjects, and non-citizen others has been displaced by a postimperial globalization of citizenship, and indirect rule within imperial possessions has been superseded by a less direct system in which

the inhabitants of the old imperial domains are governed through sovereign states of their own. . . . Indirect rule now operates, in effect, through national and international aid programs that assist, advise, and constrain the conduct of postcolonial states. (2005, 409)

Today, there exists a dense network of liberal norms that shapes the identities and behavioral patterns of states. This may be seen as a global system of indirect forms of power that operates to guide, shape, and foster specific types of not only states but also other polities, as well as individuals. It sets up standards of behavior for individuals and models of institutions to be implemented and followed by all good members of the international community.

What appears problematic in Morgenthau's framework is the grounding of politics, and of power, in a view of sovereignty as indivisible and foundational for the international. While such an analytical move may have been warranted at the time when Morgenthau wrote, it needs revision in light of subsequent changes in global politics. If we redefine sovereignty from an unproblematic foundation for international politics to an institution whose content and signifance is historically contingent, Morgenthau's view of the international will have to be revised. But in doing so, we cannot draw uncritically on the writings of Foucault. We have to allow for conflict, contestation, and agency with respect to how different societies and actors define themselves in relation to the different manifestations of a liberal governmental rationality. We have, in short, to deal with the relationship between sovereignty and liberalism.

Liberalism is a decidedly universal political project. While sovereignty has been made to constitute the universal form for the institutionalization of political authority, this very universalism is what leads to a tension between universalism and sovereignty. Sovereignty is—at one and the same time—a principle that allows for particularism, for resistance to and exit from a universal liberal governmentality *as well as* being a main target of and vehicle for universal liberal governmentality. For Foucault, sovereignty constituted an important and arguably strategic and convenient target of critique. To assert that we need to "cut off the King's head" in thinking about power is to situate an alternative reading very much in relation to sovereignty. Indeed, as we have noted, Foucault does not reject sovereignty; he sets out to identify how sovereignty is of limited analytical relevance for grasping the actual workings of power in modern society. In identifying liberalism as a governmental rationality, Foucault describes how a particular mode of thinking about and acting in the name of sovereignty has been transformed over time, resulting in a comprehensive "governmentalization" of the state.

In subsequent chapters, we seek to demonstrate that there is an "added value" to studying global politics through the lens of governmentality. Because this concerns international politics, we will have to discuss the relationship between sovereignty and liberalism carefully. Rather than being foundational for global politics, sovereignty has become redefined by the governmentalization of global politics. In chapter 3, we look at how sovereignty and protoliberal governmental rationalities combined to produce a particular definition of Russia in great power politics. In chapter 4, we show how a liberal governmental rationality is central for understanding the relationship between state and nonstate actors, and how the logic through which sovereign states govern through civil society defies the logic of sovereignty (cf. Bartelson 2006). In chapter 5, we argue that both neoliberalism and police are central features of how IOs seek to govern, in the process rendering sovereignty into an object and key task of governing. Taken together, these chapters describe a "governmentalization" of global politics that entails that the meaning and role of sovereignty are not constitutive of governmental rationalitiesbut are in fact constituted by them.

This does not mean giving governmental rationalities an ontological status more fundamental than that of sovereignty. Rather, it entails an argument to the effect that the historical process through which sovereignty *became* foundational cannot be said to have stopped. The governmentalization of the state described by Foucault, Oestreich, Raeff, and others has spilled over into the international sphere. Thus, the meaning and role of sovereignty in global politics are not given, nor are they preeminent. The continuing debate over sovereignty both as a foundational category *and* as a changing institution shows that we need to historicize sovereignty. Instead of viewing it as the "unmoved mover" of the international, we need to examine sovereignty in light of and as largely defined by the content and significance of the governmental rationalities discussed earlier. Thus understood, sovereignty assumes its meaning and role *within the context of governmental rationalities*. This transformation—from sovereignty as constitutive of world politics to sovereignty as constituted by governmental rationalities—implies that sovereignty is best described as an institution whose specific content and status vary with, and are shaped by, the specific governmental rationalities that prevail in functionally differentiated spheres of governing (security, development, economic, health, etc.).

As Jens Bartelson has noted, we "live in a world in which territorial differentiation into distinct nation-states is being challenged by a functional differentiation into distinct issue areas."

> The sovereign equality of states no longer constitutes the baseline for further stratification according to relative strength and power. In this world, there are several normative frameworks competing for both legality and legitimacy when it comes to justifying political practices, such as intervention. (2006, 474)

On this reading, global politics is much more about the tensions between and political dynamics ensuing over different governmental rationalities than it is about tensions between and political dynamics between territorially defined polities. Or, as Nicolas Guilhot argues with reference to the human rights regime, "International relations cease to be made of sovereignties relating to each other through legal rules, and become *instead a continuous space where different governmentalities overlap,* in the absence of legal mediations" (2008, 511; emphasis added). However, such a governmentalization of global politics is characterized by an "unstable politico-epistemic configuration," due to the tension between the universalist drive in governmental rationalities, on the one hand, and the resistance to and possible exit from this governmental rationality offered by the universal *form* of sovereignty, on the other.

Conclusion

While retaining the formal realist conception of politics as power struggle, we have broadened the definition of what power is and tried to specify how it operates under postmodern conditions. Seeing the constructivist conception of politics as resting on a shared understanding that is instantiated in common practices, we have also infused it with a much-needed focus on power and politics. Such a conceptualization of the international should also begin to rectify a serious shortcoming in the work of our main source of inspiration, Michel Foucault. Foucault himself never reflected on the international system in which governmental rationalities function. A conceptualization of the international as a socially embedded realm of governmentality sees the international as a structure (defined by relations of power) that generates different and changing practices of political rule (defined as governmental rationality). Such a conceptualization allows for empirical work that may tell us something about the ongoing transformation of global politics. We have provided one example of what such an analysis might look like. We will now go on to argue that the categories employed in the UN development discourse and their associated governmental rationalities find expression in the ways in which those targeted by such power relate to and respond to it. Directing the analytical focus toward the rationalities of governing, as opposed to order, enables us to offer a different take on the theme of "balancing" in international politics. The mechanisms of balancing in global politics will then appear as *internal* to the rationality by which power is applied, as expressed through specific forms of governmental practices.

3 | Governing a Great Power: Russia's Oddness Reconsidered

We have argued that governmentality may be used as a full-fledged perspective from which to analyze global politics, and juxtaposed it to traditional perspectives, which share a starting point in taking the state as the basic unit and the states system as the basic structure (chap. 2). If the governmentality perspective is to complement state-based perspectives, however, then we need to tackle the question as to what kind of status should be conferred on the state. Barry Hindess (cf. esp. 2000, 2002) points out that if we understand government in its broadest sense as structuring "the possible field of action of others" (Foucault 1994d, 341), then the modern system of states could also be seen as a discursive field, with its own rationality of government. In his 1978 lectures in *Security, Territory, Population,* Foucault explicitly mentioned the 1815 Congress of Vienna as the moment when a rationality crystallized whereby

> there will be imbalance if within the European equilibrium there is a state, not my state, with bad police. Consequently, one must see to it that there is good police, even in other states. European equilibrium begins to function as a sort of inter-state police or as right. European equilibrium gives the set of states the right to see to it that there is good police in each state. (2007, 315)

We feel that this tension between governance within "my state" and other states may be traced back to the self-reflectiveness that characterizes governmentality, as noted at the end of chapter 1. If it is only necessity, and not the rationality of governance as such, that makes "my state" the object of governance, then other states, "the foreign," are potentially an object of governance as well. In this chapter, we trace how the emerging rationality of governmentality dealt with one state that came out of another tradition of rule: Russia. We specify the practices that made for such "bad police" and the practices that were, and are, at a premium within the system of states. This we do by examining one kind of resultant classification, namely, hierarchy. On what grounds are some states accorded status as great powers?

There are two traditional views on this issue. For realists, great powers are states that can project military power. For the more geoeconomically minded realists, this status accrues as much from economic as from military power. For constructivists, by contrast, great-power status is fundamentally a question of recognition grounded in intersubjectively shared norms and values. Through all this runs an ambiguity as to whether great-power status is systemic or specific to the particular state in question.

The case of Russia is interesting here. In the eighteenth century, it was not recognized by other European states as a great power, despite its military and economic might. This suggests a constructivist reading, where Russia's lack of conformity to the norms and values of the European state system—its "semibarbarian" character—explains why it was not considered on a par with other great powers. Historical investigation reveals, however, that this reading is underspecified, in that it matters a great deal whether the norms and values to which conformity is demanded by others concern the practice of diplomacy, the conduct of warfare, or, as we will suggest, regime type. Russia was considered uncivilized primarily because it had failed to follow the liberal trend of a separation of state and society that developed in Western Europe in the seventeenth and especially the eighteenth centuries. Russia remained committed to a type of governing where the concept of society as being made up of individuals with rights and a degree of autonomy did not figure prominently. Instead, the governing logic of the police state held sway, where the application of power was focused on control and direct regulation of territory rather than as conduct and indirect rule aimed at increasing wealth in society. This feature of the Russian polity was regarded by other nations as a source of uncertainty and instability—as a sign that, if Russia should be given great-power rights and obligations, that would have to be out of necessity and based on fear rather than recognition. By specifying the claim about norm-conformity as concerning the essential characteristics of the internal logic of governing and the organization of the polity, we unearth a neglected yet central dimension of how great-power status is accorded to some states and not to others. This we do by seeing governmentality as a phenomenon on the level of global politics, with states as one of its constitutive types of polity, and thus as one type of agent whose conduct may be conducted. States are subject to what is at any given time considered to be "normal" for members of the system of states.

What Makes Powers Great? System? Materiality? Culture?

Before we can analyze the *sources* of great powerhood, we need to identify the key *functions* ascribed to great powers in the literature. As noted by Christian Reus-Smit (1999), hierarchy was present in the European states system from its very beginning. Reference was made to powers being of different ranks. Craig and George (1990, 3, 22) note that the term *great power* became a part of the "general political vocabulary" at the time of the Seven Years' War (1756–63), and that it was considered "normal and right" that there should be five great powers at this time. Vattel's classic definition, a power that can stand up to any combination of others, dates from this time.[1] Ranke's celebrated essay on the matter encapsulates the views of the German *Machtschule*. It was so dominant throughout the nineteenth century that we would argue that *great power* remained a word as opposed to a concept to its very end.[2] To Ranke as to most statesmen, great powers were states that by dint of their economic and military might were able to maintain a sphere of influence where other great powers gave them a *droit de regard*. To Ranke, it was not in question who these powers were: they were the ones who took it upon themselves to sit in all the committees that laid out the future of the European state system at the Congress of Vienna. Those who were allowed participation in only some of the committees were middle powers, and those who were not represented at all were small powers.

To Kenneth Waltz (1979) and other neorealists, the key characteristic of the existing international system is that, similarly to the way the system of the market produces functionally similar firms, it produces units that are functionally equivalent. These units are now nation-states, and they

---

1. For context, see Hurrell 1996.
2. A word may have many meanings, but it is clear from the context which meaning is invoked; with a concept, this is underdetermined by context, leaving room for ambiguity and negotiation.

differ in only one aspect: their power resources. Some states are greater than others, and this greatness may be explained by the characteristics of the system itself, which differentiates between its units only at this level. Greatness is therefore a systemic characteristic. It has nothing to do with intersubjectivity or recognition, which should be treated as questions of foreign policy.[3] Waltz's structural-functionalist analysis is strikingly similar to the kind of work carried out by, for example, Radcliffe-Brown in social anthropology, and Talcott Parsons in sociology (cf. Goddard and Nexon 2006). Their work dominated much of the social sciences up to the early 1960s. The key similarity is that the focus is on the social understood as structural traits of the system itself, what is often called "social organization." Waltz and Parsons are at one, furthermore, in how they relate to work with a cultural focus. To Parsons, such work was interesting and perfectly legitimate, as long as it was not inscribed at the center of professional sociology.[4] Similarly, fifty years later, Waltz and his fellow neorealists in IR do not acknowledge that culturally informed work has any systemically relevant business in the discipline of IR.

Hedley Bull's work on great powers is notable for retaining realist insights into the intersubjective nature of the category of great powers in the teeth of neorealism. To Bull, the existence of a category of states that are recognized as "great powers" and that consciously act in such a capacity is one of five institutions that constitute an international society. Certainly, Bull notes, with reference to sixteenth- and seventeenth-century politics, the pretense of the Habsburgs to be a universal monarchy was a relative claim, and the struggle waged by other powers against Philip II involved various discussions about hierarchy. However, "this was a hierarchy determined by the status and precedent of the receding universal society [of the Middle Ages], and not by considerations of relative power . . . or of the special rights and duties accorded to certain powers by the society of states at large" (1977, 33). To Bull, there ensued a process of rationalization and abstraction whereby it was states led by kings that were to be compared and that, as a result of such comparisons, could be "great" or otherwise—whereas formerly, the focus of such comparisons had been kings as such. The crucial question, then, becomes exactly what is to be compared. To

---

3. The discussion of which Waltz relegated to another and, unfortunately, rather less well-known work (1967).

4. Parsons argued that culture should be the domain of anthropology. Indeed, according to Adam Kuper (2000), this leading American sociologist of his day saw it as one of his crowning achievements that he was able to draw up a mutual manifesto with the leading American anthropologist, where they divided work between themselves according to these very principles.

Bull, it is "relative power," where power is understood in material and rational terms. This power may be traced in what to him were their effects: who was recognized as having a *droit de regard* in relation to a certain question of policy (such as a territorial disposition), who was empowered to make decisions with a bearing on international law (such as signing a treaty), and so forth.

Bull's argument is ambiguous, however. A great power may be great *either* because of its structural characteristics, *or* because of its status. Bull insists on a break between the standards of the emerging system of states and the situation that existed prior to that. To Bull, that shift is characterized by comparisons of factors pertaining to "the status and precedent of the receding universal society" losing their relevance, and comparisons of relative power taking their place. On the other hand, on the strength of Bull's own text it is also possible to argue that questions of status and precedent did *not* lose their relevance when it came to determining which states were in and which were out, which states were great and which small. Nor is this ambiguity unique to the work of Bull. For Weber, military and economic factors were decisive for great-power status. Yet here, too, cultural factors emerge as central. As Weber noted, "There is a close connection between the prestige of culture and the prestige of power" (1968, I, 448n6). Seeing a great power as intersubjectively constituted by the actors of a system is a very different thing from seeing it as structurally constituted by the states system. Since Weber's usage was ostensibly in line with the meaning commonly ascribed to the term *great power,* however, this seems to have gone unnoticed at the time.

The literature also includes a fully worked out constructivist argument, where the cultural factors and intersubjective meaning that lurk in Bull's argument take center stage. Christian Reus-Smit's study (1999; also see 1997) of the constitutive principles of systems of states solves the tension in Bull as to whether international society is functionally or intersubjectively determined, by doing away with the former elements and privileging the latter. This leads him to dispute Bull's claim that universal claims were a pre-Westphalian phenomenon that disappeared as international society took shape. To Reus-Smit, such claims remain among the constitutive principles of international society up to the time of the Napoleonic Wars. This is key to his understanding of great powers, for it explains the formation of the category.

> The general assumption that sovereign states differed in status, and the preoccupation with preeminence and precedence this generated, gave

old diplomacy a distinctly hierarchical character.... Toward the end of the absolutist period, this concern with standing was secularized, gradually transmutating into the idea that there were "Great Powers," endowed with special rights and obligations in international society. (1999, 109)

Note the overlap with how the state theorists that serve as raw material for Foucault's formulation of governmentality wrote about governance, and how they, too, wrote about how good governance could outweigh the sheer existence of resources. Foucault gives as one of his examples Frederick the Great's book *Anti-Machiavel*.

He [Frederick] says, for instance, let us compare Holland with Russia: Russia may have the largest territory of any European state, but it is mostly made up of swamps, forests, and deserts, and is inhabited by miserable groups of people totally destitute of activity and industry; if one takes Holland, on the other hand, with its tiny territory, again mostly marshland, we find that it nevertheless possesses such a population, such wealth, such commercial activity, and such a fleet as to make it an important European state, something that Russia is only beginning to become. To govern, then, means to govern things. ([1978] 2002b, 209–10)

And governing things, Foucault underlines, means orchestrating the human relations that set things in motion. Where IR realists emphasize resources and materiality, the governmentality perspective stresses the relations that put resources to work: not the social as static order but as dynamic governance. So there is in IR theory a bifurcation in how great powers are conceptualized. The question asked is what *great powers* are. The answer is, on the one hand, that they are simply greater in terms of the relative resources they can bring to bear on interaction with other states; and, on the other hand, that they are somehow prestigious due to some superior moral quality. The question asked in the scholarly debate about great powers is what kind of *justification* states muster when they negotiate greatness. If we look at this debate through the lens of governmentality, however, we find that the question is itself internal to diplomatic practice and cannot give us any outside analytical purchase on the question beyond hermeneutical understanding. In a governmentality perspective, when one asks where the prestige of great powers comes from, the answer would be the character of the polity. It is the regime type that renders substantive the views and perceptions of what is to be regarded as a great power. It is a question that is not internal to the system of states but that resides in the wider social realm. But if so, then the category of great power is social rather than systemic.[5] It is dependent on something intersubjective, outside of the direct grasp of any one sovereign.

An Underlying Factor: Civilization and Governance

The importance of the social realm to the question of greatness becomes evident when we scrutinize the concept of prestige itself. In both IR and social theory classifications, a distinction is made between quantity and quality. Prestige is something more than overwhelming force: it has to do with morals and ethics, with the social practices that constitute the political entity in question and how these are assessed on ethical grounds. The concept that has been used for this overall phenomenon in European tradition for the past two centuries is civilization. Within the IR literature, civilization has generally been a concern to scholars discussing the existence of a formal standard of civilization in international law (e.g., Gong 1984).[6] In social theory, it has been a concern of historical philosophy (e.g., Elias 1982). There appears to have been little theorizing about how civilization is tied up with great-power prestige. It seems to us, however, that there exists a rich literature on the question under a different heading: that of *regime type*. From the earliest Russian–European contacts, Russia's system of rule was seen as being despotic. Throughout the nineteenth and twentieth centuries, it was seen as authoritarian or even totalitarian. Parallel to the discourse on great powers—and we have in mind both the conversation between states and the analytics of that conversations here—there exists a rich and continuous discourse on the broader issues surrounding the key political question of how Russia orders the relationship between the one and the many. In keeping with the idea that the international and the domestic are two distinct realms of politics, these two discourses seem to have become disconnected, and we would suggest that

---

5. This is of key interest, for, as we will discuss at greater length in the conclusion to this book, Waltz defines *sovereignty* as the ability to take or leave stuff that resides outside of the sovereign's realm. This definition is fine in functional terms, but it cannot account for recognition. If recognition is at the heart of being a great power, then it cannot account for what a great power is, since this is an intersubjective and thus a social phenomenon. Here we reach an impasse, however, for Waltz would simply argue that his structural-functionalist analysis does not pertain to the social; cf. Goddard and Nexon 2005.

6. An IR literature on civilization in the broader sense is, however, emerging; for central examples, see Salter 2002; O'Hagan 2002; Jackson 2006; Hall and Jackson 2007; Bowden 2009.

the discourse of great powers has been embedded in the wider discourse of regime type. The distinction made in the analytics of state conversations has blinded us as analysts to the fact that the conversations between states themselves turned not only on the general questions of despotism and civilization, but, to a considerable degree, on the specific question of regime type. Here we have an underlying factor that may account for the unexplained aspects of great powerhood left by realist and constructivist readings. A power may also count as "great" by governing in a way that others see as enviable.

As did several of the analysts surveyed above, Durkheim touches on the questions of rule and governance in his treatment of great powers, without making it his explicit focus. He argues that greatness may be secured simply by setting an example—and that is a problematic position to take. As contemporary Sweden has shown, it is fully possible to share the moral purpose of a system without being among the great powers of that system.[7] It is a necessary, albeit not sufficient, prerequisite that the power in question have the material resources to socialize others into its system of governance. Once that is accomplished, however, the afterglow of superior governance may outlast superiority in resources. Consider the case of the final centuries of the East Roman or Byzantine Empire. Oikonomides (1992, 74) describes the most striking point about its relations with other powers.

> In the fourteenth century as well as the thirteenth, for all its increasing weakness, Byzantium acted as if it was still a great power of the past. Moreover—and this is even more interesting—other powers seemed to ignore reality and to accord the Byzantine ruler a special status: he was seen as the emperor par excellence, the head of a state that used to be a basic fixed point of European politics over past centuries.

It is Oikonomides that ignores reality here, not the polities in the vicinity of the Byzantine Empire. Those entities owned the legal systems that constituted them and increased their capacity to rule to the Byzantines.[8] To stick to the metaphor of the day, Byzantium was the father's house, and the state households (or, in the Greek of the Byzantines, the "economies")

---

7. The title of a book written at the behest of the Swedish state by Samuelsson (1968), *From Great Power to Welfare State: 300 Years of Swedish Social Development,* is therefore highly suggestive in more ways than one.

8. Rule, not govern; governmentality is a rationality that characterizes distinctively modern forms of political rule or government. The Byzantines did not have the means by which to govern individuals from afar in any detail. See Foucault 2000a.

of the other polities were the houses of the sons or, at best and rarely, of the brothers. And the sons looked to their father with respect, even in his dotage. If this example has limited analytical value, it is because the not-so-great powers themselves quickly came to shed their original governing structures. The process whereby the European states system became worldwide was not so clear-cut. Beginning with Turkey and Russia, European rulers came up against powers that claimed superiority or parity for their own and different governing structures. Perhaps it was the lack of social power to get these governing structures accepted that accounts for Russia's problems in being recognized as a great power.

The Case of Russia and a Different Logic of Recognition

For Russia, the emergence of governmentalized states to the west posed a problem from the very start. As noted in chapter 1, until the end of the eighteenth century, the face of governmentality was the illiberal rules-and-regulations face of police. Russia reacted by copying this rationality of government (Raeff 1983). Once the face of governmentality changed to a liberal way of governing indirectly, however, it involved renouncing certain direct means of ruling. This in Russia was seen as a potential threat to the standing of the sovereign (rather than, e.g., as an opportunity for the sovereign to increase his reach). In analytical terms, the Russian state, whose system of government thus became less effective and less efficient than those of other nineteenth-century European states, incurred a relative disadvantage. As regime type was a key criterion for gauging how heavily a certain polity weighed in the scales of civilization, the resultant widening discrepancy between Russia and the great powers was of major importance for Russia and its claim to being a great power.

In the standard work on early contacts between Russia and Europe, Marshall Poe (2000, 12–13) notes, "Despite the lore of a long scholarly tradition, Russia was not 'discovered' by Europeans in the first quarter of the sixteenth century," when early travelers like Sigismund von Herberstein arrived, for there had been continuous contact between the east Slavs and the political entities around the Baltic since Viking times, as well as more scattered contacts with the Continental powers. Poe also stresses, however, that "Muscovites knew little or nothing about 'refined' European customs before the early sixteenth century" (2000, 209–10). As we shall see in some detail, the absence of a common body of practices for official encounters is in itself a telling description of Russia's relation to the states of the emerging European system of states. The early formal contacts between Russia and European counterparts were not without problems. In 1486, a noble knight by the name of Nikolai Poppel arrived in Moscow, carrying a letter from the Holy Roman Emperor Frederick III (Karamzin [1818–24] 1998). The Holy Roman Empire came to know Muscovy as a polity separate from the Polish-Lithuanian state. Upon Poppel's return to the empire, he started to spread the word about the Russian state and about the riches and power of its ruler. Here is the official Soviet diplomatic history version of what ensued.

> In 1489, Poppel returned to Moscow, now already as the official agent of the Emperor of the Holy Roman empire. In a secret audience he suggested to Ivan III that he should petition the Emperor to confer upon him the title of king. From the point of view of Western European political thought, this would be the only means of legalising a new state and introducing it into the the common system of European states—while at the same time placing it in a certain state of dependence on the empire. But in Moscow, another point of view held sway. Ivan III answered Poppel with dignity: "By God's grace, we are the ruler of our land from the beginning, from the first of our ancestors, it has been given us by God, and as it was for our ancestors, so it is for us." (Zorin et al. 1959, 262)

Ivan III insisted on signing his written answer to the emperor with the title "Great ruler of all of Rus' by God's grace," and for the next three generations, there ensued a tug-of-war between Russian and Western courts regarding titles. Already in 1508, Ivan's son Vasiliy sent a letter to the emperor requesting an alliance in his war against Lithuania. In 1514 the emperor, somewhat belatedly, sent his envoy Georg Schnitzenpaumer back with an encouraging letter, written in German. Instead of *Tsar*, he wrote *Kaiser*. *Kaiser* may be translated into Russian as *Imperator*, and so the letter was taken by the Russian court to mean that the emperor acknowledged Vasiliy as a fellow emperor. In Maximilian's letter of August 4, 1514, however, where he confirmed an alliance against King Sigismund of Lithuania, there was no mention of the Russian ruler being a "Kaiser."

Russia was not satisfied in its quest for recognition as an empire. Of course, further to the west, there were also monarchs who struggled to establish themselves on a par with the Holy Roman Emperor. For example, under Henry VIII, England launched a campaign to be seen as an empire. The Russian trajectory differs from the others in two key ways, however.

First, the shift from seeing the king's body to seeing the territory of his state as the locus of government that we may note in England already in the sixteenth century (empire, not emperor) was deliberately held back. Russia remained very much the domain of its emperor. Second, the broad historical thrust away from thinking about polities in terms of emperors and empires, and toward thinking of them in terms of sovereigns and states, came late to Russia. Since Russia continued to pursue a policy rooted in a social reality that it no longer shared with its western neighbors, a situation ensued where Russia kept on playing the old game long after others had embarked on a new one.

Contacts were also hampered by cultural practices. For example, Herberstein noted that non-Orthodox Christians were considered unclean. This meant that rank-and-file Muscovites had a reason to stay away from them, and that the aristocrats who did meet with them, and followed the European custom of shaking hands, ritually washed themselves after the encounter. As late as the 1660s, when several European diplomats, soldiers, and merchants had been invited to the realm, a key observer spoke of their separate quarters as "the diseased parts of the state and the body politic," and it was only during this decade that ambassadors were allowed to walk the streets of Moscow. Poe (2000, 41) emphasizes, "Nonetheless, the Russian authorities realized that diplomacy and mercantile relations with European powers were necessary accoutrements of great power status." From the very beginning, then, it was a bone of contention between Russian and European rulers where in the hierarchy Russia should fit in—with Russia in principle aiming for a top position.

Invariably, the Russian hosts exposed would-be embassies to much more direct tactics of impression management than those that regulated similar occasions within Roman Christendom. Under the chapter heading "Legatus ad Moscoviam," Poe (2000, 40) notes, "Muscovite officials were quite suspicious of foreign envoys and thus took steps to ensure that they did not learn too much about Russian affairs or receive the 'wrong' impression of the tsar's realm. Accordingly, visiting ambassadors were kept in special quarters, surrounded by officially appointed attendants, and discouraged from wandering about or engaging Muscovites in discussions. Moreover, the court presented visiting diplomats with a variety of propagandistic rituals designed to emphasize the authority of the tsar, the wealth of the realm, and the subservience of the population."

For the next two hundred years—the gestation period for the European system of state—Russia remained a peripheral presence. Its resources were not plentiful enough to make it a presence on the Continent, so there was no rationalist case for great-power status here. Constructivists would emphasize that the principle on which legitimacy and recognition were sought—divine kingly sovereignty over territory—was the same, and draw attention to the doubt that ensued on both sides as to whether the other party could be considered "properly Christian." We highlight how Russia's despotic regime marked it as "barbarous." Either way, although Russia made a principled bid for great-power status, as seen from Europe, it was not a ranking power by any criterion used at the time, or indeed later. On the other hand, there were cultural and organizational borrowings during this period, and these were speeded up and diversified under Tsar Alexei (1645–76), but it was not until the reign of his son Peter that Russia undertook a deliberate process toward European socialization. After a short lag when the War of the Spanish Succession ended with the drawing up of with the Treaty of Utrecht in 1713, and Russia was not among the signatory powers, Peter launched a campaign for Russian great powerhood.

Powerful but Different

In 1613, Michael was elected tsar and initiated the Romanov dynasty. His administrative apparatus was rudimentary. Business was handled mainly by a set of *prikazy* or chancelleries, and decisions were mostly taken in the tsar's privy council. A representative council, the boyar *duma,* met on a regular basis, and the *zemskiy sobor* met from time to time. Although the basic structure of the system—a political tension between the tsar and the nobles, an administrative tension between an apparatus consisting of offices and a group of councilors—was the same as that of the other polities around the Baltic, the action capacity of Muscovy was not up to their level. Still, Muscovy was a distinct presence. In 1617, the reestablished polity concluded the Peace of Stolbovo with Sweden, and Gustavus Adolphus withdrew from Pskov and Novgorod. Russia, on the other hand, lost its access to the Baltic coast. The Peace of Stolbovo was concluded with the offices of the Netherlands and England, and the latter's envoy was present at the proceedings (Zorin et al. 1959, 293). Russia's dealings with other powers had now become a matter of major interest to key states.

In 1618, Russia concluded an armistice with Poland. On the eve of the Thirty Years' War, which was to prove pivotal in melding the states around the Baltic and those further to the south more firmly into one system of states, Russia became established as a power. Both Gustavus Adolphus and the Porte put out feelers for alliances against the Poles. Russia took an active role in supporting one party against another, among other things by providing Denmark with subsidized grain. The principle of legitimacy at this time was dynastic, so it is clear that dynastic ties and patterns of intermarriage play a particularly important role when it comes to gauging how Russia fit into European political life. As part of Russia's early initial overtures to reach beyond the Baltic, an effort was made to forge ties with the Stuarts. As to the Baltic ties, the Romanovs tried to upgrade these through marriage. The first move by the Romanovs in this direction was made in 1642, when Tsar Michael

> sent a special mission to Denmark to offer the hand of his daughter Irene to the son of Christian IV, Prince Waldemar. The instructions given to the envoys in Moscow must have seemed more than a little strange in Copenhagen: a customary overture to such negotiations, the delivery of a portrait, was to be avoided with the explanation that the taking of portraits could be dangerous for the health of Russian princesses, who in any case were to be viewed whether in the flesh or in effigy by close relatives only. The possibility of Waldemar becoming one of the latter nearly foundered at the beginning over the more serious question of his determination to remain a Lutheran, and when he traveled to Moscow on the understanding that he would not have to convert to orthodoxy only to find his prospective father-in-law a fervent proselytiser, a stalemate ensued which kept the prince under close house arrest. (Dukes 1990, 13)

In the end, there was to be no wedding. What we see here is a court that does not conform to established norms for marriage, which has not partaken in the sixteenth-century process of establishing *cuius regio eius religio* as a baseline for getting religious pluralism to dovetail with the reality of multiple sovereignties, and which does not acknowledge freedom of movement for visiting royalty.

With the Thirty Years' War out of the way, the density of contacts between Muscovy and other polities increased. According to official Soviet historiography, "Beginning from the mid-seventeenth century onwards, Russia already played a most important role in the political life of Eastern Europe, so that no international problem could any longer be solved without her participation" (Zorin et al. 1959, 293). Even if this generalization is accepted, however, what was at stake at this time was no longer what had after the Thirty Years' War become the regional issue of Baltic politics, but the European-wide system of states. This is implicitly accepted two pages later, when an observation is made about the attempt of the empire to influence the course of what has been called the First Northern War between Russia and Poland: "[This] goes to show that the Russian–Polish conflict had at this time lost its local character and become a matter of all-European importance" (Zorin et al. 1959, 295).

Anisimov (1993, 23) concurs when he usefully sketches out a tripartite journey into international society: "The first step that Russia took into the Westphalian world of international relations was its participation in the First Northern War (1655–60), a step determined by the decision of 1654 on the subjugation of the Ukraine. The next step was taken in 1686 by the Eternal Peace with the Rech Pospolita [i.e., Poland-Lithuania]." This is due not only to the way both parties now largely proceeded to draw up this treaty according to the general standard of the day, but also because Russia at this time succeeded in its long struggle to form an alliance with key powers (with the empire, Venice, Brandenburg, and Poland-Lithuania against the Porte). The third step, Anisimov argues, was taken hot on the heels of Peter's Grand Embassy of 1697–98, when he grasped the potential of alliance with states that his predecessors had considered untouchable for religious reasons, for war against Sweden, Poland-Lithuania, and the Porte. His first attempt at playing the alliance game failed, however, and the ensuing war that was waged on the Porte was called to a halt at the Congress of Carlowitz (1698–99) without Russia being present (Anisimov 1993).

These three steps all concern Russia's maneuvering toward a more central role within what by the end of the century had become the Baltic subsystem of international society. However, these steps were not accompanied by increased recognition from the major polities that made up the embryonic international society. An early example of Russia being recognized as a factor in a European disposition, but not being recognized as having a *droit de regard,* is seen in Louis XIV's campaign to put Jan Sobieski on the throne of Poland-Lithuania. Poland, and particularly its Ukrainian part, was a key conduit between international society and Muscovy. In the late 1670s, Russian overtures to Poland and Austria for help against the Porte failed, and in 1681, Russia had to sign the humiliating treaty of Bakhchisarai. Already at this time, however, Russia could muster an army of perhaps as many as 200,000—six times as many as a half century earlier (Dukes 1990, 47). These forces were trained with the help of manuals translated from Western languages, by officers imported from the West. Translations were first undertaken in the second half of the seventeenth century, and military manuals were among the first to be translated. A characteristic lag is evident in the pattern in which the powerful new administrative ethos of neostoicism spread across Europe. In the standard work on the topic, Gerhard Oestreich mentions Russia in his entry on Poland, which is reproduced here in toto.

> We may gauge the enduring popularity of Lipsius in Poland by the chronological spread of the translations. Such popularity is not surprising, seeing that the Jesuit order had great influence over Polish education. As early as 1595 the *Politics* was translated by a secretary of King Sigismund III; a new edition came out in 1604. Only a year before the outbreak of the French Revolution a translation of the *Monita et exempla politica* appeared. This work was also translated into Russian in the eighteenth century. (1982, 102)

By the end of the seventeenth century, there were two particular areas in which Russia's distance from international society was still marked.[9] The first was its lack of permanent missions to other states. Russia seems to have decided to establish a permanent mission in Sweden in 1634, but that lasted for only one and a half years and was not renewed. Instead of permanent residencies, Russia fell back on a form of representation that has similarities with the ancient Greek *proxenos* system as well as with the present system of honorary consuls when, in 1660, the English citizen John Hebdon was given the title *comissarius* to England and the Netherlands. Russia's first full-fledged resident emissary was Vasiliy Tyapkin, who took up residency in Poland from 1673 to 1677. Once Peter was on the throne, permanent missions became the rule. He sent an "extraordinary and plenipotentiary ambassador" to the Netherlands in 1699, a "resident" to Sweden in 1700, a "minister" to Vienna in 1701, and so on (Zorin et al. 1959, 344). Peter encouraged the European powers to establish permanent representations in St. Petersburg, and he himself established such missions in Paris, London, Berlin, Vienna, Dresden, Stockholm, Copenhagen, and Hamburg (Dukes 1990, 105).

The second area where cultural differences were considerable concerned the intense jealousy with which Russia guarded court procedures, both as host and as guest. In an age marked by elaborate and hierarchical court rituals, Russia was remarkable for the tenacity with which it con-

---

9. The following paragraphs are based on Zorin et al. 1959, except where otherwise indicated.

trolled every conceivable aspect of meetings between the tsar and foreign envoys and the display of hierarchy. This would begin already at the border, where an emissary would be met and escorted to the capital. Once on Russian soil, he would be presented with liberal amounts of food and drink (*korm*)—which, incidentally, made for a problem in terms of reciprocity when this style of treating foreign envoys gradually changed in the West. On reaching the capital, the visitor would be paraded in by an infantry escort; music was played, and people would throng the streets. However, no formal contact between the visiting envoy and Russians was allowed to ensue before the envoy had been received by the tsar. It was the order of the day that each visiting diplomat was ranked according to the perceived importance of the court that he represented. However, the Russian tsar was extremely cautious in his use of the term *brother* to refer to other monarchs. On occasion he would receive only the envoys of the most powerful states, leaving it to the diplomatic chancellery to take care of the rest. The Vasa kings of Sweden were held to be particularly lowly, of the order of vassals, and in the early years the tsar tried to put an end to direct contact and channel relations through the envoy from Novgorod. The discriminatory practice of receiving only what were held to be representatives of the most powerful states continued until the middle of the eighteenth century (see Zorin et al. 1959, 370).

To sum up, from its emergence in the late fifteenth century and throughout the seventeenth century, Russia considered itself great on transcendental and moral grounds: the tsar and, through him, his subjects enjoyed a superior kind of tie to the Almighty God. The problem was that this self-understanding was not shared by any other political entity. Russia's claim to being a power of the first rank (what would later be called a "great power") was noted but not taken seriously. Powers were ranked within a tightly scripted ritual-based system. Russia kept to other rituals and hence was simply not a player. Its material resources did not allow for much projection beyond its own borders, which meant that there were no other grounds to take cognizance of it, either. Russia was excluded on the grounds that its Christianity was alien (important even in the midst of severe Catholic–Protestant skirmishes) and that it was a despotate. In a historical epoch when governmentality was new, "difference" was a question of how the monarch related to his subjects, not of efficiency. And the European powers did not try to interfere with the system of rule in Russia. It was only with the Enlightenment that Russia's despotism would be characterized as "noncivilized" and be made an object of transformational attempts.

Peter's Century: Russia and the Other Anciens Régimes

Drawing on rationalist arguments, historians stress the role of the Great Northern War (1701–21) in establishing Russia as a central player in international society. Paul Kennedy (1988, 96) holds that Russia and Prussia added themselves to France, the Habsburg Empire, and Britain as great powers at the end of the Great Northern War; by 1721, "an exhausted, isolated Sweden finally had to admit to the loss of most of its Baltic provinces in the 1721 Peace of Nystad. It had now fallen to the second order of the powers, while Russia was in the first." Paul Dukes (1990, 112, 72) holds that Russia "joined Europe at the beginning of the eighteenth century" and that Poltava was "the cause of Russia's wider recognition throughout Europe." Official Soviet diplomatic history makes no specific comment here, but it nods indirectly in that direction by noting that, as Peter laid the plans for his Northern campaign, "the international situation in Europe seemed to be favorable for the realization of these plans. Western Europe's strongest powers—France, England, Austria and the Netherlands—were busy preparing for the War of the Spanish Succession and were not able to meddle in the struggle around the Baltics" (Zorin et al. 1959, 337). Anisimov argues, "The end of the Great Northern War in 1721 registered not only the collapse of Sweden as a great world power but the appearance in its place of a new empire, the Russian" (1993, 25).

It is clear that the reign of Peter the Great marked a tremendous upsurge in Russia's standing. Drawing on English diplomatic correspondence, Janet Hartley (2001) has shown just how quick and thorough was the change in other states' assessment of Russia. For example, on the eve of Peter's great embassy to the West, the English under-secretary of state in The Hague wrote to William Trumbull, secretary of state.

> Towards the end of the week we are to expect ye Empr & his Rabble here ... It were to be wishd the Czar loving ye Sea as he does, might discover ye North passage (if there be any such) into Persia, which would be a real advantage that would justify his ramble. (quoted in Hartley 2001, 54)

Hartley rightly observes, "Both during and after the Great Northern War, Britain attempted to restrain Russian ambitions through the formation of coalitions against her, which is itself indicative of a new respect for Russian power" (2001, 61–62). The leading eighteenth-century historian

Hans Bagger (1993, 36) even argued, "The Peace of Nystadt on 30 August 1721 confirmed the position that Russia had attained as a great power during the Great Northern War.... As a consequence of its new status as a great power, Russia became a European state insofar as the Russian Empire had to be incorporated into the system of European international relations." Bagger's point is that Russia's predominance in what was known as the equilibrium of the North, combined with its strength toward Austria and Turkey, was enough for it to "shake the overall equilibrium of Europe," and so "the courts of Europe could no longer ignore Russia as a semibarbarian state" but had to take it into account (1993, 36).[10] True, but neither Bagger nor anyone else has demonstrated that Russia had resources on a par with the key Continental powers (as opposed to Northern ones), or that it was an ever-present factor in the military calculations of those powers. On rationalist scores, doubt must remain about Russia's great powerhood in the early eighteenth century. For example, despite pleas from its Swedish ally, Lord Bolingbroke, who was secretary of state for the British Northern Department at the time, did not take Russia all that seriously; and Charles Whitworth, who had served as minister both in Russia and in Prussia, noted in internal correspondence in 1722, "The Czar may be a Bug-Bear to his Neighbors; But neither his Power, nor Designs can immediately affect Great Britain" (quoted in Hartley 2001, 64–65).

Furthermore, Bagger explicitly brackets how Russia was still classified as semibarbarian (as opposed to civilized) when he confers great-power status upon it. The tension identified by Bagger where Russia is concerned—between a clear military potential on the one hand and a lack of civilizational level on the other—mirrors the tension in IR theorizing of great powerhood established earlier. Furthermore, Bagger produces a quote from Russian vice-chancellor Peter Shafirov to demonstrate that Russian statesmen themselves perceived the situation in similar (if less pejorative) terms. Due to Peter's "transformation of Russia," Shafirov wrote, the European powers now sought out Russia as an ally, "despite the fact that a few decades ago, in the states of Europe people thought and wrote of the nation and state of Russia in the same way as they did of the Indian, Persian, and other nations [that had] no intercourse with Europe whatso-

---

10. The relevant compass orientations before the Napoleonic Wars were North and South. From the nineteenth century onward, an East–West division took over and has since often retroactively and mistakenly been ascribed to pre-Napoleonic times as well; see Neumann 1999.

ever, apart from a little trade" (quoted in Bagger 1993, 37; Shafirov 1973, 1–10). Shafirov, furthermore, was keenly aware of the limits beyond which Western recognition did not stretch.

> We know very well that the greater part of our neighbors view very unfavorably the good position in which it has pleased God to place us; that they would be delighted should an occasion present itself to imprison us once more in our earlier obscurity and that if they seek our alliance it is rather through fear and hate than through feelings of friendship. (Shafirov to a French colleague in 1721, here quoted from Dukes 1990, 77)

Shafirov's view was typical, and it bears out very well the limitations of material resources as a measure of great powerhood. Russia had the necessary resources and could prove itself in battle against an already recognized great power, but that was not sufficient to be recognized as a suitable alliance partner. It follows that, on constructivist criteria, where recognition is seen as intersubjective, it is impossible to accept the assessment held by so many historians, that Russia was acknowledged as a great power following the Great Northern War. When Peter celebrated his victory in 1721 by taking the title *emperor* (*Imperator*, referring to the Schnitzenpaumer correspondence as precedence), this was roundly resented, particularly by the Habsburgs (see Nekrasov 1972).[11] Although other Northern powers (except Poland) were relatively quick to acknowledge the new title, Continental powers waited until the 1740s.

An added constructivist argument against Russian great-power status in the early eighteenth century concerns the key alliance-forming practice of the day. Despite active attempts, Russia did not succeed in intermarrying with the leading royal houses of its day, targeting instead other Northern powers. In 1724, Peter married off his daughter Anna Petrovna to the duke of Holstein-Gottorp on Swedish behest. In 1745, his second-eldest daughter Elizabeth received feelers from British throne pretender Charles Edward Stuart, but these came to naught. As late as at the end of the century, when the new Russian tsar, Paul, tried to marry off his daughter to the king of Sweden, the project still stranded on the issue of religion. On constructivist criteria, an initial assessment is that we should be wary about Russia's great-power status during the period of the anciens régimes.

During the sixty years following the Great Northern War, Russia grad-

---

11. There is a parallel here to reactions when Ivan III and IV declared themselves tsars.

ually had more success in being recognized as a worthwhile ally, a power entitled to participation in peace settlements and a power mentioned in treaties as a guarantor of the peace. Russia attended its first Peace Congress at Soissons in 1728–30 (Bagger 1993, 52). In 1732, Russia concluded an alliance with Prussia and Austria, codified in the Berlin Treaty. In the War of the Polish Succession, Russia, by dint inter alia of having fielded an army of some 30,000, was definitely a player. Russia was conspicuously absent from the peace settlement, however (Craig and George 1990, 24). But come the Seven Years' War (1756–63, with the part playing itself out overseas being known in the United States as the French and Indian Wars), Russia was a key player in the basic change in alliance patterns that precipitated the war. On the rationalist criterion of objective resources and systemwide reach, this is when Russia became a great power: "By the Seven Years' War the Russian army was the largest in Europe, the establishment aimed for at its commencement consisting of 162,430 men in field regiments, 74,548 garrison troops, 27,758 men in the *landmilitsiia*, 12,937 members of the corps of engineering and artillery, and 44,000 irregulars." The Seven Years' War seems to be an important turning point also in the sense that Russia apparently restrained its military campaign short of crushing Prussia in order to keep that state in a shape where it could continue to play an important part in the workings of the balance of Europe. Russia, in other words, had entered into the management of the state system to the extent of downplaying immediate interests for what were held to be more long-term ones. The Seven Years' War is also the period when the term *great powers* emerges. We have found no indication that the shift from speaking of *powers of the first rank* to using the term *great powers* is related to the tentative entry of Russia into the category, however.

During the following decades, Russia also fulfilled the added criterion of being not only a great power, but also a "great responsible" of the system—a factor seen as crucial by the so-called English school of International Relations. Applying it to Russia, Adam Watson (1985, 70) sees Empress Elizabeth's secret negotiations with the heads of France and Austria in 1760 as the crucial date. Certainly, by dint of the role Russia played in all three partitions of Poland, this criterion was firmly fulfilled by the end of the century. If the year 1760 marked an informal breakthrough, the Treaty of Teschen concluded in 1779 was a formal one, inasmuch as Russia became for the first time a guarantor power. The importance of Teschen has been underlined particularly by German historians such as Hellmann (1978) and Oestreich (1982).

Joseph tried to round off his Austrian territory by acquiring Bavaria and so to effect a notable shift of power within the Empire. Frederick opposed him; he appealed to Russia, who joined with France in guaranteeing the peace of Teschen, which ended the war of the Bavarian succession. In this way the great power of Eastern Europe became obliged to defend the *status quo* in the Empire. The rise of Russia had taken place in the eighteenth century: she had stood united with the imperial army of Prince Eugene on the Rhine in 1735, and in the Seven Years War she had fought to crush Prussia and plundered Berlin. From now on Russia was a card to be watched in the game for internal unity [of Austria]. (Oestreich 1982, 255)

Official Soviet diplomatic history emphasizes how Russia's convention with Turkey from 1783 as well as developments in the law of the sea gave Russia a practical role in the formation of international law—definitely another breakthrough in terms of managing the system (Zorin et al. 1959, 369). By the end of the century, Russia was a full-fledged participant in the formation of alliances. For example, in 1780, Russia was a member of the League of Armed Neutrality, which also counted Denmark and Portugal. Twenty years later, a successor was formed, now consisting of Russia, Denmark, Sweden, and Prussia. In 1800, the new Russian emperor Paul ordered the College of Foreign Affairs to draw up a comprehensive analysis of Russia's current standing and future prospects in terms of foreign policy. In the report, the college characterized Russia as "the world's leading power," a "Hercules," and so on (Bagger 1993, 60).

On realist criteria, there is no doubt that Russia was a great power by the end of the eighteenth century. On constructivist criteria as well, the socialization into the state system that had taken place would appear to have been strong enough for Russia to qualify. It is of the essence for understanding the full extent of Russia's socialization to add a governance point: that the opponents of Westernization slowly but surely also started to acquire a frame of reference and to borrow their arguments from Western models. For example, Russia's conservative rallying around the well-ordered police state was a rallying around a German model.[12] There remained no doubt about its Christian credentials, the principle of legitimacy was the same as in the other powers, dynastic intermarriages

---

12. Arguments for maintaining an oligarchic constitutionalism are actually another case in point: "In eighteenth-century Russia the meaning of the word *constitution* was different from the one that the reformist movement would give it in the nineteenth century. The term meant, in fact, political system, implying the strengthening of the autocratic regime" (Medushevskii 2001, 45).

had become common. How, then, should we account for the ubiquitous European complaints about Russia's lack of civility, and continuing doubts about the extent to which it should be considered to be "of Europe"? Russia was still not seen as weighing heavily in the scales of civilization, as when David Hume complained that "the two most civilized nations, the English and French, should be in decline; and the barbarians, the Goths and the Vandals of Germany and Russia, should be in power and renown" (quoted in Horn 1945, 18–19). Variants of this complaint were heard in other forms and in other arenas. For example, in 1804, the French ambassador Hédouville complained to his foreign minister Talleyrand, "There is no other foreign court where the diplomatic corps is less informed on political dispositions and proceedings than here" (quoted in Grimsted 1969, 19).

We may answer this question by turning away from the *problématique* of order and focusing on that of governing. For starters, against the relevance of Hédouville's complaint it could be argued that, during the Napoleonic Wars, France was busy producing anti-Russian propaganda. And here the key point is exactly how this was done. The execution of the propaganda campaign tells us something about how France thought it could play on prevailing representations of Russia in the rest of Europe in order to sway opinion against that power. The slogans used—"Scratch a Russian and find a Tatar" and "Europe has to be either Republican or Cossack" are prime examples—take their power from the perceived difference in political order, in regime type, between Europe and Russia (cf. Halperin 1987, ix; Neumann 1999, 88–94). At the heart of the matter is governing.

This allows us to highlight two factors. First, as underlined by Frederick the Great and other contemporary politicians, if regarded as a police state, Russia was less successful than others.[13] Its capacity for state action was less efficient and more limited. Hamilton and Langhorn (1995, 71) point out how Peter's reforms also embraced the state apparatus. A "new college of foreign affairs was established, and unlike some of Tsar Peter's reforms survived a period of near chaos after his death and grew to have 261 members at the accession of Catherine the Great in 1762. The college

---

13. But note that Medushevskii maintains that Peter's reform, itself inspired by Sweden and other Western states, "in its turn became the stereotype or principal reform model for Russia and some West European countries in the era of Enlightened Absolutism (the administrative reforms of Frederick the Great in Prussia, Joseph II in Austria, Catherine the Great in Russia, Struense[e]'s attempts at reform in Denmark). But Peter's model of modernization was most influential in the Orient" (Medushevskii 2001, 46). For an extended comparison of Russia and Prussia as police states, see Raeff 1983.

had a president, vice president, and two chancery councilors at its establishment, and during the eighteenth century steadily lost its responsibilities for internal provincial (also Central Asian) administration, ecclesiastical administration, for tax gathering, and for the postal system, which was separated in 1782" (cf. Meissner 1956). The result was that, as late as on the eve of the nineteenth century, "compared to the smaller and more efficient foreign offices of many other European powers, the Russian ministry counted on its rolls an extraordinary large number of officials, from those of higher ranks to clerks, codifiers, translators, and copyists. The exact number of men functioning at a given time is almost impossible to ascertain because the rolls listed many persons who rarely or never served" (Grimsted 1969, 26).

Second, the order-centered discussion of Russia so far has not taken notice of the eighteenth-century process discussed previously whereby, in Europe, societies emerged and states changed their way of handling societies, from being one of direct rule to one of indirect governance. In Europe, this period saw the gradual emergence of liberal forms of governing that replaced that of the police state, and society gradually replaced territory as the object of reference for governing. In degrees that grew weaker, the further east in Europe one moved from Britain, liberalism understood as concrete social practice firmed its grip. Russia eventually had to take cognizance of the change. In summing up the reign of Catherine the Great, Bruce Lincoln stresses how one cause of her social policy was that Russia's "status as a Great Power" imposed an imperative for civil peace, which again required heightened efficiency of the Russian administration. He then adds another factor: that a number of young Russian bureaucrats held that, to a Europe dominated by Enlightenment thinking, "the premodern military and fiscal concerns of Muscovite Tsars conformed poorly to the image of a Great Power that their sovereigns hoped to project. To be sure, Russia's military needs continued greater than ever, but, as a Great Power, she also must exhibit some proper concern for her citizens" (1982, 3, cf. 175).

Thus, a new ethos of what governing a state entailed was setting a new standard, not only for what a state had to be in order to be considered well-ordered, but also, and as a corollary, for which states should be considered great powers. Liberalism formulated an imperative whereby letting go of the state's direct control of society was becoming a necessity not only for reasons of efficiency (producing a surplus that could feed state needs, including a military capacity), but also and more fundamentally for reasons of conforming to a new Europe-wide standard of governance (the need to appear "normal"). Given the penchant of nineteenth-century European thought for seeing world history in terms of stages taking place in the same order and leading to the same goal, furthermore, the lack of normality was read more specifically as insufficiently rapid civilizational development.[14] Russia was a laggard learner and, in that sense, inferior.[15]

The Concert and Communist Periods

We need not pursue the case in the same detail where the post-Napoleonic period is concerned. At Vienna in 1815, Russia's role as great power became institutionalized. Only five powers were given the right to have ambassadors extraordinary and plenipotentiary, and Russia was among them. However, Russia experienced trouble with maintaining its great-power credentials throughout what Erik Hobsbawm calls the "long nineteenth century" (1789–1917), and this may be accounted for by the factor of governance. On the strength of realist criteria, after the Napoleonic Wars, Russia was the great power par excellence. Indeed, Vattel's definition was put to the test after the Vienna settlement, when all the other great powers allied against Russia in the Quadruple Alliance, and Russia held its own with ease. However, in relative terms, Russia's strength weakened throughout the nineteenth century. Realists cannot account for this without referring to the governance factor, which lay at the heart of Russia's increasing inability to match the growth in prosperity to be found elsewhere in Europe.

A constructivist reading of Russia's tenuous standing as a great power throughout the nineteenth century would highlight how, as the principle of legitimacy shifted toward popular sovereignty, Russia led the rearguard action on behalf of kingly sovereignty. Such an account would be as apposite to discussions of Russia's great-power credentials as is a rationalist

---

14. Note that the thinking in civilizational terms was not specific to liberalism but was representative of the entire nineteenth century.
15. Cf. Neumann 1999. Where the economic basis for great powerhood is concerned, there is a sharp division of opinion between historians regarding the eighteenth century. The traditional view is that Russia was lagging steadily behind, whereas the revisionist view sees this as a myth. Bagger (1999) stresses Russia's economic modernization and export surplus, and points out that domestic stagnation set in only in the 1830s. To the revisionists, the traditionalist view is a case of illegitimately projecting the undoubted backwardness of the nineteenth century onto the previous one. This debate shall not concern us further here. We simply note that consensus has it that, by the standards of the eighteenth century, Russia was not considered by the other powers to be efficient.

one. When Britain and France shifted their stance as to what should be the constitutive principles of international society, Russia's response was to insist on the role of God and the heavenly mandate for kingly rule. What continued to tie Europe's monarchs together, Tsar Alexander argued in 1815, was that they were brothers in Christ. His proposed Holy Alliance was clearly and explicitly embedded in such a discursive universe. However, the ensuing formal and informal reactions showed that these arguments had lost not only their obviousness but also some of their persuasiveness. Russia's failure to rally the other great powers of the Congress of Europe behind a program of policing Europe against regimes based on popular sovereignty demonstrates how the discrepancy in principle of legitimacy translated into inability to act in concert.

The result was continued questioning of Russia's standing as what was seen as a "European" or even a "civilized" nation. Grimsted (1969, 3) is correct in arguing that "Russia's stature as a great European power reached its zenith because the economic, social, and political developments which were to transform the European continent in the next hundred years had not, by 1800, separated Russia from Western Europe to the extent that would be so evident in the Crimean War at mid-century."

As a more liberal type of governing took hold domestically as well as between states and established itself as "normal," Russia once again became a laggard. Where governance between states is concerned, the Congress of Vienna had marked a breakthrough in international governance. It stabilized state boundaries between European states and insulated Europe from extra-European rivalries. Much in the same way as Adam Smith had conceived of political measures as preconditions for economies to thrive, international agreement demarcated specific areas (understood as state-contained societies) for states to govern. This changed the meaning of what it meant to be a great power. As Paul Schroeder puts it, the general principles of the Concert of Europe "protected the rights, interests, and equal status of the great powers above all, but they also committed these powers to the performance of certain duties connected with those rights—respect for treaties, noninterference in other states' internal affairs, willingness to participate in the Concert's decisions and actions, and a general observance of legality and restraint in their international actions" (1986, 12–13). It became harder and less legitimate to compensate for bad governance with territorial expansion in Europe. The three partitions of Poland and the resulting territorial aggrandizement of Russia, particularly after the third division, did not increase Russia's standing as a great power in the way similar aggrandizement would have done in the eighteenth century, and in the way rationalist argument would expect.

This is generally occluded by rationalist analyses, which often conclude that, in the period from the Vienna settlement to the Crimean War (1853–56), Russia was not only secure in its great powerhood, but was even preponderant. For example, William Wohlforth (1999, 21n30) holds that the Concert of Europe, as it operated in this period, was "based on a Russo-British cohegemony." Paul Schroeder disagrees, pointing out that:

> The common view that Russia enjoyed an enormous and growing power and prestige in Europe until the Crimean War broke the bubble is a great exaggeration. After 1815, Russia never was the arbiter of Europe or exercised the dominant influence in Germany that Catherine II or Paul I had enjoyed for a time, and the young Alexander I had aspired to. (1986, 10)

The point here is that underlying not only the growing gap in relative resources but also the gap in principle of legitimacy was a difference in governance. At the heart of Russia's troubles as a great power was its unwillingness and inability to change from a rationality of direct rule to a rationality of indirect governmentality. Consider Bruce Lincoln's argument.

> If Russia was to meet the challenge posed by the rapidly industrializing West, she, in turn, had to find some way to achieve greater administrative efficiency and instil into her middle- and upper-level officials a measure of support for change. Russia's bureaucrats had to become responsive to the needs of the nation they served, and some means had to be found to enable those few who were well informed about complex social and economic issues to gain input into the tsarist policy-making process. (1982, 6)

Lincoln painstakingly traces how this process unfolded in the middle of the nineteenth century, to culminate in the emancipation of the serfs in 1861 and sweeping judicial reforms directly and explicitly inspired by European models (cf. esp. 1982, 200). However, Russia's autocratic order put a clear limit to how such moves could be taken. If all power should in theory emanate from the tsar, bureaucracy would have to maintain the principle of direct control from above. Russia's politicians could not act independently. Neither was there any way in which they could function as aggregators of societal interests apart from the tsar, and so the economic strengthening of the emerging middle class could not find any direct political expression. "As a result, just when the new social and economic groups that comprised the middle class were eroding the power of absolutism in the West, it was strengthened in Russia."

There is broad consensus in the historical literature about the logic and importance of this process. In terms of state–society relations, the problem was that Russia simply did not have the social agents necessary to mediate between the state and the population at large—and that meant that a necessary precondition for indirect rule was lacking. Geyer puts it this way.

> As a result of the new attitudes forced on the government, the reform period witnessed the first flowering of political journalism in Russia.... A common thread to all the criticism was opposition to the bureaucratic machinery of the state and demands for self-government and "openness" (*glasnost'*). No consensus existed, however, on the question of who should be responsible for self-government in the districts and provinces: aristocrats "born" to mediate between the ruler and his people? owners of private property in their capacity as the most respectable group of citizens? the educated classes as the preceptors of the people and defenders of democratic rights? (1977, 27–28)

The state could not put any of these social groups to good use, so it was basically stuck with the state apparatus. Within this apparatus, however, the regime once again ran into the elite social forces that it was not able to harness for indirect rule. The regime's lack of ability to deploy its own apparatus effectively meant that direct rule was inefficient as well. As put by Dave Alan Rich (1998, 29), "Autocracy's constructed dynastic myth left little room for state professionals. Partnership with the rising ranks of experts who filled the central bureaucracy—and sharing of authority with them—were beyond its defining tropes." Rich's example is the Russian General Staff. The military leadership's response to the reforms of the 1860s was to embark on professionalization. They succeeded in setting up a solid planning operation, but implementation proved difficult, since the tsar and his immediate family sat at the top of the military hierarchy, from which they were able to stall the process. Having failed to circumvent the royal family, the General Staff simply gave up.

> Civilian political leaders, who had sought unification of policy in the Council of Ministers after 1905, ultimately found themselves hobbled by habits of insularity and by the supreme power, Tsar Nicholas II, who

thought government his personal possession. Professional bureaucrats, the experts whose authority might have insinuated interministerial political unity, instead settled into parochialism, and none more so than the technicians of the Russian general staff. In the end, professionals were not the potential saviors of autocracy and empire but virtual guarantors of their demise. (Rich 1998, 19)

Like his predecessors, Nicholas operated according to a rationality of government that saw the tsar as the head of the household. Etymologically, we can trace this in the Russian term for state, *gosudarstvo*, which translates loosely as the "holdings of the lord." The unwillingness to let the sovereign's documents count for more than the sovereign's whim, that is, the unwillingness to subsume leadership under the law, meant that Western-style bureaucratization was held back from the top. After the assassination of Alexander II in 1881, his son and successor passed a Statute of Exceptional Measures that gave one such body, the secret police, free rein over the sovereign's subjects. Zuckerman (1996, 13) concludes from a careful reading that "the political police by the mid-1880s already operated beyond the control of the regular bureaucracy." Since these measures remained in force until the October Revolution, one may indeed describe Russia as a "police state" in these years, but in a very different meaning from what sixteenth- and seventeenth-century Europeans had meant by *police*.

The bureaucracy tended to experience the delegation of power to ad hoc organs like the secret police and those organs' subsequent tendency to ignore the bureaucracy's instructions as a direct bind not only on their own power but also on the effectiveness of the state. This may be seen, for example, in the internal fight between the Ministry of Finance and the Ministry of the Interior over the development of labor movements. Up until 1903, when the *starosta* (elder) law allowing the choice of elders from among the workers to play a role as spokesmen, forming anything approaching even a proto-union had been illegal. The new law followed a failed attempt by Sergey Zubatov, head of the Moscow secret police, to construct police-controlled worker organizations. McDaniel (1988, 65) comments that "the Zubatov experiment was the closest the Russian state ever came to a corporatist policy of creating and coopting dependent organizations, a strategy that achieved notable successes from the standpoint of the authorities in numerous other countries."

In Russia, however, the Zubatov experiment could not work: the state was too aloof, the industrialists too weak, and the workers too unused to the give-and-take necessary for cooperative industrial relations to take hold. Again, the preconditions for indirect rule simply were not present. McDaniel stresses how autocracy's choice not to accommodate social groups was deliberate, quoting, for example, the soon-to-become internal minister hailing in 1902 "the complete independence of our government" (Sipyagin, quoted in McDaniel 1988, 58). However, he also traces the impulse to govern indirectly in this debate, for one of the express reasons why the Ministry of Finance wanted the *starosta* law in the first place was

> to reduce the role of the police in the factories as much as possible. The law had its origins in the request of factory inspectors that they be allowed "to summon worker deputies and talk with them" before the police intervened. The Ministry of Internal Affairs, they claimed, did not sufficiently recognize this duty of the factory inspectorate, and unfortunately all disorders were dealt with by the police. (McDaniel 1988, 90–91)

Of course, the spokesman for indirect rule (which in this case meant drawing on factory inspectors before sending in the police), the minister of finance, was a liberal (Witte), whereas the internal minister, who was inclined toward direct rule, was a conservative. The conservative was correct in his assumption that indirect rule would undermine the regime, and so he won the debate. It is, furthermore, wholly in keeping with a governmentality perspective that it is the Ministry of Finance that sought to further governance by indirect means, only to encounter vested interests from the wielder of a key resource of direct rule—the police. We may conclude that at least some Russian bureaucrats, as well as its few liberal politicians, shared the assessment of European statesmen concerning the weakness of the Russian state. They did not, however, draw the same conclusion, or at least not in the same degree: namely, that Russia did not meet the standards of civilization necessary to pass muster as a great power.

In terms of governmentality, these studies may be generalized in ways that give them analytical purchase also today. Consider, for example, Moshe Lewin's (1987) reading of Russia's inability to reform. Throughout the nineteenth and twentieth centuries, Lewin argues, the Russian state would perceive the situation as one where Russia was losing out to Western competitors due to the relatively low productivity of its enterprises. In reaction, the Russian (or Soviet) state would ease its direct control of enterprises and encourage them to increase their own initiative. The enterprises would go ahead and do so, and then, at some point, their very success would generate demands on the state—in the form of pressure for different systems and degrees of taxation, for new legislation, for a say in decision making, and so forth. The state would not consider itself able to answer these demands without systemwide change, and would respond by simply putting an end to reforms. In a governmental perspective, this process is readily defined as one of the state refusing to accept a change away from a logic of direct rule, toward a logic of indirect governance. Society is not allowed to exist as an institutional and hence nontransparent reality. As seen from Europe, Russia clung to an outmoded and inefficient mode of state power that made it appear anything but great. Lincoln describes the result as follows.

> By 1856, the political ideologies of the West stood in unflinching, hostile array against those very precepts and institutions of autocracy that Alexander II was sworn to defend and to which the enlightened bureaucrats were committed by necessity and conviction. Europeans unhesitatingly saw in Russian autocracy the personification of that tyranny they had fought to destroy in the revolutions of 1789, 1830, and 1848, and the survival of autocracy only strengthened some of them in their opposition to Russia's claims for recognition as a European power. (1982, 175)

The tsarist state's resistance to Western pressure for a change away from police-state rule toward liberal governance was to cost it its life. General rationalist debate about whether the balance of power should be conceived as a balance of capabilities or a balance of threats has its counterpart in the rationalist debate about whether great powerhood should be assessed in terms of material or perceptual indicators. For example, William Wohlforth (1987) shows how, in the decade leading up to World War I, policymakers were led astray by their trust in numbers, which made them grossly overestimate the power of Russia. Interestingly, the state that held that power to be the most modest was Russia itself. Since Wohlforth operates within the *problématique* of order, he rests content with demonstrating the discrepancy. A focus on governing suggests that Russia's more intimate knowledge of its own weakness in this regard can explain its modesty in overall assessment of its great powerhood.

As Wohlforth himself shows, furthermore, what led foreign observers astray was precisely their inability to appreciate the full importance of the state's tenuous hold on society for its international standing, and indeed for its survival. When, in the empire's final months, the tsar turned to the ambassadors of Russia's allies, who were also representatives of the most liberal states in the system, the stock answer was that the tsar should broaden the popular basis of his government. Despite the odds, he vehemently refused. After a short socialist interregnum, a communist regime was installed. In terms of resource base, the Soviet state quickly matched the level of resources once possessed by tsarist Russia. Rationalists may account for this by pointing to Soviet disinterest in managing the system, while constructivists may point to the different principle of legitimacy on which the communists operated. Similarly, they may produce complementary accounts of how the Soviet Union regained its great-power status after emerging victorious from World War II. But how can they account for the tenacity of the view of Russian leaders as "barbarians" (cf. Neumann 1999), and the matching uneasiness of the Soviet leaders toward what they at some level obviously saw as their more highly cultured counterparts? Consider, for example, how, in his memoirs, Nikita Khrushchev compared himself to a heroine of a popular play from the 1930s, Lyubov' Yarovaya, where little Dun'ka undertakes a trip to Europe. The expression "like Dun'ka in Europe" passed into everyday language, something like "as a country bumpkin in the big city." As Khrushchev wrote, "Dun'ka's travel to Europe was of consequence and went to show that we could deal with international matters even without Stalin's orders. To use a metaphor, in foreign policy we had thrown away the boy's shorts and donned the long trousers of the adult.... We felt our power" (1993, 78).

Maybe so, but how could they account for the insecurity obvious in the need to spell out that one feels one's power from the leader of a state that perceived itself and was perceived by the other powers in the system as having the military might of a great power? Fulfilling the criterion of having enough economic strength to uphold a military might that is great in relative terms appears as a necessary but insufficient criterion of great powerhood here. Comparing Khrushchev's view with that of Shafirov, which we established as typical of Russian self-understanding in this regard around 1721, we note a continuing Russian self-understanding as being seen by (other) European powers as inferior. In Lambsdorff and Khrushchev, at least, we also see that this understanding of Russia as inferior in some regards is shared by Russian leaders themselves. By inference, Russia's status as a great power has been continuously questioned, in Russian as well as in European discourse.

Post–Cold War

With the end of the Cold War and the demise of the Soviet Union, the question of Russia's standing as a great power came up once again, particularly in institutional loci like membership of the G7 (which became the G8 when Russia was admitted), the constitution of OSCE (whose importance tapered off as Russia's claims to great-power status in its proceedings were met by partial exit by other members) and—crucially—in NATO.[16] Although there have been no explicit references to a "standard of civilization" regarding membership, claims about the cultural and political nature of the Alliance and the Cold War have always been part of NATO's narrative. In the founding treaty, the signatories had declared themselves "determined to safeguard the freedom, common heritage, and civilization of their peoples, founded upon principles of democracy, individual liberty, and the rule of law." Historically, however, they have usually been subordinated to a more narrowly "strategic" vision that identified security overwhelmingly with questions of the balance of military capabilities, exemplified in the 1967 Harmel report. In the post–Cold War period, these narratives achieved new prominence. Indeed, from about 1990, NATO documents begin to downgrade the focus on the military nature of security and on the solidarity of the Alliance in the face of an external Soviet threat. NATO was now increasingly represented as a cultural or civilizational entity whose basic identity and history should be understood less in terms of Cold War military balancing and more as the result of a deep, enduring, and profound cultural commonality (Wörner 1988, 1989).

Perhaps the clearest expression of this shift can be found in the narrative that has emerged concerning NATO's own history in relation to the Soviet Union. In secretary-general Manfred Wörner's 1991 assessment of the future of "The Atlantic Alliance in a New Era," for example, the role of the Soviet Union is drastically downplayed.

> The Treaty of Washington of 1949 nowhere mentions the Soviet Union but stresses instead the need for a permanent community of Western democracies to make each other stronger through cooperation, and to work for more peaceful international relations. The Alliance has played a major role in reconciling former adversaries, such as France and Germany, in counteracting neo-isolationism within the world's greatest power and in promoting new standards of consultation and cooperation among its members. All these elements would still have been fundamental to security and prosperity in Europe even in the absence of the post-war Soviet threat. (Wörner 1991, 5; cf. Hansen 1995)

NATO's London Declaration of July 1990 expressed a similar shift. In the

---

16. This section leans on Williams and Neumann 2000.

new context, the Allies declared, "We need to keep standing together, to extend the long peace we have enjoyed these past four decades. Yet our Alliance must be even more an agent of change. It can build the structures of a more united continent, supporting security and stability with the strength of our shared faith in democracy, the rights of the individual, and the peaceful resolution of disputes. We reaffirm that security and stability do not lie solely in the military dimension, and we intend to enhance the political component of our Alliance as provided for by *Article 2* of our Treaty" (NATO 1991, §2). Through this redescriptive logic, NATO was not rendered obsolete by the passing of the Cold War. Instead, the Alliance was now able to return to itself and to move purposefully into the new situation by building upon its true historic foundations. In 1991's "New Strategic Concept," for example, the problem of security is portrayed in the following terms.

> Risks to Allied security are less likely to result from calculated aggression against the territory of the Allies, but rather from the adverse consequences of instabilities that may arise from the serious economic, social, and political difficulties, including ethnic rivalries and territorial disputes, which are faced by many countries in central and eastern Europe. The tensions which may result, as long as they remain limited, should not directly threaten the security and territorial integrity of members of the Alliance. They could, however, lead to crises inimical to European stability and even to armed conflicts, which could involve outside powers or spill over into NATO countries, having direct effect on the security of the Alliance. (NATO 1991, §10)

The problem of security became defined largely as the emergence of specific cultural or civilizational structures. The previous understanding of the Alliance as one in which states join to meet a military threat had given way to a cultural understanding. As the military expression of a cultural or civilizational structure that exemplifies security in itself, it became possible to portray NATO as transcending the limits traditionally ascribed to alliances. However, NATO's new narrative had the power not only to represent the Alliance as a qualitatively new security community but also to define the roles that Russia could adopt in its evolving security relations with NATO, and how it was able to narrow drastically the field of politically viable options available to Russian policymakers. As early as October 28, 1992, President Yeltsin had upbraided his Foreign Ministry for having become too attached to precisely this rhetoric. "I see in our current efforts to formulate foreign policy," he argued, "the influence of an 'anti-imperialist syndrome.' We shy away from defending our own interests, apprehending that such actions would be criticized as imperialistic. But the only ideology the Foreign Ministry should follow is the defense of Russia's interests and Russia's security." However, articulating a vision of Russian "national interest" as the basis of its security policy was precisely the option that NATO's new narrative had effectively curtailed. The primary roles available to Moscow were two. If Russia wanted a constructive relationship with NATO, it would have to become an apprentice candidate for inclusion within the Western security community—a state that must be educated and socialized into the new order of which it may ultimately become a part. Conversely, if Russia should choose an oppositional stance, it would risk being cast as continuing in the countercivilizational, neoimperial role scripted for it by Western politicians and intellectuals. Given Western proclivities, both of the options available to Russia would cast its great-power standing in doubt.

Russian policy debates reflected both an understanding of there being a choice to be made, as well as considerable unease about that choice. The view that Russia was faced with a hard choice between two roles was held by several prominent spokespersons, including the Communist Party's principal thinker on foreign policy and the vice chairman of the Duma Committee on International Affairs, Aleksey Podberezkin. Indeed, Podberezkin's very point of departure was that a stark choice of foreign policy directions was being foisted upon Russia.

> The first holds that Russia's national security points out a separate path for the country.... Another approach is oriented towards bringing Western values to Russia and towards her joining "the family of civilized nations" at any price, because, as official policy tells us, there are no alternatives to this "joining." (1996, 86)

This view involved rejecting NATO and its Western civilizational mantle. A second option was to continue to promulgate the Gorbachevian argument that Russia's natural home was in Europe. A third option was to return to concepts of Russian national interest as a means of solving the problem of foreign policy in the absence of an accepted vision of Russian identity. As noted, in 1992 President Yeltsin had criticized the Foreign Ministry for being too tightly bound by the desire to avoid Russian policy being seen as "imperialist" and had called for a focus on the national interest as an antidote to just that problem. And indeed, Russia's foreign policy concept, published at the end of January 1993, reflected the ascendancy of this view. It argued that NATO's military goals remained basically unchanged. A similar shift to the language of "national interest" could be seen in direct Russian declarations on relations with NATO. By 1994, Kozyrev had shifted his position. While still holding that Russia would continue to proceed from its "principled position," that its "national and state interests in the world arena should be pursued through cooperation and not through confrontation," and that Russia and the West could work together because they were "bound together by basic democratic ideals," he also declared, "It should, however, be clear that a genuine partnership is an equal partnership. Our relations should be deprived of even the slightest hint of paternalism. . . . Partnership does not mean playing at give-away. It means, on the contrary, close cooperation based on respect for the interests of both sides" (Kosyrev 1994, 3). Indeed, no matter how a great power is understood, such equality is a prerequisite.

But this policy option also ran into dilemmas. To argue the national interest in such terms was inevitably to become open to the charge that Russia was reverting to its imperial past and that it represented a still dangerously unreconstructed state within an otherwise changed Europe. This situation left only one real option for those in Russia who did not want to give succor to the opponents of reform through opposition to NATO enlargement. That was to accept it, but on the best "national interest" terms possible, and within terms defined by the democratic community argument. The other options—either a nationalist-communist opposition that would severely damage relations with the West, or an untenable form of great power logic within the context of the OSCE—were simply not plausible paths of policy for those then in power in Russia.

The only remaining option was to fashion some kind of relationship with NATO initially by insisting on a central role in the Partnership for Peace. Russia certainly insisted, when the Partnership for Peace was introduced, that it would not let itself be treated as a country on a par with other nonmembers of NATO: it would require an arrangement qualitatively different from those offered to the other countries involved. This strategy was partially successful, inasmuch as it brought about a NATO–Russian charter, a NATO–Russian Joint Political Council, and an elaborate cooperation mechanism. But even this cannot be said to have been an unmitigated success because—significantly—there was also a Ukrainian–NATO charter and set of arrangements (Bukkvoll 1997). The result was a growing feeling of not being recognized as what Russia itself saw as a great power. Following its short war with Georgia in the autumn of 2008, Russia withdrew from the Joint Council (Pouliot 2010). The underlying tensions in NATO–Russian, and indeed Western–Russian, relations, we argue, are of a kind with previous historical tensions as outlined above, and revolve on differing understandings of what constitutes a great power.

Conclusion

From its emergence in the late fifteenth century and throughout the seventeenth century, Russia considered itself as "great" on transcendental and moral grounds. The problem was that this self-understanding was not shared by any other political entity. Russia's claim to great powerhood was taken note of but was not recognized. Russia was excluded on the grounds that its variety of Christianity was unacceptable, and that its system of rule was despotic. As Russia's ability to project power grew, epitomized by its victory over the top-ranking power of Sweden in 1721, European rulers came more directly up against Russian claims about parity or superiority to their own, and certainly different, governing structures. We have hypothesized that it was the lack of social power to get these governing structures accepted that accounts for Russia's lingering problems in gaining recognition as a great power. Symptomatic in this regard is Russian vice-chancellor Peter Shafirov's view that due to Peter the Great's "transformation of Russia," the European powers now sought out Russia as an ally, but that "if they seek our alliance it is rather through fear and hate than through feelings of friendship" (Shafirov to a French colleague in 1721, here quoted in Dukes 1990, 77).

During the eighteenth and nineteenth centuries, the Russian elite adopted various European social practices (marriage patterns, military procurement and deployment, diplomacy) and partook in the management of the state system in ways explicitly associated with great powers (being a guarantor power, participating in conferences, gaining a *droit de regard*). Still, doubt lingered in European capitals—and in some degree in Russia itself—about Russia's role as a great power.

Realists, who treat great powerhood as a matter of having and being able to project material and especially military power, may account for why Russia was increasingly recognized, but not for the lingering doubt. Constructivists, who take intersubjectivity seriously and emphasize the degree to which a power accepts confluence of norms, may explain some of the doubt. Their approach cannot, however, account for the lingering doubt in periods when Russia largely adhered to international norms. A reading that focuses on *regime types* and their representations by other powers can account for this. Interestingly, whereas this reading is something new in social theory and IR, a nontheorized prototype of it has been fairly prominent in the work of Russian historians (see Malia 1999; Hosking 2002). For example, Bruce Lincoln remarks, on Catherine the Great's reign, how one cause of her social policy was that Russia's status as a great power imposed an imperative for civil peace and a need to "exhibit some proper concern for her citizens" (1982, 3, cf. 175).

Liberal historians like Lincoln have produced analyses that dovetail nicely with the liberal reading of Russia among European statesmen during the nineteenth century and first half of the twentieth century, a reading that went on to become hegemonic as (neo-)liberalism established itself during the latter half of the twentieth century. Liberalism's hegemony was long in coming. From the seventeenth century onward, the new ethos of governing set new standards for what it meant to be a well-ordered state, but also for what it meant to be a great power. Liberalism formulated an imperative whereby letting go of the state's direct control of society was becoming a necessity not only for reasons of efficiency (producing a surplus that could feed state needs, including a military capacity), but also, and more fundamentally, for reasons of conforming to a new Europe-wide standard of governance (the need to appear "normal"). Given the penchant of nineteenth-century European thought for seeing world history in terms of stages taking place in the same order and leading to the same goal, this lack of normality was read more specifically as an insufficiently rapid civilizational development. Russia was a laggard learner and was, in that sense, inferior.

In a stimulating paper, Flemming Spidsboel-Hansen (2002, 384) has argued that "post-Soviet Russia essentially is confronted with the same basic challenge in the international arena as was Gorchakov"—meaning that in the same way that Gorchakov had to focus on rebuilding Russia's standing when he took over after the demise in the Crimean War in 1856, and that doing so involved consolidating domestically and gaining more visibility internationally, this was the challenge now facing Putin. From the very outset, Putin signaled that this was at the heart of his program, and he pursued policies that substantiated that program. After the events of September 11, 2001, the change in policy environment facilitated Putin's work, and Putin was quick to act on the new opportunities afforded him. As a result, Russia has had spectacular success in increasing its visibility. This is a precondition on the road to that explicit if elusive goal: to be recognized as a great power.

This analysis is not without bearings on the present-day situation. From the late 1980s, post-Soviet leaders themselves began to identify the root cause of their uneasiness toward the West in civilizational terms. A key slogan of the perestroika period was the need to "rejoin civilization"—which logically implied that the Soviet path had somehow led Russians away from it (Neumann 2005). With the fall of communism, the official Russian self-understanding of the Soviet past came to blame a mistaken system of governance for the lingering problems in what was frequently referred to as the "civilized world," for example, when Vladimir Putin addressed the nation at the millennium, he said that:

> Soviet power did not let the country develop a flourishing society which could be developing dynamically, with free people. First and foremost, the ideological approach to the economy made our country lag increasingly behind [*otstavanie*] the developed states. It is bitter to admit that for almost seven decades we traveled down a blind alley, which took us away from the main track of civilization.... The experience of the 1990s vividly shows that the genuine and efficient revival of our Fatherland cannot be brought about on Russian soil simply by dint of abstract models and schemata extracted from foreign textbooks. The mechanical copying of the experiences of other states will not bring progress.... Russia will not soon, if ever, be a replica of, say, the U.S. or Great Britain, where liberal values have deep-seated traditions. For us, the state, with its institutions and structures, always played an exclusively important role in the life of the country and its people. For the Russian [*rossiyanin*], a strong state is not an anomaly, not something with which he has to struggle, but, on the contrary, a source of and a guarantee for order, as well as the initiator and main moving force of any change. Contemporary Russian society does not mistake a strong and effective state for a totalitarian one.[17]

This may be read as a plea for recognition of great powerhood on new terms, with the model of governance that Russia pledges to implement at odds with key tenets of the liberal trend, where the question always is how the state may govern *less*. For Putin, the Russian state should rule in direct fashion, not govern from afar. Thus understood, Russia is, once again, developing a rationality of government that has firm precedents in Western Europe, but that has since been abandoned by West European states themselves. Seen from Western Europe and North America, then, Russia is once

---

17. For an analysis, see Neumann 2005.

again being rigged with a system of governance that jeopardizes its possible standing as a great power.

In order to account for why Russia has been seen to be a great power manqué even at the apex of its material power in the 1810s or 1940s, we need to look beyond the question of moral purpose, toward the concrete and underlying question of the degree to which Russian governance is compatible with the versions that dominate in global politics at any one given time. Even if Russia may currently be said to have adequate resources to count as a great power, for sharing in the management of the system and sharing a principle of legitimacy with other great powers (all of which may be in some doubt), the country's standing as a great power is still precarious due to its professed system of governance.

In the nineteenth century, in the wake of the French Revolution and the Napoleonic Wars, Russia decided to maintain an ancien régime while other European powers went for modernization. In the twentieth century, in the wake of World War I, Russia again parted ways with other European powers by trying to implement a socialist future while the others hung onto their bourgeois present. In the twenty-first century, while Europe appears set on a course of integration, Russia seems to be repeating its pattern by clinging to its sovereign present while others forge ahead and adopt practices of global governmentality. The problem is that this seems bound to entail a wide range of challenges of incompatibility. Russia's problem with being recognized as a great power is a social one. At its root is the question of relations between state and society. As seen from Europe, a great power cannot have state–society relations that differ too sharply from those predominant in European politics. In the final analysis, in order to achieve and maintain the status of a great power, social compatibility is needed. As long as a neoliberal rationality of government with a global reach holds sway, Russia's claim to great powerhood will remain fragile. In some degree, due to its resistance toward this rationality, Russia may even be seen as a fragile state, whose fragility is due to the inability of the state to govern by indirect means.

At the outset of this chapter, we made the point that the modern state emerged when prospective sovereigns consciously attempted to make it an object of governance. That left a residual, the "foreign" that could not be governed. As pointed out by Foucault himself, the "foreign," understood as other states, remained a potential challenge to good police in what he referred to as "my state," and so each state had an interest in how other states were governed. We saw an example of this in the way Frederick the Great criticized how Russia was ruled. The rationality of government made for a social balance of power between the states in the system. This *problématique* is still with us. Foucault needs updating on this point, however, for, as we will discuss in the remaining chapters, the governmental standard to which Russia and other states are held today no longer constitutes itself solely through practices of governance to be found at the level of any one particular state. There also exist genuinely global practices to which states are held. State politics, what used to be known as "domestic" politics, are now increasingly shaped by a globally constituted rationality of government. Thus, for a state like Russia, standing up to governmental practices has become a double challenge. It must still face the competitive pressure from practices from (other) great powers in the state system. In addition, it must increasingly try to withstand the pressure from global practices. In the conclusion to this book, we return to how, for smaller states like North Korea or Somalia, the stakes of this game have to do with not being categorized as a failed state, a rogue state, or the like. For Russia—which is, after all, able to muster more resources on its own—the stakes are more limited. First and foremost they concern the degree to which Russia will be recognized as a great power. Global governmentality works on and through states. Governmentality cannot work *through* a state before it has worked *on* it. Frederick the Great's view, that Russia is weak because it cannot govern efficiently, is still held by some politicians, and it works against acknowledging Russia as a great power. Given the increasing importance of governmental practices, if Russia continues to insist on not adopting any of these practices, the analysis in this chapter suggests that Russia is hardly likely to be seen as a great power and may even be seen as a fragile state.

4 | Nongovernmental Organizations: From Sovereignty to Liberal Governmentality

Studies of global governance were very much triggered by a related debate on the sources and effects of processes of globalization (Held and McGrew 2000; Hirst and Thompson 1996; Keohane and Milner 1996). Protoformulations about global governance-type networks and processes are found in regime theory (Holsti 1992; Krasner 1983).[1] For Oran Young (1994), for example, the vast number of international environmental regimes amount to an issue-specific "system of international governance." Moreover, studies of how transnational social movements and advocacy groups have advanced human rights norms and shaped state policy have contributed to the view of global politics as shaped by processes and networks of governance where nonstate actors play an increasingly powerful role (Boli and Thomas 1999; Keck and Sikkink 1998; Khagram et al. 2002; Price 2003; Risse, Ropp, and Sikkink 1999). Global governance thus forms a comprehensive yet heterogeneous research agenda. At its core are at least three central claims about (1) governance as a process; (2) the expanded role and power of nonstate actors; and (3) the resulting diffusion or decentralization of political authority. We critically review each of these claims and find that beneath each one there lies a specific view of power wedded to the concept of sovereignty that makes authority the analytical core of the concept of global governance.

---

1. For Krasner, regimes are intervening variables and do not qualify as a unit of analysis for the study of world politics. For Holsti and others, however, the system of regimes amounts to a "system of international governance."

Governance as a Process

Although the term *global governance* is in fact not employed in Rosenau and Czempiel's *Governance without Government* (1992), this work is widely seen as a seminal contribution to the study of global governance, as it distinguishes government as an institution from government as a task or process. In keeping with this distinction, global governance is commonly defined as a process that involves both public and private actors, with their activities coordinated through both formal and informal rules and guidelines so as to advance a common or public goal (Held and McGrew 2002; Pierre and Peters 2000; Sandholtz 1999).[2] However, while studies of global governance define their object of inquiry as a set of processes, their ontology and concomitant analytical tools are not equipped to grasp the *content* of the processes of governance itself. Studies of global governance have typically focused on the shifting roles and power of state and nonstate actors, and on the resultant changes in the institutionalization of political authority.

Here it is instructive to look at the most prolific and arguably most influential writer about global governance, James Rosenau. Rosenau asserts that global governance amounts to "social functions or processes that can be performed or implemented in a variety of ways at different times and places" (2002, 72). He formulates a typology of governance that emerges from two dimensions: "the degree to which authority is formally established" and "the degree to which authority flows in vertical or horizontal directions" (8). In this typology, the processes of governance are transformed into a focus on the "types of collectivities involved" (governments, NGOs, TNCs, IGOs). It is thus the type of actors involved, rather than the processes and practices of governance, that is of interest. Similarly, Mathias Koenig-Archibugi (2002, 50–52) focuses exclusively on the institutional dimensions of global governance as he identifies the degrees of publicness, delegation, and inclusiveness as the central dimensions for categorizing and understanding global governance. This conception of governance effectively limits the analysis of governance conceived as a process to an exploration of the types of actors involved and the authority they can bring to bear—as opposed to the substance of the processes of governance that *flows* from such authority.[3]

The central empirical claim in studies of global governance is that non-

---

2. For an early analysis of different uses of *governance*, see Rhodes 1996.
 3. See Rosenau 2002, table 3.1, "Six Types of Governance."

state actors have emerged as powerful actors in global politics, thus challenging the power and authority of sovereign states.[4] The heightened influence and power of actors representing "civil society" and its implications for the power and authority of the state are at the core of what global governance is all about (Anheier et al. 2001; Florini 2000; Held and Koenig-Archibugi 2004; Higgot et al. 2000; Scholte 2002; Weiss and Gordenker 1996; Woods 2002). Underlying the claim about the increased power of nonstate actors in shaping and carrying out governance functions is a conception of the relation between state and nonstate actors as a zero-sum game: As nonstate actors have become more powerful, states have by definition become less so. Some authors note, for example, that states can no longer "bypass the concerns of transnational actors," as these have "strengthened their bargaining position with significant moral, financial, and knowledge resources" (Benner, Reinicke, and Witte 2004, 195).

It is typically argued that there is a "relocation of authority *from* public *to* quasi-public, and *to* private, agencies" (Held and McGrew 2002, 10; emphasis added).[5] According to Rosenau (1999, 294), for example, "The weakening of states has not been followed by authority vacuums ... so much as it has resulted in a vast growth in the number of spheres in which authority has moved." Against this background, he suggests that an "appropriate ontology will highlight the extent to which the erosion of state authority and the proliferation of NGOs has resulted in a disaggregation of the loci of governance" (293). While studies of global governance excel in charting the diffusion and disaggregation of authority from the state to nonstate actors, they fail when it comes to exploring the power at work in the actual practices through which governance takes place, as well as the more specific content or logic of the relations between state and nonstate actors. The extent to which nonstate actors are directly funded by and actively encouraged by states to be engaged in processes of global governance is thus inadequately addressed. For example, Woods (2002, 31–34) provides an instructive overview of examples of how states fund, encourage, outsource, or leave space open for nonstate actors; and Risse (2002, 260) asserts, "it would be preposterous to claim that the INGO [international nongovernmental organizations] world simply represents global civil society *against* the inter-state system" and goes on to list various ways in which states actively support, fund, and encourage nonstate actors.

---

4. For a good overview and summary of this point, see Held and McGrew 2002.
  5. For one author, this amounts to a systematic "power shift" where "the steady concentration of power in the hands of states that began in 1648 with the Peace of Westphalia is over, at least for a while" (Matthews 1997, 50).

However, both Woods and Risse stop short of using these observations as a springboard for theorizing about the relations of power at work in processes of governance, including those that have bearing on the relations between state and nonstate actors.

A pervasive feature of studies of global governance is the extent to which there is, contrary to programmatic statements, a commitment to the triangle between sovereignty, authority, and legitimacy. Rosenau's formulation of "spheres of Authority" (SOAs) as the unit of analysis for studies of global governance is intended to "trace and assess the processes of governance wherever they may occur. That is, through focusing on rule systems *we will not be confined to the world of states*" (2000, 188; emphasis added). However, these processes of governance are to be analyzed "in terms of the way in which authority is created, dispersed, consolidated, or otherwise employed to exercise control." In focusing on authority as defined in terms of the "capacity to generate compliance," Rosenau is decidedly operating within the triad of power, authority, and legitimacy.[6] Hall and Biersteker (2002, 5) similarly conclude, "The state is no longer the sole, or in some instances even the principal, source of authority in either the domestic arena or in the international system."

By tying the analysis of the processes of governance to a concern with authority, studies of global governance inadvertently perpetuate the very state-centric framework that they seek to transcend: The focus is negatively defined in relation to sovereignty, aimed at analyzing to which actors power and authority have flowed from the state. The recent interest in how to render global governance more legitimate and accountable is a testament to this feature of studies of global governance. Here, the focus is on the effects of the fact (established by studies of global governance) that the practices and processes of governance do not correspond to the site of the institutionalization of political authority in the sovereign state. Addressing the "democratic deficit" and lack of accountability and legitimacy of global governance, these studies typically note that global civil society emerges as a substitute for a national "demos" to which global governance is or can be made accountable (Held and Koenig-Archibugi 2004; Nanz and Steffek 2004; Risse 2002; Scholte 2002; Fox and Brown 1998).

The literature on global governance does provide important insights. However, there are clear limits to the central concepts that guide studies of global governance. Because of the commitment to power as sovereignty

---

6. For a good discussion of the relation between authority, legitimacy, and sovereign power, see Raz 1990.

and the associated concern with the institutionalization of political authority, studies of global governance *misread* central aspects of the relations between state and nonstate actors in asserting that the power and authority of nonstate actors has increased while that of states has decreased. Studies of global governance are thus also *unable* to deliver on the claim that global governance should be studied as a process, inasmuch as its analytical tools favor theorizing about what actors "are" in terms of which actors have power and authority rather than about what these actors "do" when they engage in the processes of governing. Here we offer an analytical framework that makes the study of power integral to the analysis of the substantive content of the practices and processes of governing. In this perspective, the role of nonstate actors and the relation between state and nonstate actors will emerge in a very different light.

From Governance to Governmentality

Mitchell Dean's concept of "technologies of agency" adds specificity to Foucault's general perspective in terms of analyzing nonstate actors in global governance. For Dean (1999, 167–68), technologies of agency "seek to deploy our possibilities of agency" as a tactic or mode of governing. These technologies "engage us as active and free citizens, as informed and responsible consumers, as members of self-managing communities and organizations, as actors in democratizing social movements, and as agents capable of taking control of our own risk." Also relevant is Graham Burchell's (1996) interpretation of how civil society is defined as a sphere that is brought into the task of governing by virtue of a "contractual implication."[7] This observation is particularly interesting for the analysis of global governance, so it is worthwhile to quote him at some length. According to Burchell, this contractual implication involves:

> "offering" individuals and collectivities active involvement in action to resolve the kind of issues hitherto held to be the responsibility of authorized governmental agencies. However, the price of this involvement is that they must assume active responsibility for these activities, both for carrying them out and, of course, for their outcomes, and in so doing they are required to conduct themselves in accordance with the appropriate (or approved) model of action. This might be described as a new form of "responsibilization" corresponding to the new forms in which

---

7. Burchell borrows the term *contractual implication* from Donzelot 1991.

the governed are encouraged, freely and rationally, to conduct themselves. (1996, 29)

In this view, the ascendancy of nonstate actors in shaping and carrying out global governance functions is not an instance of transfer of power from the state to nonstate actors, or a matter of the changing sources of, or institutional locus for, authority. Rather, it is an expression of a *change* in governmentality by which civil society is redefined, from a passive object of government to be acted upon and into an entity that is both an object *and* a subject of government. Two crucial points emerge here. First, "civil society" (or the individuals or groups claiming to represent it) does not constitute a realm devoid of relations of power. These organizations' goals and modes of operations are here seen as an effect of relations of power that are integral to the practices of governing and the underlying thinking in late modern society. Second, the self-association and political will-formation characteristic of civil society organizations do not stand in opposition to the political power of the state but are instead a central feature of its exercise: Civil society organizations are constituted as self-associating units—through "technologies of agency"—whose political significance resides both in their capacity to convey and mobilize the preferences and concerns of individuals and communities, and in their capacity to carry out regulatory functions (cf. Bartelson 2006).

In reviewing the genesis of international population policy, we will show not only that nonstate actors have always been central, but also, and more important, that the type of nonstate actors, and the roles that these have assumed, are integral to and products of governmental rationalities that change over time. In our second case study, we focus on the more microlevel relations and interactions between the Norwegian government and certain NGOs in the context of processes of advocating a ban on land mines. This case shows how a focus on governmentality can yield new insights into how the roles and action orientations of nonstate actors are shaped by a governmental rationality that governs "through" civil society by harnessing their expertise and ability to channel political will-formation.

From Objects of Regulation to Subjects with Rights— The Case of International Population Policy

It is implicit in studies of global governance that nonstate actors are more powerful today than previously. Seen through the lens of governmentality, the genesis of international population policy suggests otherwise. Nonstate actors have always been central in international population policy, but there has been a marked shift in the rationality of government over time, rendering different types of nonstate actors central in different historical periods. The case of international population policy can reveal the limitations of the literature on global governance in terms of grasping the changes in the modes of governing that take place over time, how these changes are integral to shifting governmental rationalities, and how these changes accord prominence to different types of nonstate actors.

The history of international population policy shows that the power of nonstate actors in shaping global governance is nothing new, and that nonstate actors are as powerful vis-à-vis state actors as they ever were (cf. Boli and Thomas 1999). Back in the 1950s and 1960s, a small network of philanthropic institutions like the Ford and Rockefeller Foundations invested heavily in research and education about population dynamics and reproductive control (Harkavy 1995; Hodgson 1988, 1991). By the mid-1960s, they had created an international network of research institutions and had helped establish graduate training programs in demography and public health focused on reducing global population growth through family planning programs. This laid the groundwork for international population policy that was to emerge in the late 1960s (Critchlow 1999; Sending 2003; Crane 1993).

Yet, there is much more to the genesis of this policy field than this brief outline would indicate. Its formative phase was characterized by a particular governmental rationality that gave to research institutions and expert groups a special role in shaping governmental efforts. The first three decades after World War II were characterized by a "hierarchical" conception of civil society and its constituting individuals. Whereas individuals were generally seen as endowed with reason and autonomy (as consistent with a more general liberal political rationality), a great number of individuals, particularly in the developing world, were specifically *not* seen as having fully developed the capacity to act freely and autonomously (Helliwell and Hindess 2002). These individuals were defined as *objects* of government whose behavioral patterns would have to be adjusted by identifying and acting upon causal relations. Nonstate actors that could lay claim to authoritative knowledge here assumed an especially significant role, as they rendered this type of governing possible by formulating theories about the functioning of "traditional" societies and by identifying how to intervene so as to act on, shape, and speed up the transition to modernity.

Consistent with this governmental rationality, then, the relationship between state and nonstate actors was one in which *some* types of nonstate actors were identified as central. They were seen as having (saw themselves as having) a privileged and knowledge-based access to the workings of society. The framework of modernization theory and the credo of social engineering formed an integral part of this governmental rationality. As Michael Latham observes, the framework of modernization theory enabled would-be social engineers to state that:

> Complex social relationships could be placed along a progressive index. Culture, society, and personality could be evaluated on the basis of whether they emphasized universalism or particularism, achievement or ascription, oriented toward self or the collective, role specificity or diffuseness, and affective and non-affective relationships. (2000, 33)

With the "traditional" and the "modern" being placed on an evolutionary, progressive scale, modernization theory identified the genesis of Western society as the model upon which traditional societies could and would develop—assisted by Western expertise and know-how. This formed the governmental context within which a host of nonstate actors who were engaged in knowledge production became central in establishing international population policy. In an important report from a survey trip to the "Far East" organized by the Rockefeller Foundation in 1948, it was emphasized that "careful observation and testing of a wide variety of ameliorative efforts" should form the basis for the Foundation's efforts to invest in the field of population (Balfour et al. 1950, 112). The authors of the report emphasized that because of the magnitude and sensitivity of the population problem, "The role of the private agencies lies in encouraging teaching, research and experiment and demonstration to increase knowledge and ultimately to foster its wide dissemination. Study should be emphasized as opposed to direct ameliorative action" (1950, 112). It was with these considerations in mind that the single most important institution in shaping international population policy—the Population Council—was set up by John D. Rockefeller III in 1952 (Sending 2004; Hauser 1954).

The Population Council was to invest heavily in the production and dissemination of knowledge. It also sought, through funding from the Ford Foundation and the Rockefeller Foundation, as well as private donations from John D. Rockefeller III and the Scaife Foundation, to establish a resource base of "trained personnel" that could "rationally" approach and seek out solutions to what was held to be a fact beyond dispute: high population growth rates in the developing world were slowing down economic growth and undermining other development efforts, thus threatening to undermine the U.S.-led projection of liberal values to the developing world.

The Population Council was involved in establishing or funding specialized research programs in family planning and related fields at a range of academic institutions: the University of Chicago, Columbia University, University of Michigan, University of Pennsylvania, Boston University, Princeton University, Cornell University, the University of Minnesota, and Dartmouth College (Critchlow 1999, 240). This was in keeping with what had been the rationale for the very establishment of the Population Council. As formulated in the first five-year program of its Demographic Division, the identity of the Population Council was closely linked to a conception of knowledge and expertise as a prerequisite for governing, where those to be governed were seen as objects in need of guidance from those with access to the workings of society.

> [The] intelligent resolution of the world's population problems requires the interests and initiative of trained people in the countries concerned, especially in underdeveloped areas. The Council has therefore worked to develop a small body of persons in important countries who can provide authoritative guidance on population problems to both the governments and the public, in their own language and in terms of their own values. (Population Council 1958, 1)

Starting in 1953, the Population Council established a fellowship program for the study of demography or a related topic at U.S. universities. By 1958, 69 fellowships had been awarded to individuals from 21 countries. During the 1950s, nearly half of these fellows attended Frank Notestein's course on the demographic transition, which he gave at the Office of Population Research at Princeton University (Caldwell and Caldwell 1986, 12). By 1961, 140 fellowships had been granted,[8] and, by 1968, the Population Council had awarded no less than 529 fellowships, 404 of which had gone to students from the developing world.[9]

Both the research centers established at various universities and the Population Council and the Ford Foundation in fact provided direct tech-

---

8. Frank W. Notestein, 1961. Letter from Frank Notestein to Dana Creel, The Rockefeller Brothers Fund, September 22, 1961. Rockefeller Archives Center (RAC) RAC, IV3B4.2 Box 4, "Demographic Division 1957–1966," Folder 41.

9. See also Notestein 1968.

nical assistance to developing countries, thus assuming direct policy (and political) roles. The population research centers at the universities of Michigan, Harvard, Johns Hopkins, North Carolina, Chicago, and Pittsburgh were all directly involved in providing technical assistance, in giving courses and seconding personnel to help establish population programs in the developing world.[10] The involvement of U.S. universities in the formulation and execution of population policies was also transmitted to Asia. For example, in 1972, representatives of twenty Asian universities met in Jogjakarta, Indonesia, "to discuss the role that universities *should* play in formulating and carrying out national population policies" (Demeny 1972, 249; emphasis added). The role of knowledge-producing actors was central to this governmental rationality, as these made it possible to identify objects whose behavioral patterns could be altered by acting upon causal relations.

During the three decades stretching from the end of World War II to the early 1970s, the individuals who were targeted for intervention to reduce population growth were defined as objects whose behavioral characteristics could be changed by delivering modern contraceptive technology through family planning programs. The *types* of actors central for such a rationality of political rule were those who could lay claim to authoritative interpretations and explanations of societal structures and the behavioral patterns of individuals, as well as those who could produce contraceptive technology (Sending 2003). These experts were not only central in shaping the rationale and thinking for these governmental efforts, they were also heavily involved in implementing them, by establishing and running family planning programs in the developing world. They were politically well-connected and elitist in orientation, and saw themselves as an integral element of the U.S. foreign policy of combating communism (Critchlow 1999).

Then, in the final two decades of the twentieth century, came a new governmental rationality. Civil society now became conceptualized in "horizontal" terms, and individuals were defined as objects of government *as well as* being persons with rights and autonomy. Other types of nonstate actors emerged as central in shaping and performing governance functions: Actors claiming to represent affected individuals and constituencies of "civil society" came to assume key governing roles, in service delivery, advocacy, and expertise. Here, governing increasingly operated

---

10. Population Council. 1965. Minutes, meeting at the Population Council October 5–7, 1965. 1. Rockefeller Archives Center: Folder 2364, Box 128, IVB4.6 "Population Subject File."

through affected individuals rather than *on* them, as they became seen more and more as key actors to ensure effectiveness in program delivery and to confer legitimacy on governmental practices.

In contrast to the formative phase of population policy, this new "reproductive health and rights approach" in the 1990s was formulated and advanced by a transnational women's health movement, loosely organized and coordinated through certain key NGOs in the United States. In 1980, Judith Bruce had published an article with a title that signaled the emergence of the individual subject in family planning research and population studies: "Implementing the User's Perspective." Bruce initiated her discussion with an instructive critique of established policy.

> The individual's perspective and experience have often been viewed as discretionary and dispensable items, rather than as determining factors in the effectiveness of a birth planning programs. (1980, 29)

This call for establishing "the individual as the analytical focal point" was aimed at establishing a different conceptualization of the individual woman, one in which she would emerge as a *subject* endowed with rights and autonomy rather than as a mere object of regulation based on social science knowledge. As this type of research expanded considerably during the 1980s, it marked the emergence of individuals as *subjects* whose preferences, rights, and action-orientation must be made an essential feature of governmental efforts.[11] A decade later, this research had coalesced with other strands of research and with rights-based women's health advocacy to form an integrated epistemic-political platform focused on advancing "reproductive health and rights."

More generally, from the 1980s onward, modernization theory lost its sway over development policy. Rational, knowledge-based planning and social engineering had been replaced by a conceptualization that saw development as best promoted by establishing an institutional framework within which the self-regulating mechanisms of the market and of civil society could be realized. Moreover, especially with the end of the Cold War, human rights norms had become something of a normative master

---

11. For an overview of population research on the associated concepts of "quality of care," "user perspective," and "unmet needs," see Bongaarts and Bruce 1995; Bruce, Jain, and Mensch 1992; Dixon-Mueller and Germain 1992. For research originating within public health and medicine, particularly within the World Health Organization, see Barzelatto 1988. For an overview of how this research was incorporated into and supported an already established network of women's health advocates, see Dixon-Mueller 1993 and Sending 2003.

discourse (Risse, Ropp, and Sikkink 1999). It was on this basis that a women's health movement emerged to advocate for a "reproductive health and rights" approach in the context of the UN-organized International Conference on Population and Development (ICPD) in 1994. This new conceptualization of individuals as subjects whose preferences and rights were central to governmental efficacy is integral to the new governmental rationality that gave a new *type* of nonstate actors a central place in shaping and carrying out international population policy.

Organizations representing the subjects of population policy were invited to assert their views and goals directly through the ICPD process. As Donald Critchlow observes, "the mobilization of grassroots groups meant that power shifted from elite interests, which had played a critical role in the shaping of family planning programs policy in the first three decades following the Second World War, to social movements organized at the community level" (1999, 185). In our view, the emergence of this new type of actors is better understood as a shift in governmental rationality. The changed conceptualization of the task of government and the concomitant relations between governmental practices and the objects of government served to privilege a new and different set of nonstate actors.[12]

The reproductive health and rights approach was formulated and advanced by a set of actors who assumed roles qualitatively different from those of the research institutions that had established the policy field of population. The very names of the key women's organizations involved in the ICPD process indicate that their self-understanding derived from a political project of advancing and expressing the preferences, rights, and concerns of women: the Women's Environmental and Development Organization (WEDO), the International Reproductive Rights Research and Action Group (IRRRAG), Development Alternatives with Women for a New Era (DAWN), Women's Global Network for Reproductive Rights (WGNRR), National Feminist Health and Reproductive Rights Network, Women Living under Muslim Laws, Medical Women's International Association, Women and Development Unit, and Catholics for Free Choice.

In preparing for the ICPD, organizations like the International Women's Health Coalition (IWHC), WEDO, DAWN, and others entered into relations with governmental agencies in the United States that involved what Burchell calls a "contractual implication." Claiming to represent and safeguard the rights and autonomy of individual subjects in the

---

12. Ottaway (2001) points to the same change in types of NGOs being accredited to the ECOSOC during the course of the 1990s.

developing world, these actors assumed identities and action-orientations in keeping with the belief that governing is most effectively pursued by enrolling actors who can ground governmental efforts in such a way as to render their content consistent with the self-identity of these individuals as autonomous actors.

In keeping with such a governmental rationality, the women's health movement organized to perform a series of activities integral to the task of governing in late modern societies. These efforts were welcomed by the U.S. State Department. Timothy Wirth, Under-Secretary for Global Affairs, actively encouraged the involvement of these nonstate actors as the United States set out to formulate a new policy on population.[13] For example, in 1993 the IWHC served as secretariat for a meeting in New York that produced the declaration "Women's Voices '94—Women's Declaration on Population Policy," signed by individuals from all continents and published in *Population and Development Review* (IWHC 1994b).

In January 1994, 215 women's health advocates from seventy-nine countries met to formulate a common position in Rio de Janeiro. Referred to as the "feminist prepcom," the meeting represented a central arena for the formulation of a common position and resulted in "The Rio Statement."

> The participants strongly voiced their opposition to population policies intended to control the fertility of women and that do not address their basic right to secure livelihood, freedom from poverty and oppression; or do not respect their rights to free, informed choice or to adequate health care; that whether such policies are pro- or anti-natalist, they are often coercive, treat women as objects, not subjects, and that in the context of such policies, low fertility does not result in alleviating poverty. (IWHC 1994a, 4)

Through those and other networking activities in advance of and during the ICPD process, the women's health movement was able to influence the views and positions advanced by the official delegations, not least because these delegations often included representatives from the NGOs involved in this effort to establish a reproductive health and rights approach.

While the formative phase of the policy field of population was marked by investment in social scientific knowledge as a tool to conceal or present as "rational" a set of intrusive governmental practices, the formulation and advancement of the reproductive health and rights approach

---

13. Interview with Barbara Crane (USAID), March 26, 2000; Ellen Marshall (U.S. State Dept.), April 20, 2000; Adrienne Germain (IWHC), August 1, 2000.

was marked by a rationality that gave to the self-associating political subjects in civil society—in the North and the South—a clear role in identifying and justifying a new policy approach. When viewed from within the problematics of sovereignty and the triad of power, legitimacy, and authority, these developments can be read as a case of how nonstate actors representing civil society can exercise power at a global level. It can be interpreted as a changing institutionalization of political authority: a new set of actors—women's health organizations—were able to define a sphere of political authority through reference to the legitimacy of human and women's rights. However, we feel that this is a somewhat shallow interpretation. Not only did these women's groups establish close ties with the old breed of nonstate actors that had established this policy field, such as the Population Council, and also with key countries, such as the United States; they also, and much more importantly, were allowed to perform these central functions, thanks to a new conceptualization of individuals and of society as objects of government.

We have here, more generally, a case of how a new governmental rationality defines the autonomy of individual subjects as a prerequisite for legitimate and effective government. The political will-formation found in civil society represents a central locus of government to the extent that it renders these forces responsible by involving them in formulating and carrying out these governmental functions. In the words of the Commission on Global Governance, "in their wide variety, they [NGOs] bring expertise, commitment, and grassroots perceptions that should be mobilized in the interests of better governance" (Commission on Global Governance 1995, 254). In this sense, the literature on global governance itself forms part of the governmental rationality that characterizes contemporary global politics: In identifying nonstate actors as crucial actors in global governance, and particularly in identifying new sources and modes of conferring legitimacy to governmental practices that involve nonstate actors, the literature on global governance forms part of and underwrites governmentality in terms of the thinking and knowledge underpinning this form of governing.

Handmaidens of State Do-Gooders—The Case of "Contractual Implication"

The literature on global governance and on "global civil society" frequently highlights the case of the ban on antipersonnel land mines as a key example of successful transnational network advocacy (Cameron et al. 1998; Price 1998; Thakur and Maley 1999). A global governance-style interpretation of the case of Norway in the global advocacy against antipersonnel land mines may have immediate appeal. Certain Norwegian NGOs allied with other NGOs and over time managed to persuade, or "shame," or otherwise induce the Norwegian government to support, politically and financially, the NGO-initiated advocacy for banning land mines (Neumann 2002a).[14] This would seem a standard case of the power of NGOs vis-à-vis states, and a testament to a transformation of the dynamics of global politics.

However, in the Norwegian case, such an interpretation would in fact be misleading. This was not a case of a transfer of power from the state to nonstate actors. Our analytical perspective enables us to focus on the microlevel relations and interactions between the state and nonstate actors, making it clear how a governmental rationality was at work that defined the will-formation, expertise, and advocacy residing in "civil society" as key to effective governing.

The Norwegian government invested heavily in the anti–land mine process, both financially and politically. The government's funding to NGOs involved in the field of development more generally has increased dramatically over the past two decades. Between 1981 and 2002, official funding of Norwegian developmental NGOs rose from NKr 204 million to NKr 2,374 million (approximately US$390 million).[15] Although NGOs are heavily dependent on the state for funding and operate within a broad sociopolitical consensus, this should not lead to the conclusion that the greater reliance upon NGOs for policy advocacy and policy execution merely represents an "extension" of the state into civil society—as if the state in some way "controls" civil society.[16] Probing more deeply into the mechanisms by which the Norwegian state and Norwegian NGOs acted and related to each other in the process of advocating for a ban on land mines, we will see that their relationship is characteristic of a form of government involving a "technology of agency" by which nonstate actors are

---

14. For a discussion of the mechanisms of shaming, see Schimmelfennig 2001.

15. Statistical Database, Norwegian Agency for Development Cooperation (NORAD). Reprinted in Tvedt 1998, which also includes an analysis of the institutional system of Norwegian development assistance, including the role of NGOs. See Neumann 1999.

16. Ronnie Lipschutz (2005a), in his otherwise robust analysis of civil society organizations—employing elements of the same theoretical perspective that we do here—seems to infer, from the fact that the state does to some extent control civil society organizations through funding mechanisms, that the "capillaries of power" extend from the state and into civil society.

enrolled to perform governance functions by virtue of their technical expertise, advocacy, and capacity for political will-formation.

Together with Norwegian People's Aid (NPA), the Norwegian Afghanistan Committee became a central player in the process that resulted in full-scale official activism at the international stage against antipersonnel land mines. Official funding to Norwegian People's Aid increased by more than NKr 255 million (approximately US$41 million) between 1991 and 1996, largely because the Ministry of Foreign Affairs encouraged the NPA to take up mine clearance in certain countries. Jan Egeland had served at the Geneva headquarters of the Red Cross. Before becoming its media face in Norway as well as in Geneva, he had worked with land mine issues. As state secretary in the Norwegian Ministry of Foreign Affairs (MFA), he was heavily involved in the issue of land mines. Egeland, who was serving in a Social Democratic government, turned to the NPA, aware that they had the backing and the financial resources to follow through on the initiative.

The NPA was enrolled not only as an object but also as a subject of government, with all the attendant pros and cons: "The NPA was keen, I was actually a bit worried about how keen they were, they are willing to do everything for everybody.... Our civil servants had to make sure that the NGOs recruited professionals, but *we also wanted the enthusiasm that the NGOs could provide.* They also had the major comparative advantage of knowing what the mine situation was out there in the field."[17] As early as in 1989, the Norwegian Afghanistan Committee (NAC) had started to work on mine clearance after two of the organization's staff members and nine others had been killed in a car explosion in Peshawar the previous year. When the UN started to work on mine clearance in Afghanistan in 1989, they approached the Norwegian MFA, which decided to finance this work. In this context, the NAC was to become a central actor in shaping official Norwegian policy, as described by a representative of the NAC.

> The NAC was an important decision shaper where Norwegian Afghan policy was concerned. We were always asked when new initiatives were afoot. We had regular meetings, for example the annual meetings on disaster aid allocation as well as informal ones, and quite often they took place when our local representative in Peshawar was in Oslo. Actually,

---

17. Interview with Jan Egeland, adviser to the foreign minister and then junior minister, 1990–97. At the time of the interview, September 21, 1999, he was working as special adviser to the Red Cross. Emphasis added.

> the MFA people around Peshawar also discussed with them on location, and we had good contacts with the Norwegian military personnel—you know how ex-pat circles work, you talk to compatriots you would never have approached at home even if you had been neighbors. They [the MFA] would show us stuff they had received from the UN with a view to hearing how this looked from out in the field. Actually, a meeting never went by without them putting out at least one of these feelers. The MFA rarely asked us just like that, however, they were a bit invisible in the way they asked their questions.[18]

In fact, the Norwegian state was drawing on the practical knowledge of the NGOs, the lion's share of whose work they had financed in the first place. In the late 1980s, however, the NAC also took part in parallel activities centered on Peshawar: the setting up of a Mines Advisory Group that was eventually to become the International Campaign to Ban Landmines (ICBL). What kind of governmental rationality can be said to characterize the close relations between NGOs and the state? Egeland's reading of this relationship is instructive.

> This circle [around the NPA], which also consisted of the Norwegian Red Cross, their Geneva office, Norwegian Church Aid and their international branches—the Lutheran World Federation and the World Council of Churches—began to argue in favor of a total ban. Suddenly, I was on the defensive. I had seen the need for this, I had put the NPA on the case, I had even provided the money, and then there they were! I remember sitting down to a TV program on mines, you know, rest a little on my laurels, and there was this person from the NPA being interviewed out in the field in Cambodia saying now the Norwegian state must wake up and see the enormous need etc. etc. . . . I was called names, you know reactionary, all that, by the people who thought of themselves as progressive activists.[19]

This statement seems to indicate that the relation between state and nonstate actors was one of criticism from the outside, where nonstate actors represented the liberal-progressive forces of a "global civil society" against the traditionalism of states. Interestingly, however, Egeland goes on to tell how he approached this criticism.

> So I thought it was time to follow up on my previous good experiences

---

18. Interview with Kristian Berg Harpviken, September 24, 1999.
19. Interview with Jan Egeland, September 21, 1999.

and simply talk to them. This was when I initiated a series of meetings, but there I had to argue the case for why a total ban was unrealistic. This I had not done before. I had been neither in favor, nor against, because the idea of a total ban had not existed as such. . . . So why, they said, why cannot we be the first ones to be in favor of a total ban? Well, I said, because Canada and Belgium are bordering other NATO allies only [and not Russia, as does Norway]. In Norway, the MoD and the [MFA] department for security affairs were in the driver's seat, and to put it mildly, I had no power of instruction over them.[20]

The critical role played by nonstate actors in this case was directed at a different part of the state apparatus, the Ministry of Defense (MoD). As a representative of the Norwegian state, Egeland was at pains to mediate between the humanitarian goals that he supported and the "high politics" of disarmament represented by the MoD. We see this opposition again in the framing of the international process as one where a global movement (representing "global civil society") to ban land mines involving a plethora of actors was working under a humanitarian banner, in opposition to a UN-based disarmament process where states, and particularly the great powers, were in charge.

In fact, the genesis of the Norwegian involvement in the work to ban land mines shows how nonstate actors can be used to create space for political agency by *different* parts of the state. Officers in the Norwegian Army had been involved in training mine clearance for some time, and they were the ones that had the technical expertise to do this. However, the MoD was not the place to start advocating for a ban on land mines. When these officers began getting involved in the work of the NGOs against land mines, Egeland and the MFA could use both the local knowledge and technical expertise of these ex-military officers *and* the critical and progressive advocacy of the NPA and NCA to advance the "humanitarian" cause against the more traditional military views found elsewhere in the state apparatus.[21]

The following description of the relation between state officials and NGO representatives suggests how the relative autonomy and opposition of NGOs were central to their standing as politically significant subjects through which to govern: "We were opponents and collaborators at the same time. We needed their expertise, which was of a kind that we our-

---

20. Interview with Jan Egeland, September 21, 1999.
21. Interview with Kristian Berg Harpviken, September 24, 1999. Interview with Jan Egeland, September 21, 1999.

selves did not possess, and so it was nice to be able to draw on theirs."²² This suggests that while nonstate actors have increasingly been enrolled to assume active, responsible roles in performing governance functions, their critical attitude and more idealistic goals have also generated some friction.

The ways in which the MFA and the NGOs interacted during the land mine process is indicative of a more general development. The relations between the state and nonstate actors have been redefined as an integral part of a shift whereby nonstate actors are defined as both objects of government by the state, and subjects whose self-associating features, criticism, and mobilizing capacity are to be put to use in processes of governing. For example, back in 1975 the Norwegian Ministry of Foreign Affairs had established a "Humanitarian Emergency Committee" to advise the government on how to respond to humanitarian emergencies. It included all the major NGOs working on humanitarian and development assistance. Starting in the early 1990s, the state secretary in the MFA started to chair the meetings of the committee. Crucially, this meant that the function of the committee changed from advising to coordinating and mobilizing. The participating NGOs came to be seen, both by themselves and by representatives of the state, as actors that were operating in tandem with the state, and as responsible and mobilizing actors within civil society.

In the early 1990s, the Norwegian government issued a report that outlined a qualitatively new relation between the government apparatus and NGOs. It stated that NGOs filled an important but "supplementary" role in relation to official development institutions, especially in geographical and issue areas where the government could not or would not get directly involved. The report then went on to emphasize that NGOs would in the future be included as "active partners" in the formulation and planning of Norwegian development policy.²³ This identification of NGOs as "active partners" in the government's official policy is reflected in the increased funding for NGOs in this period.

There can be no doubt that the transnational movement to ban antipersonnel mines was instrumental in swaying the policy of the Norwegian state on land mines. Neither can there be any doubt that Norwegian NGOs played a central role in agenda setting and decision shaping. These NGOs played to their different strengths to get an effective lobbying campaign under way: the NAC using its early contacts with the rest of the

---

22. Interview with Leif Arne Ulland and Jørn Gjelstad, September 10, 1999.
23. Utenriksdepartementet 1991–92.

"epistemic community" of mine specialists to sensitize other NGOs and also the state to the issue, and the NPA using its close links to the labor movement as well as a wide range of politicians and NGOs with an interest in humanitarian work.

Our analytical perspective both challenges and provides an "added value" to the literature on global governance. It challenges the view that nonstate actors have become more powerful at the expense of the state. But it also provides an analytical framework that explicitly aims to theorize the ways in which states relate to nonstate actors. A governance focus that considers only how the knowledge and expertise produced and brought to bear by NGOs as a case of how nonstate actors challenge state supremacy and control misses a fundamental point. The expertise and knowledge embedded in NGOs must be examined in terms that also consider how different types of actors and organizations fit into and correspond to a more general rationality of government. Note, for example, the following description of the genesis of NGOs' activities during the past decade.

> The NGOs were learning on the job. Since protocol 2 they had been adjusting their language and their behavior.[24] In the early days, they were slogging around, but now they had shaped up, started to look out for what was effective, they appeared streamlined and diplomatic in their approach.[25]

We can extract two important theoretical points from this description of how NGOs have been "adjusting their language and their behavior" and how they had previously tended to simply "slog around" but had now "shaped up" and become "effective" and "streamlined and diplomatic in their approach." First, this indicates what we also discussed in the case of population policy: that different governmental rationalities generate different action-orientations of nonstate actors. The transformation in governmental rationality implied in the greater emphasis on governing through free and autonomous subjects generates new types of NGOs, as well as new action-orientations among existing ones. As brought out in the quote, these actors have assumed responsible, effective, and diplomatic attitudes. Second, it suggests that NGOs are defined as responsible

---

24. Protocol 2 here refers to the 1980 UN Convention on Certain Conventional Weapons, "Protocol II on Prohibitions or Restrictions on the Use of Mines, Booby Traps, and Other Devices" Amended in 1996.
   25. Interview with Leif Arne Ulland and Jørn Gjelstad, September 10, 1999.

and "streamlined" actors that perform crucially important governmental tasks in international settings by virtue of being defined as *subjects* of government. It is precisely their ability to act as responsible vehicles for political will-formation and as sources of expertise that renders them central actors in such processes. As they are brought into the task of governing, the state also emphasizes their autonomous capacities. For example, a centrally placed higher official underlined that it was vital for the MFA to "professionalize" the NGOs in the land mine case, yet retain their "enthusiasm" and draw on their expertise on the ground.[26]

This case is specifically not one that conforms to the notion of co-optation. These actors are not brought into the fold and thereby deprived of their autonomy as recognized representatives of "civil society." No, it is precisely their status as actors who have expertise central to the task of governing and, far more important, the fact that they appear to be autonomous political subjects with a capacity for political will-formation that make them key subjects of, and allies in, governmental tasks. It is thus not the functional role of the state that has changed, but the intermeshing of the networks that has become so much denser that it qualitatively changes how the state goes about seeing to that function—how it recruits its personnel, organizes its work, and shapes the plethora of actors central to governmental functions.

Looking specifically at the case of the land mine campaign, Richard Price has maintained that the success of the NGOs challenges the central role of states. As our presentation has shown, however, such generalizations need further specification. The change in operating mode of states surely does suggest that new actors emerge to play important roles. When subsumed within an analytical framework focused on governmental rationalities, however, the changing institutional forms of the state are considered as being internal to and derived from a far more general political rationality of rule.

Conclusion

Studies of global governance have certainly produced a range of new insights about how political institutions, such as the sovereign state, have been affected by the forces of globalization. These studies have shown how the multilayered and polyarchic networks that comprise states, NGOs,

---

26. Interview with Jan Egeland, September 21, 1999.

IGOs, and transnational corporations have become central sites for the formulation and implementation of governance. Crucially, the literature on global governance concludes that nonstate actors have become more powerful and that states have become less so, with resulting changes in the institutionalization of political authority.

We have argued here that the literature on global governance fails to deliver on its claim to focus on the processes of governance, that it conceptualizes the relation between the state and nonstate actors as a zero-sum game, and that, contrary to programmatic statements, it perpetuates a concern with the sovereignty-authority-legitimacy triad. We have offered a different perspective that partly challenges and partly supplements this literature. Studying global governance through the lens of governmentality enables us to see how different governmental rationalities are defined by certain rules, practices, and techniques, and how such rationalities of rule generate specific action-orientations and types of actors. Our two case studies have shown how, in late modernity, the changing institutional forms of the state might be better understood within a more general framework of a change in governmental rationality. Both the types of actors—state and nonstate—involved in shaping and performing governmental tasks, and the various institutional forms of the state and of political authority, should be analyzed *within* a focus on governmental rationalities.

We have applied this theoretical perspective to two cases: on international population policy and on land mines. This has made it possible to criticize the literature on global governance on key accounts. We have found that civil society is increasingly defined as a field populated by political subjects whose autonomy, expertise, and ability to responsibly channel political will-formation has become crucial to the tasks of governing. We have identified a governmental rationality whereby political power operates *through* rather than *on* civil society. Governing is performed *through* autonomous subjects, not *on* passive objects.

5 | International Organizations: Liberalism, Sovereignty, and Police

International organizations (IOs) have been a consistent focal point for contrasting views on such fundamental issues as international order, the prospects for international cooperation, and the sources of potential changes in state interests (Ruggie and Kratochwil 1986; Keohane 1984; Moravcsik 1999; Risse 2000). The contrast between theorists privileging power on the one hand and those privileging norms on the other is notably evident in this literature (see chap. 2). Indeed, during the past decade, international financial institutions such as the World Bank, World Trade Organization (WTO), and the International Monetary Fund (IMF) have become the targets of political protests on a scale not seen before (Corry 2006). IOs feature in current academic debates about global governance, often as an empirical focal point for analyses of how great powers govern (Drezner 2007), how they help regulate and constitute the social world of states (Barnett and Finnemore 2004), and the sources and effects of their "organized hypocrisy" (Weaver 2008).

The debate about IOs has centered primarily on whether they are actors or arenas, whether they are controlled by states or are in part autonomous. Studies of IOs have had little to say about global governance as a set of interrelated *processes*. Since IOs are presumed to be central arenas, actors, nodes, and mechanisms in governing efforts characterized by being decentralized and networked, this lacuna should be rectified. In this chapter, we take up this challenge by employing the same analytical perspective as in our analysis of NGOs in the previous chapter. We want to move beyond a focus on IO identities as actors and look more closely at the work and role of IOs within the context of global governance. In so doing, we seek to expand and supplement the perspective on IOs presented in Barnett and Finnemore's *Rules for the World* (2004). Their analytical framework draws on a broad range of accounts of the primacy of liberalism in global politics and the processes of bureaucratic rationalization in modern society and is developed in support of their key claim that IOs often have autonomy from and authority over states. By subjecting liberalism and bureaucratic rationalization to a *governmental reading*, however, we supplement Barnett and Finnemore's account in an attempt to understand more about the role of IOs in processes of global governance. This we do by shifting the focus away from the character of IO identity and toward the actions of IOs as they engage in governing at the transnational level.

We pay special attention to the role of IOs as central vehicles in producing and disseminating universal grids or frames of reference for the evaluation, rating, and discussion about how societies should be governed. Studies of the role and power of global best practices, including many that draw on the concept of governmentality, gloss over the production and specific content of these standards. Instead, they focus on how such standards and best practices (good governance, privatization, anticorruption) constitute an important source of power as they subject states to an ever-denser web of surveillance techniques and performance evaluations that cannot be ignored (Fougner 2008; Jaeger 2008; Löwenheim 2008; Zanotti 2005).

However, documenting and theorizing how liberally oriented norms and principles are reaching out to more and more areas—often with IOs in a lead role—and may constitute a liberal governmental rationality with a global reach is not our central aim here. Instead, we explore one aspect of the content and functioning of governmental rationality that has been overlooked: the relationship between episteme and governmental rationality. For Foucault, what characterizes liberal governmentalities is how "the rationality of the governed must serve as the regulating principle for the rationality of government" (2008, 312). Therefore, much hinges on the authoritative interpretation and definition of what is and what is not "the rationality of the governed," and how the attendant rationality of government is linked and applied to the governed. Building on this reading of Foucault, we investigate several aspects that appear central to how governmental rationalities may be said to operate at the global level. First, we consider how sovereignty is interpreted and how it functions within a more generally liberal episteme of governing.[1] Sovereignty, we argue, is

---

1. We read Foucault's (1980, 121) much-quoted exhortation to the effect that "we need to cut off the King's head, in political theory that has still to be done" not as a chastisement of those

constitutive of the episteme within which IOs operate—defining not only the level of analysis but also the level at which IOs generally operate. Second, we show how the changes over time in what is considered "rational" take us beyond combinations of liberal and neoliberal forms of governing. Looking at the World Bank, we find that what it does is far from merely defining or enacting a script of neoliberal governmental reason. Instead, it reintroduces policelike elements under the name of state building, thus elevating state control and capacity—state sovereignty—to a central position within a generally neoliberal governmental rationality. Third, we focus on how IOs are involved in defining the standards against which states are measured, resulting in new categories of statehood—fragile states, for example—deemed in need of special forms of intervention and care.

International Organizations in Global Politics

When IOs have formed a focal point for debates in IR theory, it is not only because they represent a central phenomenon to be explained and understood in a sovereignty-based international system. It is also because there seems to be an implicit assumption that it is the degree of autonomy and actorhood of IOs that is the litmus test for various theories. Realists, for example, answer the question of IO autonomy and agency in the negative. They hold that IOs merely reflect hegemonic positions or distribution of power in the international system (Krasner 1976; Waltz 1999; cf. Gilpin 1981; Lenin [1917] 1953). IOs are epiphenomenal. Rationalists, by contrast, building their case from within economic theory, hold that IOs do in fact have a degree of autonomy (or, in the language of principal agent theory, "slippage"), and that they help resolve collective action problems by reducing transaction costs and helping to identify "Pareto-improving" cooperative solutions (Keohane 1984; Young 1989). In this sense, IOs are able to change the behavior, but not the interests, of states (Moravcsik 1999). By contrast, constructivists and many institutionalists see IOs as autonomous from and partly authoritative toward states by virtue of their expertise, the liberal goals they advance, and their bureaucratic features.

---

who study sovereignty (after all, he himself was in the habit of doing so) but of those who thought that sovereignty is all there is (in IR, neorealists would make for a good example). As noted in chapter 1, the work on governmentality was, among other things, an answer to those who had criticized him for not studying the state, and he answered in the spirit of "I don't want to say that the State isn't important; what I want to say is that relations of power . . . necessarily extend beyond the limits of the State" (1979, 38). We concur, and in this book we have tried to go beyond Foucault's own haunts.

For this reason, IOs can "teach" interests to states and more generally have authority to set the agenda for global governance, defining what counts as legitimate and effective policy responses (Finnemore 1996; Barnett and Finnemore 2004; Sharman 2008).

Debates about the role of IOs in IR theory have, then, largely focused on the question of their relative autonomy from member-states. For realists, such autonomy does not exist. For rationalists, such autonomy rests either with the skilled leadership of certain prominent individuals (Young 1989) or with the ability of IOs to reduce transaction costs and help identify the "Pareto-improving" solution (Keohane 1984). Once established, IOs can in this view have autonomy only by virtue of the "slippage" or lack of control by principals (states) of their agent (IO). For scholars working in the tradition of David Mitrany (1943) and Ernst Haas (1991), IOs can have autonomy if they are able to institutionalize learning patterns within the organization and so serve as a hub for knowledge and expertise considered important for states, not least under conditions of uncertainty (Haas 1992). Barnett and Finnemore (1998, 2004, 2005) have presented the most comprehensive account of IOs as genuinely autonomous and authoritative bureaucratic organizations. They arrive at this position by identifying two general features of modernity—rationalization and liberalism—and argue that IOs embed and build on both as sources of authority.

The contrast between these two positions may be further clarified by comparing two of the most sophisticated accounts of the role of IOs in recent years: Barnett and Finnemore's (2004) *Rules for the World* and Drezner's (2007) *All Politics Is Global*. Both works frame the issue of determining whether, how, and why IOs are *actors* or *arenas*. For Barnett and Finnemore, IOs are actors, by virtue of their bureaucratic features of setting goals and producing policies *for* states. For Drezner, by contrast, states—and powerful states in particular—still call the shots and set the terms for what IOs do and how global governance operates. For this reason, these analyses form an important part of the research on global governance discussed in chapter 4, where a concern for the contents and dynamics of global governance is substituted for a focus on the power and authority of specific actors in relation to other actors. Whereas many students of global governance have focused on the role of various forms of nonstate actors (corporations, NGOs, etc.), students of intergovernmental organizations arguably perpetuate the—largely implicit—assumption that studies of global politics should focus on the relative distribution of power between different types of actors, be they empires, great powers, states, NGOs, corporations, or IOs. True to the proposal that governmentality represents a third option here, we explore instead how states, IOs, and NGOs are implicated in and shaped by rationalities of governing, paying special attention to IOs as sites for the negotiation and formalization of universal categories and practices of rule. In short, we argue that IOs have indeed become more powerful, and we support Barnett and Finnemore's central claims in this regard.

While acknowledging that IOs draw their organizational culture from their political environment, Barnett and Finnemore focus almost exclusively on how IOs have authority over and thus autonomy from states. This analytical move is made possible by applying a broad definition of power as the "production, in and through social relations, of effects that shape the capacities of actors to determine their own circumstances and fate" (Barnett and Finnemore 2004, 29). Curiously, however, this broad definition of power, which includes not only direct compulsory power but also the type of productive power that we focus on here, is studied from the vantage point of IO power *over other actors*.[2] In fact, their analysis seems based on a reading where the defining features of modernity—rationalization and liberalism—are primarily vested in IOs and not in other types of actors. Clearly, if "IOs use their authority to both regulate and constitute the world" (Barnett and Finnemore 2004, 9), then they are not doing so in isolation or in a vacuum, as if IOs were the sole actors to be characterized by a culture of rule-following, expertise, and the advancement of liberal goals. There is something fundamentally important about the operating environment of IOs that gets lost here. Barnett and Finnemore describe in great detail the bureaucratic and liberal features of IOs and make due reference to the role of states in advancing and setting up IOs in this way. But they lose sight of how IOs operate in a sovereignty-based system and the way in which that affects how IOs operate as well as how powerful they are.

We do not contend that Barnett and Finnemore are mistaken in characterizing IOs in this way. Rather, our concern is the extent that IOs share their bureaucratic and liberal features with a host of other actors. In order to investigate this, it is not particularly helpful to frame the question of IOs in terms of their identity and relative authority over and autonomy from states. For Barnett and Finnemore, the social take on IOs is a way toward better understanding their properties as actors.

---

2. Note the discrepancy between Barnett and Finnemore 2004 and Barnett and Duvall 2005, where the implications of the understanding of power on display in the latter work in some degree point up the fairly uncomplicated approach in the former.

We can better understand what IOs *do* if we better understand what IOs *are*. International Organizations are bureaucracies, and bureaucracies are distinctive social forms that exercise authority in particular ways. Perhaps most influential and least noticed are the ways in which IOs use their authority to both regulate and constitute the world. (2004, 9)

The extent to which the explanatory thrust is focused on the agentic or actor-specific properties of IOs is made clear by their programmatic statement that "understanding how IOs are constituted socially allows us to hypothesize about the *behavior* of IOs and the *effects* this social form might have in global politics" (Barnett and Finnemore 2004, 9–10). It is exceedingly difficult to find where to draw the line between actorhood or arena, however. Perhaps we can get a better view of what IOs are through a focus on what they *do* when they engage in global governance. Thus understood, IOs may very well be *both* bureaucracies with a considerable degree of autonomy and power over states (Barnett and Finnemore 2004; Mortensen 2008; Woods 2006) *and* agents controlled by principals (states), where some states are more powerful than others (Drezner 2007). But these debates derive much of their significance from a prior concern with the question of who has power: states, NGOs, or IOs. In a sense, the debate mirrors what was said in the previous chapter concerning the relationship between states and NGOs in discussions about global governance.

Crucially, we want to draw attention to the paradoxical relationship that IOs have to sovereignty. IOs have sovereign states as their core epistemic entry point and target for governing: they seek to govern and act on *states;* and while these states are measured, evaluated, and acted upon from within a largely liberal and neoliberal political rationality, there is always an inescapable institutional state focus on what IOs generally do. In this sense, IOs are heavily structured in their operations by the institution of sovereignty, even as they are authoritative and autonomous from states. Moreover, IOs generally cannot avail themselves of sovereign powers, and so they are compelled to govern sovereign states "through freedom." The power of IOs thus rests very much with their ability to establish and disseminate authoritative standards, best practices, and performance ratings, and to couple these with aid allocations, as we discuss later. Stripped of the background condition of sovereignty, liberal forms of governing cannot, as they can in the domestic realm, lean on and operate in tandem with sovereignty.

Episteme and Government

In his interpretation of Foucault's work on governmentality, Mitchell Dean holds that understanding the transformations in the episteme of governing, from *raison d'état* to liberalism, is central to understanding its rationality.

> The point at which population ceases to be the sum of the inhabitants within a territory and becomes a reality *sui generis* with its own forces and tendencies is the point at which this dispositional government of the state begins to meet a government through social, economic, and biological processes. This government through these processes would come to generalize the pastoral government of religious communities to the entire population within the state. (1999, 96)

Dean here summarizes how Foucault's discussion of pastoral power—expressed in the shepherd/flock game—was generalized and universalized once the episteme changed into one where the social was understood as a sui generis reality. This perspective brings up a fundamentally important question regarding the episteme within which IOs operate: What is the concrete content of the episteme from within which IOs seek to govern, and how does that episteme affect the governing and mode of operation of IOs? Does it differ from that of states—and if so, in what way? Focusing on the role of sovereignty within the episteme of the IO mode of governing, we discuss in greater detail the role and content of sovereignty within the governmental rationality of one specific IO: the World Bank.

Liberal governmentality rests and operates "through freedom." Further, Foucault holds that the emergence of liberalism as a distinct form of governing has been defined by how the market performs the role of a "test" for whether one is governing too much. The "thin phenomenal layer of interests" that guides interactions of individuals, the interplay of interests, is placed between the ruler and society, thereby transforming the goal and functioning of power from sovereignty to biopower (2008, 46). The establishment, at the global level, of a range of different indicators, standards and ratings setting clear criteria and standards for how government should relate to and regulate the economy constitute, in our view, an operationalization of such a test at the global level. But does liberalism merely entail that governing must respect fundamental principles of human rights and the alleged spontaneous equilibrium that markets produce—that the market is a domain whose own laws and dynamics must be respected? Far from it. Foucault notes that, in the regime of liberalism, freedom "is not a ready-made region which has to be respected. . . . Freedom is something which is constantly produced" (2008, 65).

Here, IOs play a central role in governing the globe inasmuch as they are involved in setting up authoritative indexes and grids through which societies are analyzed, rated, and compared with regard to everything from the capacity of the state and human rights records to the costs of doing business. Laura Zanotti, for example, has described how the good governance agenda of the UNDP and the World Bank represents a "global project of state engineering that addresses, but does not limit itself to, state institutions"—a project that also seeks to harness civil society to strengthen and help regulate the state (2005, 471). Other studies have identified a global governmentality at work through "world opinion" as a functional and semantic conduit for postsovereign modes of governing at the global level already at the founding of the UN (Jaeger 2008). Still others have drawn attention to the elaborate web of "systems of examination" where actors are measured, evaluated, and made responsible for their actions within the indexes largely formulated and promulgated by IOs (Löwenheim 2008).

We concur with this interpretation. Global ratings and indicators are a relatively recent phenomenon in global politics. Originating within economic governance in the postwar era, there is today a plethora of different global indicators and ratings that amount to a truly global "audit culture" (Strathern 2000) where more and more areas of the social are presented and rendered intelligible within a liberal framework aimed at producing and consuming freedom. As Michael Power has noted about this "audit explosion," this entails a transformation in the reference point for governing, because "the standards of performance themselves are shaped by the need to be auditable. . . . Audit becomes a formal 'loop' by which the system observes itself" (1994, 36–37). First developed in the 1940s under the leadership of John M. Keynes and later made a standard at the global level, national accounts were one of the first global indicators to make possible international comparisons, in this case, of the finances of various countries. Today, however, countries are not evaluated by themselves or others solely on the basis of macroeconomic indicators from national accounts. As a World Bank report put it, governments now also "pay attention to the laws, regulations and institutional arrangements that shape daily economic activity" (World Bank 2008, v). The report goes on to note, however, that "until very recently, . . . there were no globally available indicator sets for monitoring microeconomic factors and analyzing their relevance." This was the basis for the Bank's establishment of the "Doing Business" reports, with ten detailed indicators of the microeconomic regulatory frameworks of 181 countries, aimed at providing "an objective basis for understanding and improving the regulatory environment for business" (v).

Moreover, these indicators, and the ratings and recommendations that ensue, enter the vocabulary of states, amounting to what Ian Hacking calls the "looping effect." This takes place in no small part through the establishment of what Michael Powers calls "rituals of verification," whereby standards for auditing produce new practices aimed at documenting and making visible what states do and how they do it (1999). For example, in 2006, the Egyptian investment minister saw these indicators as useful because they "create a forum for exchanging knowledge. We have checked the best performers. . . . So we just ask them 'What did you do?' We need to capitalize on their experience." For the minister of planning of Ghana, the indicators similarly served to "spur us on to examine other areas where we currently fall short and see how we can improve things." The Mexican secretary of the economy claims that it has "helped [Mexico] to obtain a more objective view of the country as a whole."[3] For the *Financial Times*, who reported on all this, such indicators were a "public good [that] may become as indispensable to reformers and to academics as national income accounts."[4]

Against this background, we can say that studies of global-level governmental reason have been supplemented in their accounts by the view of IOs presented by Barnett and Finnemore, where IOs have the authority and autonomy to regulate as well as constitute the social world within which states govern. In short, IOs are central to the production of the freedom through which states govern: IOs authoritatively define what the market is, how it should be regulated and set up, and what governments should and should not do. While we agree with the overall thrust of this interpretation, it fails to capture the fundamental importance of sovereign states *within* an expanding liberal governmental reason at the global level. We can see this through an analysis of how sovereignty and the state is interpreted within the World Bank's Country Policy and Institutional Assessment (CPIA).

---

3. Available at "More on Doing Business," http://www.doingbusiness.org/Media/db.aspx.

4. *Financial Times*, September 6, 2006. Quote from "More on Doing Business." http://www.doingbusiness.org/Media/db.aspx.

CPIA at the World Bank—Sovereignty in a Liberal Governmentality

One of the more significant yet less publicly known global ratings is the Country Policy and Institutional Assessment (CPIA). This is an annual exercise where the Bank evaluates and rates recipient countries on everything from macroeconomic policy to social policy. It plays a central role for how the World Bank, through the International Development Association (IDA), allocates funds and tailors policy responses. The World Bank's mission is to "promote economic development, increase productivity, and thus raise standards of living in the less developed areas of the world [by providing finance] on terms which are more flexible and bear less heavily . . . than conventional loans" (World Bank Press Release no. 621, 1960). For 2005, IDA eligible countries were those with an income per capita of less than US$1,025. As of 2006, eighty-one countries, comprising about 2.5 billion people, were eligible for IDA loans.

Country assessments were initiated in the 1970s as a "tool to guide the allocation of IDA lending sources" (World Bank 2005a, 1), originally as an assessment tool adjacent to the Bank's Structural Adjustment Programs that were then being introduced. In this period, the assessment exercise covered mainly economic issues, such as financial policy, trade, taxation. Since 1977, the IDA funds have been dispersed on the basis of the Performance-Based Allocation System (PBA), where "performance" has been assessed by what is now known as the CPIA (IDA 2004, 1). While the CPIA is principally aimed at enabling aid allocations, the Bank also considers it central to a host of other aspects of Bank operations: It informs the Country Assistance Strategy (CAS), which details Bank operations at the country level; it provides the foundation for Bank Country Teams in their "policy dialogue" with developing countries; and it provides important background data for a host of research activities and evaluations performed by the Bank (IDA 2006).

At the core of the CPIA are the sixteen indicators that are used to rank a country's performance in four "clusters" or thematic areas: (a) economic management, (b) structural policies, (c) policies for social inclusion and equity, and (d) public sector management and institutions. For each of the sixteen indicators, countries are ranked on a scale from 1 to 6, where 1 is defined as "very weak performance" and 6 as "very strong performance." According to the guidelines for the exercise, in rating countries on the different criteria, the scores "should reflect a variety of indicators, observations, and judgements that are based on country knowledge originated in the Bank, analytic work or policy dialogue, or work done by partners, and relevant publicly available indicators" (World Bank 2005a, 4). The guidelines for the CPIA are highly detailed. For example, criterion 12, "Property Rights and Rule-based Governance," comprises three dimensions: (a) legal basis for property rights, (b) predictability, transparency, impartiality, and enforcement of laws regulating economic activity, (c) crime and violence as impediment to economic activity. Moreover, assessment of performance on each criterion is guided by a description for each score.

The significance of the CPIA resides in part in its universalist underpinnings—in how it defines a global grid of intelligibility for governing not just the economy but society more generally. Like the Doing Business Indicators and others, the CPIA sets up standards and best practices for governing that are universal not only in coverage but also in logic by assuming that there is an optimal policy regardless of context. Ravi Kanbur, former economist at the Bank, points out how the CPIA signals a view of the world, and of the processes of "development," that is distinct in its universalist assumptions.

> The twenty categories are the same for each country, the guidelines for what gets a high score in each country are the same in every country, and the weighting scheme across the twenty scores (equal weighting) is the same for every country. What could be the logic behind this uniformity in country treatment? (2005, 12)

The very logic of the assessment posits that the development process is or will be *similar* in all countries. The CPIA thus imposes a global standard, leaving little room for national policy maneuver or for the exploration of different models of development. In this sense, the CPIA is a perfect example of a liberally oriented global governmentality—setting authoritative standards that developing countries ignore at their peril. If we pause to consider what the CPIA really measures, however, it is clear that the central— arguably constitutive—*entity* of the episteme of the CPIA is that of sovereign states. The guidelines for how Bank staff are to evaluate countries explicitly state that the criteria are intended to capture factors that are within a country's control: "The criteria focus on policies and institutional arrangements, the key elements that are within the country's control, rather than on actual outcomes (for example, growth rates) that are influenced by elements outside the country's control" (World Bank 2007, 4).

As much as the CPIA renders specific a liberal governmental rationality that operates at the global level, therefore, it does so by operating from within, or on the basis of, an episteme where sovereign states are the key reference point and target of analysis. This does not mean that sovereignty dictates or sets the terms for this episteme: only that sovereign states occupy a central position within the social world that the Bank seeks to assess and govern. The significance of sovereignty within the CPIA is nowhere clearer than in the specific contents of the criteria used. Of the four thematic clusters, cluster (d) on public sector management and institutions covers, for example, "rules-based governance" (criterion 12); "quality of budget administration" (criterion 15); and "transparency, accountability, corruption" (criterion 16). All of them are focused on government policies or state "behavior" measured in terms of whether the state apparatus maintains a distinction between public and private (corruption etc.), whether state institutions uphold and follow established rules, and so on. Indicator 9 ("Building Human Resources") refers to "universal access to good preventive and curative health services," to "good national health strategy and effective regulation," to "policies and resources to allow prevention and treatment of all forms of malnutrition," and "cost effective use of public resources." Clearly, to the extent that liberalism or neoliberalism is about "governing less," then—as far as the developing countries are concerned—how the World Bank evaluates and seeks to act on and govern aid recipients cannot be understood as solely being liberal or neoliberal on a par with how such governmental rationalities operating within the nation-state context function.

The management of the World Bank justifies the strong focus on performance with reference to the incentives that it gives to recipient countries: rewarding the performance of client countries helps establish a structure of incentives for client countries to "do the right thing." The CPIA can be seen to define a global grid of indicators within which all actors can readily factor in global standards in their decision making. At a 2006 seminar, "Measuring Governance: Possibilities and Pitfalls" at the Center for Global Development (CGD) in Washington, DC, the former finance and foreign minister of Nigeria was asked to give a perspective on being subjected to such in-depth measurement methods by the Bank.

> I want to say that from the perspective of a person on the ground, having these indicators . . . these measurements are crucial. . . . If you are in the process of doing reform, there has to be some way of being able to measure where you're going, the trends, the results . . . and if you don't have that, then you have a dialogue of the deaf. And the more objective the indicators are, that is the more it comes from some organization or

body that is not necessary, yourself, the more people will look at this. So I think it is, crucially important, to have these indicators. (Okonjo-Iweala 2006, 14)

Still—and this goes to the fundamental difference between national-level and global-level governmental rationalities—the World Bank (and other IOs) operate in a world of sovereign states, and as much as sovereignty is relativized, trumped by, or "shared" with donors (bilateral and multilateral), it is an inescapable feature of the parameters within which IOs evaluate and seek to govern, or act on, states. This is clearly brought out in Best's analysis of the principle of "national ownership."

> The emerging discourse of ownership thus feeds into a conception of self responsibility that greatly resembles a Foucauldian logic of self-government. The goal of global economic governance is to ensure that member states and the individuals within them take responsibility for their own economic well-being by fostering an entrepreneurial spirit. Their progress towards that end is to be carefully measured through the application of the global standards that define the norm and monitored through the logic of transparency. The IMF and World Bank's new global strategies have thus begun the work of translating into the global realm the logic of liberal governmentality. (Best 2005, 21; see also Hindess 2004, 35)

This is also a reflection of the modus operandi between Bank Country Teams and recipient governments: by mandate and through convention, Bank staff interact with governmental officials in developing the Country Assistance Strategy (CAS) and the Poverty Reduction Strategies (PRS). Moreover, the CPIA—as a tool for governing—leans heavily on sovereignty expressed in terms of money allocated to the state and the conditions that the World Bank attaches to its grants and loans, where governments must commit to specific policies, in order to be eligible for funding. The principle of ownership is thus in itself a testimony to the "governmentalization of sovereignty" in development discourse, as ownership and participatory processes function as an entry point for Bank officials to peg governing attempts to the expressed needs of the poor. In the Bank's own publications, we find material that indicates that its officials decide what to look for before they enter the field, and then simply report back on what they had already decided to find. For example, in the Colombian case study in the *World Bank Sourcebook,* the recommendations given by fifteen Bank staff representatives before the participatory exercise started are almost identical to those given by the Colombian "participants" after the exercise.[5] Logically, it may be that World Bank personnel were able to assess the situation as if from a local perspective. When viewed in the light of how the *Sourcebook* itself describes what it calls a participatory process led by the Bank itself, however, it seems quite clear that what we have here is a case of governmentality.

At one level, all of this is self-evident and straightforward enough: state sovereignty is obviously central to global politics. While many studies have shown in great detail the extent to which sovereignty is trumped, relativized, and reconfigured in fundamental ways by processes of globalization and the doings of the World Bank and other IOs, this should not detract attention away from how sovereignty organizes thought and imposes categories of thought and action, including for IOs themselves (see Bourdieu 1999).

Sovereignty is often glossed over in studies of governmentality at the global level—as if Foucault's call to study the practices of rule rather than the institutions of the state has been interpreted to mean that one can ignore the state and the institution of sovereignty in analyses of contemporary rationalities of power. Sovereign states—even exceedingly weak and poor ones—form the basic units and the frame of reference for how IOs "see the world" and act in it (see Broome and Seabrooke 2007). The central point is to understand how sovereignty is part of the episteme within which IOs operate. Exploring the relation between this episteme and liberal governmental rationality gives us a handle on the sui generis governmental rationality espoused by IOs.

Does State Building Equal Neoliberalism plus Police?

For Foucault, the emergence of neoliberalism entails that freedom is substituted for competition as the guiding principle of governing. It is worth quoting him at some length here, as he identifies a central implication of the shift from liberalism to neoliberalism.

> There will not be the market game, which must be left free, and then the domain in which state begins to intervene, since the market, or rather pure competition, which is the essence of the market, can only appear if it is produced, and it is produced by an active governmentality. There

---

5. http://www.worldbank.org/wbi/sourcebook/sbhome.htm. Accessed January 20, 2009. We were directed to this source by reading Trinborg 2007.

will thus be a sort of complete superimposition of market mechanisms, indexed to competition, and governmental policy.... The market economy does not take something away from government. Rather, it indicates, it constitutes the general index in which one must place the rule for defining all governmental action. One must govern for the market, rather than because of the market. To that extent you can see that the relationship defined by eighteenth century liberalism is completely reversed. (2008, 121)

While the term *neoliberalism* as a political idea or ideology must not be confused with neoliberalism as a governmental rationality, it is striking that both the World Bank and the IMF have been the central targets—along with the WTO—of protests against globalization interpreted as "the spread of neoliberalism." While it is not always clear what is meant by *neoliberalism,* critics share a concern with the "rolling back" of the state often advocated by the World Bank and the IMF. Here, the state is generally seen as an obstacle to economic growth and development, whereas the market and civil society are conceptualized as the progressive forces that would be unleashed if the state got out of the way (cf. Ferguson 2006, 95–97). Understood as a governmental rationality, neoliberalism is different, in that it concerns an important shift in terms of the state now emerging as much more important for the detailed intervention to help set up markets—or competition—within the state and in society in general. Thus conceived, neoliberalism is about making the entire social body driven by competition, for which state intervention is necessary.

As explained by Ferguson (2006), the modernization programs of earlier periods placed the state as in the position as "developer" and society as in some way "backward." Under neoliberalism, by contrast, the state is seen as the obstacle to progress and evolution: "Where the first paradigm saw the development problem as too much society and not enough state, the second sees it as too much state and not enough society" (97). As Ferguson is quick to point out, however, these two models are not very different, as both operate with a very crude hierarchy, or dichotomy, between state and society. If we read these two models of development in a governmental framework, the role of the state is central also in the neoliberal version. Here, governmental action emerges as essential to the functioning and spread of markets and the "pure competition" that they entail.

In the era of structural adjustment programs, states and governments may have been seen as obstacles to progress and growth. Today's World Bank policy, however, presents a view of the state that is markedly different, seeing effective and robust states as central to the objective of the Bank. During the latter half of the 1990s, state characteristics—defined in terms of good governance—emerged as the central explanatory factor for why aid was effective in spurring growth in some countries and not in others (Burnside and Dollar 2000; Collier and Dollar 1999). It is this research that underpins the standards embedded in the CPIA, where governance is by far the most significant factor affecting overall country score and thus also aid allocations. This research has found that aid is used most effectively in countries that have good governance. While governance is central to all aspects of the CPIA, it is particularly cluster (d), as discussed earlier, that covers this dimension. Crucially, the Bank defines governance in terms reminiscent of the household episteme of governing that underpinned police and *raison d'état:* as "the manner in which power is exercised in the management of a country's economic and social resources" (World Bank 1994, xiv, quoted in Steets 2008, 7). The CPIA is gradually updated and "has evolved well beyond the 'Washington Consensus' to take into account a wider range of policy areas" (World Bank 2007, 3). This expansion to a "wider range of policy areas" is in part a reflection of the research on aid effectiveness, and the CPIA specifies and operationalizes the contents of the good governance agenda.

As shown in the CPIA standards, the prevailing consensus within the World Bank is that there exists a host of factors associated with higher aid effectiveness and economic development—and these factors all have to do with how the state governs itself and society. The interpretation of the role of the state within the liberal or neoliberal outlook that characterizes the World Bank thus contains central elements of sovereignty. The World Bank and other key IOs in the field of development build on OECD-DAC principles where state building is defined in terms of three pillars: "the capacity of state structures to perform core functions; their legitimacy and accountability; and ability to provide an enabling environment for strong economic performance" (OECD-DAC 2005). Here, governing by IOs aims to restore and help build sovereignty, to establish a state whose structures can perform "core functions," *and* to have this state govern in a way that is clearly modeled on the market as it is to define and establish an "enabling environment" for the market to operate in. State building entails a significant change in the role accorded to the state, where development and security policies have been merged to produce a much stronger focus on the state's ability to control its territory and govern its population (Cammack et al. 2006). While the CPIA does not explicitly focus on the security apparatus, it is used—as we discuss in the next section—to identify which states are deemed "fragile" and in need of special forms of intervention.

In providing a detailed list of which state policies are considered most important for generating development, the CPIA serves as a bridge from the economic realm to the state. It helps furnish decision makers with a set of "actionable" indicators that transform client countries from being primarily economic entities into also administrative, legal, social, and political entities. The CPIA, we submit, is an operationalization and specification of precisely what the "social," the "political," and the "administrative" of its client countries are, and how to act on them. Thus, we must take care to avoid relying on a domestic analogy that might lead us in the direction of seeking to find the same governmental rationality within IOs as is found within sovereign states. While several studies have found governmentality flourishing well beyond the established liberal democracies of the West—for example, in China (Sigley 2006)—the character of governmentality at the *global* level is arguably transformed by the existence of sovereignty. Foucault's basic narrative is one about how the image of the household gradually lost out to the image of an independent society with the market as the reference point for governing. The story unfolding at the global level, by contrast, is one where the image of the household—of the government spending its resources wisely, regulating its economy wisely—is being superimposed on the preexisting image of a liberally oriented governmentality at the national level. Foucault writes of the evolution of a mode of thinking about "governing less" that gradually takes hold, in the form of a liberal art of government.

What we have described here is, if anything, a process whereby IOs—*in casu*, the World Bank—expand their assessments and governing beyond the original economic mandate and into the realm of the state (see Barnett and Finnemore 2004; Best 2005). In this sense, IOs and other actors *actively* seek to set up and build a global grid of performance indicators and benchmarks—not in order to govern more intrusively, if such a word can be used, but rather to expand the reach of IO governing techniques. The standards set out in the CPIA—in the form of measures of social inclusion, public expenditure, and so on—go well beyond the mechanisms of the market, and so it is not sufficient to label this simply a liberal or neoliberal governmentality. Instead, it is a test that captures virtually all aspects of a *state's* sphere of competence—everything from financial policy, trade, environmental standards, and corruption, to health, human rights, and labor regulations. In that sense, global-level governmentality (as opposed to a globalization of or convergence of liberal or neoliberal governmentality at the national level) embeds the image of the society as an extension of the household found in the police state: Governments "own" their societies—that is, they are inseparable from and responsible for them—much as individuals are responsible for their health. Consider the following description of the function of the World Bank's "Doing Business Indicators" (2009, vi).

> It functions as a kind of cholesterol test for the regulatory environment for domestic business. A cholesterol test does not tell us everything about the state of our health. But it does measure something important for our health. And it puts us on watch to change behaviors in ways that will improve not only our cholesterol rating but also our overall health.

Here, states are equated with individuals whose health is in their hands to manage and sustain, much as the territory of the Prince was for him to nurture and control. The *Index of Economic Freedom* notes in a similar vein that "this index exists . . . to remind forgetful politicians of the benefits of economic freedom. [*The Index*] follows the simple tenet that something cannot be improved if it is not measured" (quoted in Löwenheim 2008, 260). Our central point is that we have to get a grasp on how states are conceptualized within IOs if we are to understand the specific rationality by which IOs seek to govern and act on states. The image of the state within the World Bank is one where state control and state regulation are seen as central to effective economic governing, and where the ideal state combines key elements of neoliberal and policelike qualities. We do not want to suggest that the World Bank and other IOs are operating within an episteme modeled on *Polizeiwissenschaft*, nor to argue that they do not advance a view of progress and development emerging from the market and "civil society." We do want to suggest, however, that most studies of the governmental aspect of IOs development operations (e.g., Rojas 2004) have overlooked how sovereignty and state capacity and control are not obliterated by a neoliberal governmental rationality but have instead been reconfigured within it as a central means to achieving adequate government modeled on the principle of competition.

Fragile States and Global Governmental Reason

We have noted that various practices of screening, and evaluation have been established at the global level, all focusing on efforts to produce states whose policies and institutions are to be geared toward a special relation involving the state, civil society, and the economy. Here we have tried to identify a distinct and often overlooked sovereign theme running within this liberal governmental reason. We next examine how some states have come to be defined as "fragile" or "failed." Such a category did not exist before the mid-1990s. In 2008, Stepputat and Engeberg-Pederson reviewed the fragile states agenda and found that:

> The notion of fragile states is emerging as a focus to forge stable and manageable relations with states that do not conform to established images and expectations of states. These attempts are mainly donor-driven, and few states' incumbents are likely to present themselves as representing "fragile" or "failed" states. But maybe this will change as policy fields and budget-lines crystallize around the notion of fragile states. (1)

Indeed, there is already a "looping effect" at work in the sense that this new category affects the self-understanding of states (Hacking 2001). When addressing the UN Security Council in 2006, president of Liberia Ellen Johnson-Sirleaf, noted, for example, that "Liberia is still a fragile state."[6] Afghan president Hamid Karzai similarly told an international conference in 2004 that "drugs in Afghanistan are undermining the very existence of the Afghan state" and that "the problem for us is too huge to be able to face or challenge alone."[7] Thus understood, the category "fragile" or "failed" state is a productive one, in the sense that once a state is so defined, that changes donor aid allocations and policies toward that state. For one thing, international credit rating companies, such as Moody's and Standard & Poor's, adjust their rating and make it more expensive to borrow money on the international financial markets. What primarily interests us here, however, is not so much the existence or strength of such a "looping effect" but rather the governmental rationality that can be said to characterize efforts to define, understand, and address state failure and state fragility in global politics.

Barry Hindess (2004, 33) notes how liberalism can be seen as a governmental rationality that has always extended beyond the confines of the state.

---

6. UN Press Release, March 17, 2006. http://www.un.org/apps/news/story.asp?NewsID=17845&Cr=liberia&Cr1=&Kw1=fragile+state&Kw2=&Kw3= (accessed on January 8, 2009).

7. "Drugs 'undermining existence of Afghan state.'" Press release, Agence France, March 31, 2004. http://www.aegis.com/NEWS/AFP/2004/AF0403D1.html (accessed on January 8, 2009).

> Liberalism has been concerned with regulating the conduct of the aggregate population encompassed within the system of states, and ... it addresses this task by allocating responsibility for the government of specific populations to individual states ... and promoting within states appropriate means of governing the populations under their control.

Central to Hindess's interpretation of liberalism as a global governmental rationality is the idea that liberalism operates, as Foucault put it, by using the market "as a test." This test effectively places some groups in the realm of being governed "through freedom" while others are in need of other forms of rule (Hindess 2004, 28). Against the backdrop of the thickening web of global indicators and best practices that partly supplements, partly competes with nationally constituted "repertoires of evaluation and justification" (Lamont and Thevenot 2000), it seems important to examine how such a test is set up and whether some groups or activities are seen to require nonliberal forms of governing. In this context, IOs are central to the production and institutionalization of authoritative tests for states. At the World Bank, this test is the CPIA, which not only defines a hierarchy of states according to performance but also uses this performance rating to allocate funding among countries and thus to institutionalize performance as the central determinant of funding and attention relative to "needs" (in this case, poverty levels).

As we have seen, however, it is hard to detect a clear liberal or neoliberal governmental rationality in how the CPIA defines statehood. Certainly, the CPIA contains a test, where some states are deemed to exhibit poor performance: a state is defined as "fragile" if it has an overall score of 3.2 or lower. Given the weight accorded to governance in the CPIA, fragility is here defined in terms of "lack of capacity" and/or "lack of political will" (Steets 2008, 32). The reference to lack of capacity clearly indicates a concern with states as sovereign, capable of controlling and regulating the territory and the social body. The somewhat elusive reference to political will, by contrast, apparently places "will" in relation to a certain standard of governing in accordance with liberal principles. In this sense, fragility here draws on both an image of sovereignty and an image of liberalism.

While those states that are considered fragile receive less funds, ceteris paribus, than other states because of their low performance rating, there is little indication that the categorization as "fragile" subjects these states to particular forms of either liberal or nonliberal rule. The "test" according to which some states are deemed unfit for liberal rule, therefore, seems today to be of little import. An evaluation by the Independent Evaluation

Group of the World Bank concluded that since the establishment of the Low Income Countries Under Stress (LICUS) task force in 2002, "the objectives and scope of the LICUS initiative have shifted from general aid effectiveness concerns to state building and peace building objectives. . . . State building and peace building have not been well defined, however, and remain somewhat abstract, especially from an operational point of view" (IEG 2006, 7–8). Indeed, key policy documents from all IOs with a focus on state building seem to share the same liberal interpretation of fragility as defined largely in terms of lacking capacity, institutional resources, and individual skills (OECD 2007; UNDP 2007). In short, the practices through which IOs seek to address state fragility seem to be the very same methods and strategies used for nonfragile states. We find little differentiation in terms of rationale or form of governing between fragile and nonfragile states. Certainly, the Bank has developed more flexible, dynamic methods to engage with fragile states so as to be able to capture and act on dynamic factors on the ground.

If we broaden the perspective from the CPIA and the World Bank, however, a different interpretation of failed and fragile states emerges. It should be noted that both state failure and fragility have at least three distinct roots, and the World Bank focuses primarily on the first two of these. The first is that of human security and postconflict peace-building. The experiences with Somalia, Rwanda, and the Balkans ushered in a period of reflection at the UN and elsewhere on how to help prevent internal conflicts through both military and developmental means. The second is the concern with development effectiveness, where the poorest developing countries (least developed countries, or LDCs) were constituted as a separate category of states lacking those characteristics that would enable more liberally oriented governing modes to be effective.

While these two trajectories together established fragile states and failed states as significant challenges for combating poverty and building peace, the third trajectory—already present in discussions about global threats and insecurities—emerged as a highly potent response after the terrorist attacks of September 11. This latter interpretation conceptualizes fragile and failed states not in terms of the challenge they pose to their inhabitants but as regards the challenge to the security and welfare of other countries and global governance efforts more generally. The U.S. National Security Strategy of 2002 puts it bluntly: "America is now threatened less by conquering states than we are by failing ones" (NSS 2002, 1). Similarly, the European security strategy, published the following year, declares, "State failure is an alarming phenomenon that undermines global governance, and adds to regional instability" (EU 2003, 4). In keeping with this threat assessment, the United States established a new command, AFRICOM—one of whose objectives is to work to prevent unstable and fragile African states from becoming sources of instability for the region and for the world.

Consider how Stephen Krasner, then serving as Director of Policy Planning at the State Department, and Carlos Pascual, a Brookings Institution researcher involved in Brookings' Weak States Index, laid out a strategy for state building to advance U.S. interests.

> The United States and the rest of the world need to develop the tools to both prevent conflict and manage its aftermath when it does occur. Such efforts will entail not just peacekeeping measures, but also influencing *the choices that troubled countries make* about their economies, their political systems, the rule of law, and their internal security. Weak countries are unable to take advantage of the global economy not just because of a lack of resources, but also because they lack strong, capable institutions. To promote sustainable peace, Washington and its partners must thus commit to making long-term investments of money, energy, and expertise. (2005, 153–54; emphasis added)

In his report *In Larger Freedom,* prepared for the UN Summit in 2005, then secretary-general Kofi Annan argued that the very purpose of the UN as defined in the Charter was being threatened by fragile states: "If states are fragile, the peoples of the world will not enjoy security, development, and justice that are their right. Therefore, one of the great challenges of the new millennium is to ensure that all States are strong enough to meet the many challenges we face" (UN 2005a, 6). The references to fragile and failed states have made their way into broader debates about the effectiveness of global governance, so fragile and failed states now occupy a central position in discussions about global threats and their governing. Indeed, one significant outcome of the 2005 UN Summit was the acceptance by UN member-states of what has become known as the "responsibility to protect." The outcome document establishes that the "international community, through the United Nations . . . has the responsibility to use appropriate . . . means to help to protect populations from genocide, war crimes, ethnic cleansing, and crimes against humanity." Further, this may, as a last resort, involve "collective action" in accordance with Chapter VII; and such a responsibility is triggered when "national authorities are manifestly failing to protect their populations" (UN 2005b, 30). Invoking language drawn from the discourse on conflict prevention and state building, the document goes on to assert, "We also intend to commit ourselves, as necessary and appropriate, to helping States build capacity to protect their populations ... and to assisting those which are under stress before crises and conflicts break out" (30).

The definition of fragile states as central to the protection of civilians against genocide and crimes against humanity as well as global threats such as terrorism, organized crime, and weapons of mass destruction seems to fall outside of the scope of a liberal governmental rationality. Our central contention is that the significance of the term *fragile states* must be grasped at the level at which it was formulated: the global security discourse, broadly defined. At this level, the postulation of a category of fragile states serves various significant purposes, some of which provide a new approach for dissecting and describing the rationality of political rule that characterize *global* governance. The rationality of this global-level political rule must be distinguished from the convergence of governmental rationalities that we may observe in various different areas in different countries. (One interesting example here could be the pervasiveness of liberal governmental rationalities in China.) At this global level, fragile states serve the purpose of bringing together disparate elements from development and security in the concept of prevention and in a broad concept of security. Both these features can be analyzed in terms of the police rationality of governing.

As a governmental rationality, police is focused on prevention. It concerns both *securité* (security) and *sureté* (safety); it operates through detailed regulation, with lists of things to do and not to do, without any clear, overarching principles of prioritization. Indeed, as Mariana Valverde has pointed out, police powers have never ceased to be a central component of governing, despite claims to the contrary by Foucault and others. What rendered police logic a target of critique by Adam Smith and others was merely that some central aspects of the social body were beyond the reach of the "gaze of government."

> Liberal thinkers such as Adam Smith gained their renown by insisting that economic and social processes were to some extent self-governing and thus opaque to the gaze of government: to that extent—and only to that extent—they broke with the police logic. (Valverde 2003, 236)

Valverde goes on to provide an account of the role of *licensing* as a distinct governmental technique that is policelike in its logic but is central to liberal forms of governing in contemporary society.

> The legal technology of the license allows governments to ensure that certain spaces, activities, and people are under constant surveillance and are subject to immediate disciplinary measures, but without state officials or centralized state knowledges being involved in this micromanagement. (2003, 236)

The global-level rationality of governing brought out through the discourse of failed states is strikingly similar in form to that of the licensing as laid out by Valverde. Global governance discourse increasingly conceptualizes states as entities that are "licensed" to survey, regulate, and discipline their territories and populations in such a way as to avoid instability and risks. Here, the global presence is rarely felt because the UN and other IOs are only exceptionally (as in "peace operations") involved directly in such policelike governing. Instead, they set up best practices, norms, and benchmarks for how population and territory need to be attended to in a very different way. There is thus a sui generis character to global governmentality: it can be seen as licensing *to* states that are increasingly measured, evaluated, and always at risk of being branded "failed" or "fragile."

Conclusion

We noted earlier that Hindess interpreted liberalism as operating both at the domestic and at the international levels, thus seeing liberal government as an overarching governmental rationality at both the state and the global levels. This view of the global governmental logic of liberalism can be compared with that provided by Foucault in one of his rare remarks on the international. In his lectures in 1978, Foucault discussed the "European equilibrium" that constituted the external dimension of police within the state (see chap. 3). He argued that there was a "close relationship" between police as a governmental rationality aimed at "good use of the state's forces" and the European equilibrium of states that became institutionalized with the Treaty of Vienna (2007, 314). According to this logic, each state has to be assured of the capacity of other states to order and police their own territories and populations. Foucault noted that, with this interplay of external competition and internal police, the following dynamic emerged.

> In the end, there will be imbalance if within the European equilibrium there is a state, not my state, with bad police. Consequently, one must see

to it that there is good police, even in other states. European equilibrium begins to function as a sort of inter-state police or as right. European equilibrium gives the set of states the right to see to it that there is good police in each state. (2007, 315)

Whereas Hindess identifies an overarching liberal governmental reason or logic that both allocates governmental responsibility to states *and* seeks to govern populations within each of them, Foucault stresses that the ensuing equilibrium is a result of the partly contradictory logics of internal police and external balancing. We should thus be sensitive to the difference between global- and national-level rationalities of government. Our argument has been that there is a global and liberally oriented governmentality at work in and through IOs, and that this liberal governmental rationality sets up sovereignty as central for the articulation of governmental power. We have, moreover, argued that, at the level of the global governance discourse, fragile and failed states are central to and reflective of a distinct "police character" to global governance, where prevention and detailed regulation is at work and always aims to "govern more." Finally, inasmuch as UN member-states have agreed on their responsibility to protect and are also committed to state building, state sovereignty emanates from the global-level rationality of governing, according states both license and responsibility to govern liberally and effectively.

Conclusion: Liberal Sovereignty in the Global Polity

We began by introducing the concept of governmentality and the possibility of developing it as a perspective on global politics overall (chap. 1). Since this perspective may strike most IR scholars as being a rather novel one, we read it against Hans Morgenthau's perspective (chap. 2). We found that, primarily due to the shared Weberian roots where the understanding of power is concerned, the two perspectives are largely compatible. This we took to mean that insights produced by means of the governmentality perspective could be used to update what Morgenthau called politics among nations and saw as an ideal type of global politics. Chapters 3 to 5 offered new insights into how an increasingly effective liberal rationality of government is establishing itself worldwide, exerting structural pressure on the state to govern indirectly. This in turn means that the state is forced to evolve new practices, which often include establishing new interfaces with NGOs, IOs, and other agents. With these insights in hand, we will now attempt to draw up a new ideal type.

We begin with a brief stock-taking exercise where we highlight the continued importance of sovereignty to global politics. Then we try to locate the place of sovereignty in global politics understood in a governmentality perspective, touching base with mainstream IR understandings en route. Like Waltz, we understand sovereignty as a question of the kind of relations that exist among units. Given such an understanding, the question of exactly which practices are at any one given time constitutive of sovereignty arises. This also means, however, that a change in sovereignty may be understood and analyzed as a change in the practices that constitute sovereignty. However, if there is a change in which practices are constitutive of sovereignty, then that gives rise to the question of why such a change comes about. Our answer is that the current change, the stirrings of which may be traced back to the aftermath of the Napoleonic Wars, is due to the ever-increasing structural pressure exerted by liberalism. Liberalism may thus be understood as a selector of why certain practices become constitutive of sovereignty (and, inversely, why some cease to be so).

Liberalism also tells a story about how the world should be understood as a global polity. This story is prescriptive: it dictates a need for spreading liberal practices that may then realize the global polity of the liberal story. Since these practices have emerged and are growing in number and importance, the liberal story about the global polity can be said to be a success story. Consequently, our ideal type of global politics revolves around a global polity (as opposed to Morgenthau's system of states) and a process whereby rule goes from depending first and foremost on direct means, to depending first and foremost on indirect ones. This means that governmentality is a key mode of power for global politics—but it does not mean that power understood as a game of wills (sovereignty) and power understood as domination disappear. Furthermore, sovereignty persists as a principle, but since liberalism constitutes a rationality of government that is above and beyond each single sovereign unit, this is a sovereignty unlike from the one envisaged in Morgenthau's ideal type.

Finally, we discuss an interesting paradox: that liberalism dictates governing less, whereas what we are now seeing is that global governmentality entails *more* global rule than before. This points to a weak spot in liberal self-reflection, but it should not impair the usefulness of our ideal type. That usefulness hinges on the degree to which our ideal type is suited as a point of departure for empirical studies of the sui generis character of global governmental reasoning and global governmental practices.

A caveat is in order. We freely acknowledge that the ideal type we formulate below cannot grasp the full complexity of the phenomenon under study. As seen in Weber's own practice, complex phenomena are better understood through a combination of different ideal types. Furthermore, the general thrust of Foucault's formulation of the concept of governmentality was not so much aimed at capturing a set of coherent ideas and attendant techniques of governing. Rather, governmentality, and liberalism for that matter, were for Foucault "characteristic ways of posing problems" (Dean 1999, 49). Our aim here is to capture a central and generic feature of world politics by formulating an ideal-typical description, while also acknowledging that such a description will always have to be supplemented by other ideal-typical features. We seek to formulate an analytical tool that can capture how present-day liberal governmentality relates to and may condition sovereignty as a defining feature of global politics.

Politics

As discussed in chapter 1, Foucault culled his governmentality perspective from a reading of how a nontransparent network of relations between subjects, what was to become known as "society," emerged in Europe from the sixteenth century onward. The emergence of society posed a key challenge where the governing of subjects was concerned, for it added a nontransparent layer between the sovereign and his subjects. We hypothesized that today something similar may be about to happen on the global level. In chapter 2, we discussed how such a way of framing global politics would fit in with how the international and the global have traditionally been understood in the discipline of international relations. We concluded that Foucault's understanding of politics is very close to realist icon and Weber student Hans Morgenthau's understanding of politics as intensity. This is due to the influence on both Weber and Foucault of Nietzsche's understanding of power. Like Morgenthau, Foucault bases his thinking on how there is a choice between understanding politics either as emanating from the nature of things ("everything is political") or as defined by the existence of adversaries (as did Carl Schmitt). Foucault concludes that it is "a question of saying rather: nothing is political, everything can be politicized, everything may become political. Politics is no more or less than that which is born with resistance to governmentality, the first uprising, the first confrontation" (quoted in Snellart 2007, 390). Politics, then, is intensification of a specific set of social relations.

Here we have a crucially important difference between Foucault and Morgenthau. While the two share a view of politics as intensity, they are grounded in two very different understandings of power. Morgenthau's analyses of world politics were based on a psychological understanding of power. Early on in his career, Morgenthau developed a view of power defined by the individual's psychological "desire for self-expression in and recognition by the community" (Koskenniemi 2004, 444). This view stayed with him. It is this very individualized conception of power that underwrites Morgenthau's identification of "national honor" as central to the dynamics of world politics. While Foucault's understanding of power may, like Morgenthau's, be traced back to Nietzsche, it is not only much broader. It is an attempt at accounting historically and sociologically for the existence of and changes in what is for Morgenthau simply an ontic presupposition. Thus, while politics is a process for both—anything can be made political—a governmentality reading offers a more sociological reading of the political. It treats social relations as endogenous. These relations are relative to the specific forms of power that are embedded in and operating through governmental practices, and they may be analyzed empirically.

As we shall see, however, Foucault's suggestion that politics is "born with resistance to governmentality" and that sovereignty is but the governing practices attached to it is too restrictive for an attempt to theorize about world politics. To capture essential features of the political at the global level, we have to treat sovereignty as a principle, not a practice. This also means that what constitutes the political at the global level cannot solely be written off as resistance to governmentality but must include a central focus, namely, the principle of sovereignty as a system-defining feature.

Politics, then, is process. It may take in anything as its subject matter; it may intensify anything social. The key point for forging an ideal type of global politics is to note that governance, and institutions of governance such as the state, are parasitic upon the social. Foucault's reading of how this works in early modern Europe did not start from ideas or ideologies as such, but from how things came to be experienced as problematic by the people involved.[1] The first thing to look for is how questions about a certain emerging phenomenon are posed, how a certain problem emerged historically. Specifically, Foucault was interested in "the *practices* on the basis of which these problematizations are formed" (1992, 11). Theorizing about historical shifts should start in historical reflection, not in some abstract analytical thought experiment. As Colin Gordon has observed, Foucault is highly skeptical of attempts to "deduce the modern activities of government from essential properties and propensities of the state." Instead, he saw the nature of the institution of the state as a function of changes in practices of government (Foucault 2000a). Practices, not institutions, are his point of entry for the analysis of the functioning of power.

Retrospectively, the problematization in this book emerges as what global governmentality is and how it shapes the global polity. Chapters 3 through 5 are our contributions to a growing literature that seeks to identify and analyze such governing practices in the international realm. As Foucault's concepts are tailored to address phenomena within a different

---

1. This goes for any Foucauldian problematization.

type of social system, however, we must move beyond Foucault's work in order to systematize and generalize from these findings.[2]

If the practices that have come to characterize global politics are neither reducible to nor intelligible within a state system, then surely we need to cast our net wider than is commonly done in IR theory, if we want to theorize the global polity.[3] However, we must still be able to capture defining features of the state system. Crucially, we must address the traditional defining principle of that system—sovereignty—head on. Sovereignty must be treated as a principle, not as a practice. In fact, global governance theorists typically skirt the issue of sovereignty by introducing "spheres of authority" as a new unit of analysis, or by focusing almost exclusively on the distinction between public and private (or state and nonstate) actors (Rosenau 1999, 2002; Börzel and Risse 2005; Scholte 2002). Such a focus on the cast of actors (private and public) involved in governance occludes the question of how sovereignty defines the specific character of the international realm. Such studies of how the power of epistemic communities, advocacy networks, private corporations, civil society organizations, and so on may shape policy outcomes are valuable, but it is not clear how they contribute to *global* governance—only that they may contribute to specific processes. The tendency of this literature not to reflect systematically on the sui generis quality of the international is a flaw shared with much of the constructivist literature of which it is a part (for a key exception, see Wendt 1999). In an effort to address this lacuna, we will now sketch a Weberian ideal type of global politics that seeks to supplant the one offered by Morgenthau.[4] Such an ideal type will have to reflect the continued importance of the states system, but it must also reflect the changes in practices that we have documented here.

At the heart of Morgenthau's ideal type was the system of states, understood as consisting of discrete units (territorial states), each with universality and a claimed monopoly of violence. Between and among these units, there was anarchy. Note that the basis for Morgenthau's ideal type was Eu-

---

2. Cf. Kalm 2008. For a different view, see Lipschutz 2005b.

3. If we do not, as do public choice theorists (e.g., Shepsle and Bondchek 1997), simply bracket all this as stuff that has been "delegated" by states.

4. As argued most recently by Patrick Jackson (2010b), ideal types may be quite literally utopian, in the sense that the world they describe does not exist and never did, but nonetheless, "at the most basic logical level it is quite impossible to disentangle [an existing] world from the practical knowledge activities that we use in constituting and studying it. All knowledge is therefore ideal-typical, whether or not we are explicit and rigorous about spelling out our value-commitments and the kinds of analytical oversimplifications to which they give rise" (147).

rope and the European experience. By extrapolating from this specific historical experience, he shut out the key extra-European experiences of being at the receiving end of colonialism and empire. One precondition for Morgenthau's giving pride of place to sovereignty lay exactly here. Sovereignty was hardly as central to the extra-European experience as it was to the European one (cf., e.g., Hobson and Sharman 2005; Salter 2002; O'Hagan 2002). Outside of Europe and North America, up until the 1960s and arguably also after that, empire was more important than state, and suzerainty more important than sovereignty. Given the exponential increase in importance of polities that are not European and not Western since Morgenthau offered his ideal type, even in Weber's and Morgenthau's own power political terms we have here an additional reason for updating.

Morgenthau defined politics as an ideal type revolving around intensity. It was, moreover, conditioned by and centered on sovereignty so as to be flexible and, we think, analytically powerful. This notwithstanding, politics was nonetheless reduced to the mediation between an inside of steadily growing sources of instability and imprudent politics (mass nationalism, etc.) and an outside of constant anarchy. Retaining key insights from Morgenthau's formulation of politics as intensity within the framework of the changes we have identified in global politics calls for a framework that avoids the possible reductionism entailed in linking politics to a specific institutional form. We need an alternative. Given that Morgenthau's ideal type centered on sovereignty, and that the changes in sovereign practices have been extensive since his time, we choose sovereignty as our point of departure.

Sovereignty

As a preliminary step, we recognize the distinction between sovereignty as the principle that constitutes the state as a given unit of the international system and sovereignty as the form of power that is traditionally said to go with it. Sovereignty as a constitutive principle was traditionally linked with anarchy: it was the principled, ideal-type relationship that existed among states. In such a relationship, the only mode of power said to be present was what Foucault termed "sovereignty" and understood as a strategic game of wills, where the outcome was unknown (see table 1 in chapter 1). For this to happen, A and B must be fairly evenly matched, and A and B must have an adequately mutual understanding of the world and of the situation, if they are to engage in a game.

There is nothing to indicate that sovereignty, understood as the principle that constitutes the state and the states system, should dictate that *all* practices that states engage in would be permeated with the mode of power that Foucault calls sovereignty (citing relations among sovereign states in early modern Europe as an example). It follows that there is nothing *inherently* sovereign about the practices that make up sovereignty. It is the quality of the *relation among* the units, understood as a self-reflective recognition, that defines sovereignty (Reus-Smit 1999). Changes in practices will change relations among actors on the whole. So, once states compete or cooperate not primarily over survival, but over how to govern phenomena ranging from international trade to the prevention of war to the threat of irreversible climate change, it follows that relations among them will change. And with this, sovereignty also changes. Historically, a key example is the change wrought by the emergence of popular sovereignty in the nineteenth century, but depending on what is considered a large enough change to be of importance, one may speak of any number of changes in sovereignty (Weber 1995).

At this point, it is useful to touch base with Kenneth Waltz's (1979) much-quoted work on sovereignty. Waltz's study of present-day international politics as the interaction of like state units within a self-help system may (and, as convincingly argued in Goddard and Nexon 2006, should) be read as an ideal-type study of how the principle of sovereignty defines the state system, which in turn defines global politics. As Goddard and Nexon are quick to point out, however, Waltz picks and defines his concepts with a view to identifying "covering laws" (and he is famously unspecific where specifying their area of validity is concerned). Covering laws must by definition be resistant to change in what is covered, making them useless if what we are looking for is social change. This means that Waltz's ideal type of international politics is not Weberian, for it does not allow for the fact that the values that went into forging it are time- and space-specific. For example, Waltz (1979, 67) writes that a state is sovereign when "it decides for itself how it will cope with its internal and external problems, including whether or not to seek assistance from others and in doing so to limit its freedom by making commitments to them." This definition is helpful if the task is to make an analytical distinction between sovereign and suzerain systems. For our purposes, however, where the point is to discuss historical changes in the preconditions for the actions of polities, it is less helpful, for it does not invite discussions of what "deciding for itself" may entail socially.

Waltz's definition of sovereignty does not revolve on there being any special scope for decisions. The point is, rather, that there should be *some* scope. If there is no scope for fighting an ultimatum, for taking or leaving a proposed alliance and so on, then there is no sovereignty. But if sovereignty does not turn on any specific degree of leeway or on any specific practices being followed, then it must turn on the proposed *status* of units (states) relative to one another. If we compare Waltz's definition of sovereignty to Foucault's understanding of power we see clear similarities. Power, Foucault insists, exists only when there is room for resistance. When one of the units (in Foucault's discussion, individuals) has no leeway, then the relationship is not one of power. To both Waltz and Foucault, there has to be some scope for agency for there to be a power relation. To Waltz, that power relation is sovereignty. To the late Foucault, however, the mode of power he named *sovereignty* that traditionally suffused the principle of sovereignty is only one of three modes of power (the two others being dominance and governmentality). What characterizes sovereignty as a mode of power in relation to the other two is exactly that the result of the transaction is not given beforehand. We would argue that this must be because the units have some kind of similar status. In this way, Waltz's and Foucault's understandings of sovereignty are quite similar.

If we treat sovereignty as a mode of power among others, and acknowledge that sovereignty is the principle that constitutes the state as a given unit of the international system, then we see that sovereignty still exists in global politics—even if certain practices that constitute it are now characterized by governmentality and dominance (rather than by sovereignty). Sovereignty still plays a role as an ordering principle of relations among states, but it is a changed ordering principle, a changed sovereignty. The crucial thing is that the mode-of-power sovereignty and the ordering-principle sovereignty are no longer identical. Consider the traditional view, as spelled out by John Mearsheimer.

> [Anarchy] is an ordering principle, which says that the *system* comprises independent states that have no central authority over them. Sovereignty, in other words, inheres in states because there is no higher ruling body in the international system. There is no "government over governments." (2001, 30)

We disagree entirely. It is the key thesis of this book that there does exist a rationality of government with matching principles that adds up to government over governments. Sovereignty may remain as an ordering principle among states, but the practices that constitute it are permeated not only with the mode of power that is sovereignty, but also with other modes of power, notably governmentality. Early sovereignty, in the shape of classical *raison d'état*, rested on a form of governmental reason that was inward looking, as the sovereign reflected on the management of his own household. Governmentalization today is focused on the state, but it comes from both the inside *and* the outside of the state. Put differently, the international game in Putnam's "two level game" (1988) has become more important for the domestic game, as the international game now formulates standards for governing that states ignore or defy at their peril. Moreover, the international game provides domestic actors with resources for shaping and reconfiguring governing practices (Sassen 2008). A key example of this dynamic is found in how a global governmentality sets up standards for governing that target states based on the principles of competition found in markets and the political will-formation found in civil society. Together, these practices guide, discipline, and reconfigure the state (see chapter 5).

We can see how practices characterized by the mode of power strategy are challenged by an increase in the number of global political practices that follow the other two modes of power in how Serbia was treated after its 1999 defeat in war. When Kosovo was first put under a mandate system and then made a sovereign state, Serbia was given an ultimatum that it had no choice but to accept. Still, Serbian sovereignty has continued. In Foucauldian language, since that situation was one where Serbia could have done anything, and yet the ultimate outcome was already a given, the mode of power at work here was discipline.

Similarly, in this book we have discussed several cases where governmentality has been effective in securing state action that would not otherwise have taken place. None of this is to deny that sovereignty, understood as a mode of power, is still a very important mode of power within the global polity. But it is not alone in characterizing the practices that constitute the state as a given unit—not alone in characterizing sovereignty, that is. We may thus hypothesize that because of the historically established place of sovereignty in the international system, governmentality (but also discipline) does not challenge or undermine sovereignty, but rather steps in to give it a new form. In so doing, these forms of power produce a more differentiated set of states and other polities, thereby conditioning sovereignty and taking us beyond Waltz's image of international politics, where all relevant units were said to be the same.

We are making no claims about the newness of this situation. Throughout history, ultimatums have been issued, with no real possibility for variation in outcome. To take two examples from Waltz's own century, consider Denmark. When, in April 1940, that country was militarily occupied by Nazi Germany, the Danish state decided *not* (repeat: not) to regard this action as an infringement of sovereignty. Danish sovereignty from 1940 to 1943 was definitely simulated, but, according to Waltz's definition, it was still sovereignty.[5] A less clear-cut but nonetheless illuminating example occurred in 1957, when the Danish state allowed the United States to emplace nuclear weapons on its territory (on Greenland) despite the official nuclear-free policy—the reasoning being that if Denmark did not allow this, the United States would simply grab that territory (Petersen 1997). Our claim is that, whereas such situations as these were exceptional, in the sense that they were not quotidian, today another mode of power than sovereignty—governmentality—has become an everyday and ubiquitous presence in global politics. An ideal type that does not acknowledge the difference of this situation relative to one where dominance is only exceptionally at work is in need of updating. If power in contemporary global politics "flows primarily from the deployment of specialized knowledges for the regularization of populations, rather than the ability to kill" (Wendt and Duvall 2008, 612), then it stands to reason that we need a broader vocabulary, one that can explore changes in the relationship between sovereignty as a form of power, and sovereignty as an institution.

Given the logic of Waltz's argument, there does, however, exist an easy answer to this challenge. It is to argue that, since anarchy and sovereignty are still the defining principle, the units that are being differentiated by this principle are still recognizable as being states. We concur about the primacy of states in global politics, but—again with reference to our studies—we would argue that states are no longer similar enough to be thought of as one class of unit. As Ian Hurd (1999, 404) has argued, the authority of the institution of sovereignty itself is prima facie evidence that the international system is not anarchic because sovereignty is also a governance institution—it constitutes "international governance without an international government." Again, the issue is not to "falsify" Waltz's ideal type, for ideal types cannot be falsified. The question is the pragmatic one of whether, and in what degree, and in which areas, they are handy tools for empirical research. With particular reference to our empirical analyses of states, NGOs, and IOs, we argue that, in order to be use-

---

5. For a good overview, see Lund 2003.

ful today, an ideal type of global politics should include an account of how sovereignty is transformed.

We may observe in the practices of international relations how sovereign states are *themselves* becoming an object class of governing (see chap. 5). Contrary to what some may hold, it is not the case that sovereignty disappears (Hardt and Negri 2004) or is necessarily weakened (Rosenau 2002; Held and McGrew 2002). On the contrary, sovereignty may be increasingly conditioned by and rendered effective by means of the vehicles of other modes of power than sovereignty. As we saw in chapter 4, the role of civil society in contemporary global governance is not antithetical to sovereignty but is a central expression of how the state is governmentalized not only through its pegging to the liberal episteme of a separation between state and society, but more generally through the governmentalization of a global civil society (Bartelson 2006). We may say with Guilhot (2008, 511) that "international relations cease to be made of sovereignties relating to each other through legal rules, and become instead a continuous space where different governmentalities overlap, in the absence of legal mediations." We will now try to specify and generalize this into an ideal-typical feature of global politics by suggesting that liberalism, understood as a rationality of government, acts like a practice selector—the mechanism whereby certain practices are made constitutive of sovereignty, and not others.

Liberalism as Practice Selector

The only way to investigate structural phenomena is through their effects. The effects we are looking at here are practices (cf. Andersen forthcoming). Practices are the stuff of global politics. One key development is that a tightly defined bundle of practices that used to constitute state sovereignty now pop up at the global level, where they are being complemented, and even hybridized and occluded, by other practices. Having discussed some exemplary principles in this regard, the next step should be to identify the principle or logic of practice configuration. We suggest that *liberalism is a selecting principle that articulates and disarticulates certain practices with sovereignty.* Liberalism, in one form or another, has increasingly been the rationality of European governing since the Congress of Vienna. As that governing has gone global and gained in importance, liberalism has become more and more dominant for global politics overall.[6] In early modern Europe, liberalism was preceded by *raison d'état*, which was a totalizing form of governing that clustered around practices of coercion and punishment. The tools of governing were certainly direct. This changed when political economy was added to the calculus. When "society," understood as a semiautonomous, separate sphere, was acknowledged as having an existence, this was the key precondition for liberalism to emerge. At the global level, however, the story is a different one.

The parallel between what is happening today on the global level and what happened in emerging states in early modern Europe is a quantitative one: there was and is an increase in governmentality. However, we note an important difference in what kind of situation governmentality supersedes. In early modern Europe, governmentality followed *raison d'état*. Whereas the trajectory of governing in early modern Europe was from "more is more" to "more is less," its present-day trajectory on the global level is from "little is fine" to "more is more." Instead of going from more to less governing, we are now going from less to more. "Global governance" is about spotting more and more phenomena that are said to have transnational origins and effects, and then making them into objects of governing. Debates about the role and efficacy of IOs tend to revolve around how they can be made more effective by establishing global governing practices that address what was first defined as global threats and challenges (for a key example, see UN 2005).

As a result, we have a situation where the trajectory of government at the global level has gone from interstate diplomacy, balancing, and cooperation to a more integrated, more assertive mode of governing. A liberal political reason seems to override and give concrete form and content both to states' governing practices and to those "spheres of authority" that operate at the transnational level. Enter path dependence. To the degree that global governmentality is shaped by what came before, that shaping will play itself out along rather different paths than the one that led from *raison d'état* to governmentality in early modern Europe. Consequently, we cannot simply assume that the liberal rationality of government that is now growing stronger at the global level will be like the one Foucault found in his tentative genealogy of European states. For our ideal type to work, we need to postulate some kind of *typical* constellation of articulation of practices that we may then name the "global liberal rationality of government." If that

---

6. As Foucault put it, liberalism is the "condition of intelligibility of biopolitics." Biopolitics, in turn, "requires that the conditions of life of the population be made visible and assayed, and practical knowledge be made available to improve them" (Wendt and Duvall 2008, 618).

constellation cannot be assumed to be like the one we know from early modern European history, we will need some other candidate.

Returning to Morgenthau's ideal type, which is the one that we seek to update, it is exemplarily parsimonious in naming practices. Morgenthau claims that all practices involving the use of force and taxation, as well as everything to do with authority, are to be found on the state level. He is less specific when it comes to practices found on the international level. Beyond the claim that they are by definition not practices of force, taxation, and authority, little has been said about them. When it comes to practices, then, Morgenthau's international level is simply a residual category, not a social one—which means that Morgenthau has nothing to offer on this score. Morgenthau's conceptualization of the international as a residual category is intimately connected to Morgenthau's view of politics as grounded in what he holds to be the individual psyche.

Turning to Morgenthau's critics, we see that Wendt (1999) has added the most effective retort to date on how sovereignty is a social phenomenon with a history and is thus malleable to change. State systems may be more or less mature depending on the maturity of the social quality of the principle of self-help. Here we concur. From our perspective, however, Wendt's approach has an important limitation. Since the state system explicitly remains Wendt's object of analysis, his conception of the social does not stretch beyond state interaction. By limiting "the social" to understanding states as subjects and treating the relations between them as intersubjective, Wendt deliberately cuts himself off from analyzing the wider social setting(s) within which state relations are undeniably embedded. That is an admissible limitation if the object of analysis remains the state system, but it is also a guaranteed way of missing changes that originate in social interaction between and among other agents than sovereign states as traditionally conceived. If the major drama of today's global politics concerns how states themselves change as a result of changing global practices, then it follows logically that Wendt's approach will not be able to capture this.[7]

With no guidance from either Morgenthau or his critics, we opt for

---

7. Actually, as a consequence of our hypothesis that the key changes are to be found in what kind of practices states engage in, so that global politics is now so much more than the workings of the states system, this book has been an attempt at putting the states system in its place. While we agree that the states system remains very important to global politics (and, consequently, began our construction of an ideal type by approaching sovereignty), our errand in this book is to theorize global politics overall.

identifying our typical constellation of articulation of practices by asking not about the status of subjects of governance but about the status of the global object of governance itself. To the extent that a global polity exists, and is defined or constituted by a liberal governmental rationality, we are in a position to posit a more specific relation between sovereignty and liberal political reason in world politics.

The Global Polity

Where Morgenthau took the state system as the centerpiece for his ideal type of international politics, it follows from our choice of theorizing global politics in its entirety that we must have a wider focus. We opt for the global polity, understood as global interactions as a whole. This section will discuss how the global polity may be understood in terms of agents and practices. Roland Paris (2003, 442) observes that we may treat the world as a single society, kept together by a (rudimentary) global culture. We concur—but without giving that object some kind of theoretical status, we cannot proceed to draw up an ideal type. Jens Bartelson's (2006) work on the status of global civil society is useful in this regard. Having established that, historically, the concept of civil society was offered as a way to establish new, legitimate authority as an alternative to existing illegitimate authority (the corollary of which is that the concept of civil society emerges after, and as a function of, the state, rather than before it), Bartelson (2006, 373) reaches the conclusion that the primary function of theories of global civil society "is to constitute the global as a political space, and their secondary function is to turn that global space into a governable realm by justifying the exercise of authority within it."[8] More specifically, "the concept of global civil society can be used to justify the exercise of governmental authority within an emergent world polity to the extent that it provides a substitute for a truly transnational demos" (Bartelson 2006, 373–74). As governing practices and reflection and debate on those practices have the global as their central frame of reference—global governance—we may detect a global polity in the making.

Attempts to theorize global politics with a starting point that breaks with sovereignty typically start either with empire or with the general con-

---

8. Bartelson (2006, 385) clearly states, "I believe that the concept of global civil society performs analogous functions in the world polity as the concept of civil society once did within distinct national polities in 18th-century Europe." Foucault (2003) saw the rise of political theory as the handmaiden of monarchical power in its struggle with the aristocracy.

cept of a polity. Higgott and Ougaard (2002, 2–13; cf. Corry 2006, 8) postulate that a global polity has four elements: (1) interconnectedness between whole societies (rather than just international diplomacy), (2) a thick network of international institutions, (3) the weakening of the nation-state, and (4) the heightened relevance of discourses of globality. As Olaf Corry points out, however, Higgott and Ougaard share with other theorists such as Ruggie (1998, 179) and Walker (e.g., 1993) a propensity for "bashing" the importance of the states system rather than presenting competing theorizations of global politics. As a result, the global polity is given the status of a negation of international politics rather than a positive phenomenon.

> The intention of theorising a global polity from a clean theoretical slate in relation to more conventional IR theory thereby falls rather flat because the institutions and actors of a global polity are not seen to be significantly affected by or constituted through global polity discourse. They remain state, inter-state or non-state. With a notion of discourse as constitutive of a global polity, this would be different. (Corry 2006, 66)

Corry's positive understanding of a global polity begins where both Bartelson and we ourselves began: with Foucault's reading of how, during the sixteenth century, European kings had to grapple with the emergence of societies. Corry generalizes from this to the effect that it is the real object that is to be governed that takes precedence. The subjects that deliberately, and conscious of one another, attempt to govern some object are drawn together in a polity because of those very attempts. Corry thus defines a "polity to have been constructed whenever a set of actors or 'governance-subjects' agree upon the existence of one or more common 'governance objects' that significantly impinge upon the identities of those actors" (Corry 2006, 101).[9] Such a governance-object may be a society, but it may also be the environment, or global interactions understood as a whole: the global polity.

This is very useful, but we would take issue with Corry's reading on one point. We are at one in stressing the parallel between what happens now and what happened in Europe from the sixteenth century onward. As did the emerging state then, a global governance-object now invites emerging governance-subjects. This is but one side of the story, however.

---

9. Corry (2006, 103) also notes the precondition that "the governance-object must play a significant role in relation to the identities of the actors if they are to be deemed to be a part of a polity."

As noted earlier, Foucault (quoted in Senellart 2007, 390) also underlined how politics is "no more or less than that which is born with resistance to governmentality." Empirically, neither the states of early modern Europe nor the sundry polities that attempt to govern the global polity today need much encouragement. Historically, there was never a dearth of agents wanting to demand tribute, monopolize force, and lay down the law. Governance-objects and governance-subjects are co-constitutive. How any one historical sequence involving them plays out is an empirical question. It follows that ontically, the starting point for our ideal type cannot be the global polity understood as an agent. It must be the global polity understood as the relational practices of governing.[10]

Saying that the global polity consists of practices specifies the object of our ideal type, but it still does not yield that typical constellation of articulation of practices that we set out to identify. This is where it is helpful to highlight power. Like any relationship, the relationship between governing agents and the global polity is permeated with power. The relationship may be stylized by specifying the practices at work not only, as was traditionally done, in terms of sovereignty, but also in terms of the two other modes of power postulated by Foucault: discipline and governmentality. Governmental practices, then, make up but one bundle of the practices by which the global polity is governed. They coexist with a bundle of disciplining practices, and of sovereign practices. The rare circumstances where sovereignty has the ability to decide on the exception or the "ability to kill" kicks in should not be made central to an ideal type. The competence to decide on the exception, it seems, falls not so much within the purview of sovereignty but within liberal political reason. Morgenthau puts it this way.

> The appeal to moral principles in the international sphere has no concrete universal meaning. It is either so vague as to have no concrete meaning that could provide rational guidance for rational action, or it will be nothing but a reflection of the moral preconceptions of a particular nation and will by the same token be unable to gain the universal recognition it pretends to deserve. (Morgenthau, quoted in Koskenniemi 2002, 438)

In 1951, Morgenthau wrote this prescriptively, seeking to dissuade policymakers from engaging in dangerous utopian foreign policy endeavors. Sixty years later, such appeals to moral principles have become part of

---

10. Like Morgenthau's choice of sovereignty as a base for his ideal type, this is of course a value commitment.

global political practice through the policies of the UN, the World Bank, and other IOs with regard to human rights, development, and peacebuilding (Barnett and Finnemore 2004). It is in this sense that the global social space is tilted toward and rendered material through liberally oriented governmental practice. Because of this social fact, it is necessary to treat the political, and sovereignty, as something that is internally linked to liberal governmental reason.

We are not alone in grounding our investigation of the global in this way. Even a brief look at those developments within international law where there are parallel efforts to identify a global polity by way of theorizing the object of lawmaking is heartening in this regard. The most apposite example may be developments within the emerging subfield of global administrative law.

> The distinction between domestic and international law becomes more precarious, soft forms of rule-making are ever more widespread, the sovereign equality of states is gradually undermined, and the basis of legitimacy of international law is increasingly in doubt. (Krisch and Kingsbury 2006, 1)

As a result, empirical developments in disparate loci of global life (public–private networks, UN security council sanctions, refugees, and environmental governance are given as examples) simply do not fit the dominant traditional understanding of international law. Together, we have here a body of administrative measures that "operate below the level of highly publicized diplomatic conferences and treaty-making, but in aggregate they regulate and manage vast sectors of economic and social life" (Kingsbury, Krisch, and Stewart 2005, 17). Global administrative law is an attempt to link and accord a new theoretical status to these developments by looking at them as "dispersed practices" (Krisch and Kingsbury 2006, 1–2). The importance of this effort for our undertaking is twofold (besides being the common starting point in practices): first, the very same problems that prompted our attempt to update Morgenthau's ideal type may be observed within a different international discourse as well; and second, the lawyers provide a rich array of empirical examples from their own field that complement our own.[11]

---

11. Their theorizing is less helpful. Kingsbury, Krisch, and Stewart (2005, 43) evoke the "simplified ideal types" of international society evolved by the English school of International Relations—pluralist, solidarist, and cosmopolitan—to characterize the state of their field. As these are all ideal types of an international society whose principal members remain states, however, this approach rather begs the question (cf. Corry 2006).

The legal experts who are busy codifying global administrative law take part in what we have argued is a central, and distinguishing, feature of global-level governmental reason: By cataloging and systematizing knowledge that used to be local with a view to making it global, they take part in the spread of a typical sovereign practice—law—to the global polity. Read in this way, the emergence of more than one hundred courts claiming extraterritorial jurisprudence (the most central of which is the International Criminal Court, or ICC) may constitute a challenge to state sovereignty, but it may also be viewed as constitutive of the global polity.[12] Logically, there will be nothing extraterritorial about these courts once their reach is indeed global.[13]

Liberalism and the Global Polity: From Direct to Indirect Rule

Global governance is a sui generis governmental rationality. It is characterized by a drive to *govern more* in the sense of covering more and more geographical and functional domains. For example, one central feature of global governance would be the efforts to establish practices that can curb money laundering and stop the trade in blood diamonds and illicit weapons. Moreover, states are now increasingly targeted as objects of governing (see chap. 5). Sovereignty is conditioned through a globally issued "license" to regulate and control the flow and circulation of goods (as well as "bads") within and across their territory. Failure to regulate and control territory and population results in different forms of sanctions and assistance to help reestablish proper governance structures for the benefit of managing global threats and insecurities. Indeed, contemporary state

---

12. The ICC may also try individuals from states that are not signatories if the alleged crime took place in a country that has ratified the ICC statute. In this sense, the ICC approaches universal jurisdiction. See Ruggie 2004.

13. Admittedly, we leave out the region level here. In a state system that was supposed to be sovereign, *extraterritoriality* meant extrastate. Obviously, a regional court will be extraterritorial in this way, without necessarily having the potential to become global. On this point, we take issue with Valverde, who simply notes that courts have traditionally been a sovereign practice. Within a state, this is definitely true, since courts orchestrate a battle between two parts that are said to be similar, and privilege the state in looking after procedures and guaranteeing outcomes of court cases. But how do we conceptualize the existence of courts on the global plane? Should we simply say that they work through sovereignty, since states have accepted them? That is logical, but it also questions the wisdom of referring to the international courts themselves as being a "sovereign practice."

building, as a case of global governance, is not about restoring the ability of the state to rule its territory in a postconflict situation as much as it is about establishing liberal democratic states (cf. Bellina et al. 2009; Bhuta 2008). Due to the funds and advice they receive from external actors, such states have less scope for refusing to adopt liberal practices, as they are not in a position to contest or significantly modify the liberal templates (democracy, rule of law, market economy) that define state building in a liberal world. Their sovereignty is characterized by the high content of governmentality, and perhaps even dominance, in their dealing with stronger states.

Indeed, global governance is modeled on such a neoliberal governmental rationality. This governmental rationality is about *governing less*—about acting on the conditions and organizations of the freedom of subjects to guide actions in a particular direction. Consequently, money-laundering regulation, trade in blood diamonds, indications of state fragility, human rights norms, labor standards—all are primarily governed through practices "pegged to the rationality of the governed" in the form of governing practices that are modeled on, or at a minimum do not challenge, the interests and dynamics of markets and the free association of civil society. The drive to govern more within global governance, then, can thus be said to be mainly about the *extension* of a particular governmental rationality that is modeled on governing less to be effective within and beyond states.

Taken together, these two features of global governance raise fundamental questions about the concept of the political and the constitution of actors within it. If the goal is to govern more in the sense of venturing into more and more areas, and this proceeds through a logic of governing through freedom, then we would expect to see political fault lines being redrawn. Here, we want to draw attention to two dimensions: first, how the liberal governmental rationality is prone to a peculiar mode of expansion that extends a mode of governing—programmatically governing less—to new areas. The rub is that such an extension logically entails governing more. Since humans are not "born free," but, on the contrary, have to be socialized to be what liberal ideology at any one time calls "free," liberal global governance means that there must be more governing now, for there to be less governing later. More governing entails new constellations of actors and also a possible retreat from the political. Depending on the degree and direction these developments take, we get a new hierarchy of states and other actors, where some are judged to conform to standards, some fall short of them (so-called fragile states), and some directly threaten a liberal governmental rationality (terrorists, rogue states, transnational criminal networks).

This process is intensified by the increase in practices that are made relevant to it. During the past two decades, a range of new governing initiatives have emerged at the global level, seeking to govern areas hitherto seen as the province of the market. Perhaps the most prominent of these efforts is the UN Global Compact. The goal of the Global Compact is to transform market actors, corporations, from being profit-seeking actors within a legal framework, to become profit-seeking actors "with a conscience" in terms of taking on broad principles for their own mode of operation that are aligned with and supportive of human rights norms, labor standards, anticorruption, and dealing with climate change. As a practice of governing, multistakeholder governance brings on board actors with different, often conflicting, interests. In the barest possible terms, then, in order to govern more, the state enrolls new actors on its side (NGOs, TNCs, etc.). As a result of these new liaisons, the state becomes less centralized and more network-based. For Ruggie (2004), the Global Compact is a key part of the emergence of a new "global public domain." In our reading, it rather constitutes one manifestation of the combination of "governing more" (i.e., governing more areas) and "governing less" (i.e., indirectly). It results in a transformation of the content of governing practices, not only from being direct to being indirect, but arguably also from being "political" and hierarchical in the sense of deciding authoritatively on the ends and means of governing, to being far more horizontal, voluntary, and thus also less "political." It is governing through the lowest common denominator (Hindess 2005).

There will be discontents, actors that are held by the leading states to be problematic, or even bad. We know from the workings of a liberal rationality of government on the level of the state that there will always be cases where illiberal practices have to be used (traditionally, against women, in prisons, in asylums, against indigenous groups, against children, etc.). While there seems to be no necessity when it comes to *who* will at any one point be marginalized in this way by liberal rule, given that the liberal mode of governing has to break in its objects, there will always be those who will not or cannot conform. We have no reason to think that the same will not be the case with liberal governmental rationality at the global level. When we looked at the historical case of Russia we saw that what has characterized and still characterizes Russia, as compared to states further to its west, is exactly a maximization of direct rule and an aversion to indirect rule (chap. 3). What we have here is a case of continued resistance to a liberal rationality of government, observable by the fact that so few governing practices in Russia may be classified as belonging to the governmental mode of power. And yet, the Russian state is constituted by enough (if few) governmental practices to be simply "problematic." It does not yet have a high number of disciplinary practices to be classified as a fragile state, a failed state, a rogue state, or the like (though it did during the Soviet period). And as noted in chapter 5, states are increasingly subject to global-level evaluations, ratings, and surveillance. Global efforts at producing a governable space beyond the state, then, are highly significant, not least when it comes to which actors are categorized as not conforming to a liberal governmental rationality. The practices whereby states deemed fragile or failed are governed can be *aliberal* and authoritarian; or they can, as we suggested in chapter 5, be reminiscent of that early illiberal form of governmentality that early modern Europe knew as police.

What constitutes a challenge or threat to a liberal rationality of government—a categorization that may have dire effects for the agent so classified—has been broadened in recent years to such an extent that climate change, epidemics, corruption, migration patterns, and poverty now operate as central markers for global risk and security. This process accelerated with the publication of the report of the Commission on Global Governance in the mid-1990s and reached its present peak with the UN secretary-general's report *In Larger Freedom* (UN 2005). Here, the governing practices of sovereign states are themselves subject to intense scrutiny with regard both to their pastoral care for their own populations *and* for their global responsibility to control the circulation of objects and threats within their territory. If a state fails on these criteria, or if its reliance on disciplinary practices is deemed too high by leading liberal states, it is reclassified as a fragile or even failed or rogue state, and so loses its sovereignty license. Liberalism is at work as practice selector, defining which actors fail to conform to governmental practices. It also defines the precise configuration of governing practices (sovereign, disciplinary, liberal) that are to be applied by leading liberal states to failed actors.

Fragile states are, by definition, seen by the leading states as being transformable by means of strategic, governmental, and disciplinary practices. Then there are the actors who are held to be the "other" of liberal governmental rationality. Such "bad actors"—terrorist networks, transnational criminal networks, and rogue states—are theoretically noteworthy for three distinct reasons. Rogue states are the constitutive outside of the liberal order, they are reminders that a liberal order issues "sovereignty licenses," and they are an illustration of what it means to see politics as intensity. First, in contradistinction to actors defined as problematic (a fragile or even failed state), these actors' *intentions* (rather than their capacities and institutional form) are accorded much greater significance. Their identity is defined by their alleged intention to destroy or challenge a liberally inclined political order. They define the limits of what is permissible by a liberal rationality of government. A second reason why rogue states are noteworthy is what their existence tells us about sovereignty. The classification of "bad actors," and the tangible effects of that classification, are testament to there being a global governing space whose content and limits are defined by something *other* than the institution of sovereignty itself. Global politics is certainly still very much about the rivalry and competition among states, but it takes place within a liberally tilted two-level game. A third reason for taking note of rogue states here is that the governing practices deemed appropriate for these actors fall outside the realm of liberal governmental reason precisely *because* their intentions are antithetical to, are deemed to be fundamental threats to, liberal forms of rule. The existence of "rogue states" in liberal discourse is a testament to the fruitfulness of seeing politics as intensity, for it is the very insistence on a set of political standards (liberalism) that fuels resistance to liberal rule and thus intensifies the entire issue of relations between liberal and rogue states.

Conclusion

For the first time, market economy, democratic rule, and human rights norms have become institutionalized at a global level (Simmons, Dobbins, and Garrett 2008). To take a key example, understanding the scope and significance of the typical liberal governmental practices involved is now central to understanding how China is governed (Sigley 2006). Developing countries are targeted by multilateral and bilateral donors who seek to govern through freedom by setting up new liberal rules and institutions and by building skills and capacity to promote the emergence of liberal modes of governing.

As Weber (1949; cf. Jackson 2010a) himself put it, once values have been established, even a Chinese should be able to follow the argument of an ideal type. That way of putting it was, of course, itself an example of value-laden assumptions, for by "Chinese," Weber here clearly meant anybody with an entirely different value system. A hundred years ago, that was a reasonable assumption to make for a European intellectual. It stands as a telling reminder of the need to update our models and our way of presenting them that today, no self-reflective intellectual anywhere is likely to make such an assumption. The world has indeed shrunk. That was one of our key reasons for undertaking the job of looking for contemporary ideal-typical features in the first place. Another reason, however, was that our stylization of a new, global rationality of government should serve as a baseline for further empirical research on the specific rationalities that operate within the discourses of which global politics consist.

Today, one such discourse is exactly the Chinese discourse on politics. Feng Xu (2007) has argued that the 1970s change in China from simply discouraging more births to making the population a specific object of government and aiming for its containment and qualitative enhancement is but one example of a turn to governmentality. Farquhar and Zhang (2005, 320) note, as a further example, how, "in the 1980s, a great deal of national government support was withdrawn from hospitals, medical schools, and clinics, and there was a rapid shift to fee-for-service models of payment. In the 1990s, there has been a massive growth in health insurance schemes." As mentioned in chapter 1, the spread of insurance was a key element in the governmental individuation and self-government in Europe in the eighteenth and nineteenth centuries. Farquhar and Zhang also detail how, over the past thirty years, the care of the self in Beijing has gone from being a state-run affair toward being a whole plethora of different activities organized by individuals. Such investigations may serve as stepping-stones of further empirical work that may specify how important, relative to discipline and sovereignty, governmentality as a mode of power is becoming in Chinese politics, or in other areas of global politics for that matter, and how other rationalities of government compare with global governmentality in specific locales.[14]

We would not have attempted to forge this specific ideal type if we had not concluded from the empirical analyses that a global governmental rationality, characterized by these traits, is increasingly being established as the standard for governing. This standard changes sovereignty, understood as the principle that constitutes the state as a given unit of the inter-

---

14. What these rationalities are is an empirical question that may, for example, be analyzed genealogically. Given the importance of regions in global politics, we would also have thought that comparisons within and between regions would yield interesting differences. It would be an immanent test of our ideal type whether it would be useful as a starting point for genealogical and comparative analyses of the kind suggested here.

national system, by enmeshing states in a number of practices that are not strategic (characterized by a gaming mode of power where the outcome is uncertain) but rather governmental (characterized by a mode of power whereby an already given rationality makes a state govern itself according to this very rationality when it would not traditionally have done so). If governmentality fails, leading liberal states may even employ practices characterized by domination (a mode of power where the outcome is given). A liberal rationality of government determines whether, how, and on what actors sovereignty is to be bestowed (who should be licensed as sovereign). In other words, real existing liberalism serves as a practice selector for sovereignty. It conditions and subjects sovereignty as an institution, which means that it is a systems-defining feature of global politics. We would maintain that sovereignty is still systems-defining, but that sovereignty is undergoing empirically identifiable transformations. Furthermore, sovereignty may be central to defining global politics, but it is not alone in doing so. It is liberalism, understood as a rationality of government, that is central. Sovereignty is only one, albeit the most important one, of the kinds of relations that are transformed by liberalism.

Nothing in the spread of such liberal standards and governmental rationalities should be taken to imply that political struggle and debate are no longer central. Politics is as intense as ever—among other things because global politics, understood as politics that potentially are significantly shaped by and have effects on politics everywhere, is imbricated in a growing number of political relations. In summarizing his lectures on biopolitics, Foucault noted,

> In the modern world, . . . a series of governmental rationalities overlap, lean on each other, challenge each other, and struggle with each other: art of government according to truth, art of government according to the rationality of the sovereign state, and art of government according to the rationality of economic agents, and more generally, according to the rationality of the governed themselves. And it is all these different arts of government [that] constitute the object of political debate from the nineteenth century. *What is politics, in the end, if not both the interplay of these different arts of government with their different reference points and the debate to which these different arts of government give rise?* (2008, 313; emphasis added)

Thus, whereas sovereignty once could be seen to constitute and organize other forms of power, the reverse is increasingly the case. More and more, politics is not so much about the strategic interplay between sovereigns as it is about the interplay between different governmental rationalities, one of which is that of sovereignty itself. Guilhot's (2008) noted description of the human rights regime fits in with this interpretation. We have found the same in our analyses of the interplay between states and NGOs. Greater state interaction with other actors such as human rights activists, anti–land mine activists, feminists, and the like is the effect of a form of state and a form of state policy that arises when sovereignty is replaced by other forms of power. When what is subject to political struggle and contestation is increasingly the content of different governmental rationalities, the state evolves a series of new interfaces with other kinds of actors, NGOs among them.

The global practices established to prevent and manage violent conflicts, to regulate financial flows, and to address environmental changes, health pandemics, and organized crime bring a focus on sovereign states as the primary loci of implementation. States become the main interlocutors in global debates about, and efforts to respond to, perceived collective threats and challenges. At its most extreme, the very same governmental rationality that conditions state sovereignty by authoritatively defining the appropriate mode of governing also helps set up and bolster the capacity of sovereign states for governance, state building being a key case in point.[15]

The changing meaning and role of sovereignty within the global governance discourse bear an affinity to how neoliberal forms of rule are supplanting and supplementing liberal forms of rule. Liberal governmental rationality entailed a view of the market as a distinct, quasiautonomous, and natural sphere with its own laws and mechanisms. Neoliberalism, by contrast, entails a fundamentally different view of the market. Market mechanisms and competition more generally are seen by neoliberalism as something that has to be *actively* constructed. Neoliberalism acknowledges the tension in liberalism between holding that people are born free and that people have to be made free by opting firmly for the latter alternative. Neoliberalism thus entails a different, engineering episteme whereby markets are both more fragile and contingent, thus requiring active establishment and management. Note, however, that a new tension creeps into neoliberalism, for it also sees markets as being more central to governing in the sense that market mechanisms can and should be actively set up, to enable them to pervade state practices.

---

15. We detect a reconfiguration of sovereignty within a global governmental reason that combines neoliberalism and police that we intend to analyze further in forthcoming work.

In light of this, we may specify the ongoing transformation of sovereignty as follows. Whereas sovereignty was once constitutive of international politics, it now assumes a meaning akin to the market, for within neoliberalism it is no longer seen as a universal and quasinatural institutionalization of political authority. It is rather conceptualized as something that needs to be actively nurtured, shaped, and assisted. We may see this within development and security discourses, perhaps most prominently in the case of fragile and failed states. However, nurturing is never held to be finished: it applies also to (neo-) liberal states themselves. In all these cases, liberalism serves as a practice selector, a global rationality of governing by dint of which practices are judged.

To sum up, an increasingly tangible global rationality of governing is changing the category of the state. Characteristically, the state is evolving new interfaces with a plethora of other agents. This complicates relations among states as well, to such a degree that relations among states ("international relations") are becoming more and more enmeshed in global politics. Global politics needs to be theorized in ways that can give pride of place to these changes, but without denying the continued importance of the state. This book has been our attempt at doing just that.

References

Adler, Emmanuel. 2002. Constructivism and International Relations. In *Handbook of International Relations*, edited by Walter Carlsnaes, Thomas Risse, and Beth Simmons. London: Sage.
Albert, Mathias, and Lena Hilkermeier, eds. 2004. *Observing International Relations: Niklas Luhmann and World Politics.* London: Routledge.
Althusser, Louis. [1970] 1971. *Lenin and Philosophy and Other Essays.* London: New Left Books.
Andersen, Morten S. Forthcoming. Empire, Population, Power: A Case for Turning to Practices in the Study of IR. Ms.
Anderson, M[atthew] S[mith]. 1993. *The Rise of Modern Diplomacy, 1450–1919.* London: Longman.
Andreas, Peter. 2003. Redrawing the Line: Borders and Security in the Twenty-First Century. *International Security* 28 (2): 78–111.
Anheier, Helmut, Marlies Glasius, and Mary Kaldor, eds. 2001. *Global Civil Society.* Oxford: Oxford University Press.
Anisimov, Evgeniy Viktorovich. 1993. The Imperial Heritage of Peter the Great in the Foreign Policy of His Early Successors. In *Imperial Russian Foreign Policy*, edited by Hugh Ragsdale. Cambridge: Cambridge University Press.
Ashley, Richard. 1981. Political Realism and Human Understanding. *International Studies Quarterly* 25 (2): 204–36.
Bagger, Hans. 1993. The Role of the Baltic in Russian Foreign Policy. In *Imperial Russian Foreign Policy*, edited by Hugh Ragsdale. Cambridge: Cambridge University Press.
Balfour, Marshall, Roger F. Evans, Frank W. Notestein, and Irene B. Tauber. 1950. *Public Health and Demography in the Far East.* New York: Rockefeller Foundation.
Barkin, Samuel J., and Bruce Cronin. 1994. The State and the Nation: Changing Norms and the Rules of Sovereignty in International Relations. *International Organization* 48 (1): 107–30.
Barnett, Michael, and Raymond Duvall. 2005a. Power in Global Governance. In *Power in Global Governance,* edited by Michael Barnett and Raymond Duvall, 1–32. Cambridge: Cambridge University Press.

Barnett, Michael, and Raymond Duvall, eds. 2005b. *Power in Global Governance.* Cambridge: Cambridge University Press.

Barnett, Michael, and Martha Finnemore. 2004. *Rules for the World.* Ithaca: Cornell University Press.

Bartelson, Jens. 2006a. The Concept of Sovereignty Revisited. *European Journal of International Law* 17 (2): 463–74.

Bartelson, Jens. 2006b. Making Sense of Global Civil Society. *European Journal of International Relations* 12 (3): 371–95.

Barzelatto, Jose. 1988. Continuity and Change. In *Research in Human Reproduction. Biennial Report of 1986–1987, WHO Special Programme of Research, Development and Research Training in Human Reproduction*, edited by Egon Diczfalusy, David Griffin, and Jitendra Khanna, 11–16. Geneva: WHO.

Baudrillard, Jean. [1977] 2007. *Forget Foucault.* Cambridge: MIT Press.

Bellina, Severine, Dominique Darbon, Stein Sundstøl Eriksen, and Ole Jacob Sending. 2009. Legitimacy of the State in Fragile Situations. Research report for OECD-DAC Fragile States Working Group. Paris: OECD.

Benner, Thorsten, Wolfgang Reinicke, and Jan Martin Witte. 2004. Multisectoral Networks in Global Governance: Towards a Pluralistic System of Accountability. *Government and Opposition* 39 (2): 191–210.

Bhuta, Nehal. 2008. Against State-Building. *Constellations* 15 (4): 517–42.

Biernacki, Richard. 1995. *The Fabrication of Labor: Germany and Britain, 1640–1914.* Berkeley: University of California Press.

Bigo, Didier. 2006. *Policing Insecurity Today.* Basingstoke: Palgrave.

Boli, John, and George M. Thomas, eds. 1999. *Constructing World Culture: International Non-Governmental Organizations since 1875.* Palo Alto: Stanford University Press.

Bongaarts, John, and Judith Bruce. 1995. The Causes of Unmet Need for Contraception and the Social Content of Services. *Studies in Family Planning* 26 (2): 57–75.

Bourdieu, Pierre. 2004. *Esquisse pour une auto-analyse.* Paris: Raisons d'agir.

Brekke, Torkel. 2002. *Gud i norsk politikk. Religion og politisk makt.* Oslo: Pax.

Broome, Andre, and Leonard Seabrooke. 2007. Seeing Like the IMF: Institutional Change in Small Open Economies. *Review of International Political Economy* 14 (4): 576–601.

Bruce, Judith. 1980. Implementing the User's Perspective. *Studies in Family Planning* 11 (1): 29–34.

Bruce, Judith, Anrudh Jain, and Barbara Mensch. 1992. Setting Standards of Quality in Family Planning Programs. *Studies in Family Planning* 23 (6): 392–95.

Bukkvoll, Tor. 1997. *Ukraine and European Security.* Chatham House Papers. London: Royal Institute of International Affairs.

Bull, Hedley. 1977. *The Anarchical Society: A Study of Order in World Politics.* London: Macmillan.

Burchell, Graham. 1991. Peculiar Interests: Civil Society and Governing "The System of Natural Liberty." In *The Foucault Effect: Studies in Governmentality*, edited by Graham Burchell, Colin Gordon, and Peter Miller, 119–50. Chicago: University of Chicago Press.

Burchell, Graham. 1996. Liberal Government and Techniques of the Self. In *Foucault and Political Reason*, edited by Andrew Barry, Thomas Osborne, and Nikolas Rose, 19–36. London: University College, London.

Burnside, Craig, and David Dollar. 2000. Aid, Policies, and Growth. *American Economic Review* 90 (4): 847–68.
Caldwell, John, and Pat Caldwell. 1986. *Limiting Population Growth and the Ford Foundation Contribution.* London: Frances Pinter.
Cameron, Maxwell A., Robert J. Lawson, and Brian W. Tomlin, eds. 1998. *To Walk without Fear: The Global Movement to Ban Landmines.* Ontario: Oxford University Press, Canada.
Campbell, David. 1992. *Writing Security: U.S. Foreign Policy and the Politics of Identity.* Minneapolis: University of Minnesota Press.
Cassirer, Ernst. 1989. *Zur Logik der Kulturwissenschaften: fünf Studien.* Darmstadt: Wissenschaftliche Buchgesellschaft.
Checkel, Jeffrey. 2001. Why Comply? Social Learning and European Identity Change. *International Organization* 55 (3): 553–88.
Collier, Paul, and David Dollar. 1999. Aid Allocation and Poverty Reduction. In *Policy Research Working Paper no. 2041.* Washington, DC: Development Research Group, World Bank.
Commission on Global Governance. 1995. *Our Global Neighborhood.* Oxford: Oxford University Press.
Connolly, William. 1985. Taylor, Foucault, and Otherness. *Political Theory* 13 (3): 365–76.
Connolly, William E. 2004. The Complexity of Sovereignty. In *Sovereign Lives: Power in Global Politics,* ed. Jenny Edkins, Veronique Pin-Fat, and Michael J. Shapiro. New York: Routledge.
Cooper, Andrew F., John English, and Ramesh Takur, eds. 2002. *Enhancing Global Governance: Towards a New Diplomacy?* Tokyo: United Nations University Press.
Corry, Olaf. 2006. Constructing a Global Polity. PhD thesis, University of Copenhagen, Department of Political Science.
Craig, Gordon A., and Alexander George. 1990. *Force and Statecraft: Diplomatic Problems of Our Time.* 2nd ed. New York: Oxford University Press.
Crane, Barbara. 1993. International Population Institutions: Adaptation to a Changing World Order. In *Institutions for the Earth: Sources of Effective International Environmental Protection,* edited by Peter M. Haas, Robert O. Keohane, and Margaret A. Levy, 351–93. Cambridge: MIT Press.
Critchlow, Donald T. 1999. *Intended Consequences: Birth Control, Abortion, and the Federal Government in Modern America.* New York: Oxford University Press.
Dean, Mitchell. 1999. *Governmentality: Power and Rule in Modern Society.* London: Sage.
Dean, Mitchell. 2007. *Governing Societies: Political Perspectives on Domestic and International Rule.* Buckingham: Open University Press.
Dean, Mitchell, and Barry Hindess. 1998. Introduction: Government, Liberalism, Society. In *Governing Australia: Studies in Contemporary Rationalities of Government,* edited by Mitchell Dean and Barry Hindess, 1–19. Melbourne: Cambridge University Press.
Debrix, Francois. 1999. Space Quest: Surveillance, Governance, and the Panoptic Eye of the United Nations. *Alternatives* 24 (3): 269–94.
Deleuze, Gilles. 1999. *Foucault.* London: Continuum.
Demeny, Paul. 1972. Asian Universities and Population Policy. *Studies in Family Planning* 3 (10): 249–50.

Desrosières, Alain. 1998. *The Politics of Large Numbers: A History of Statistical Reasoning*. Cambridge: Cambridge University Press.
Desrosières, Alain. 2004. For a Politics of the Tools for Knowledge: The Case of Statistics. In *Politics and Knowledge: Democratizing Knowledge in Times of the Expert*. University of Bergen, Norway, June 21–22.
Dilling, Lisbeth, and Hans Mikkelsen. 1983. *Dansk politihistorisk bibliografi 1682–1938*. Copenhagen: Politihistorisk Selskab.
Dillon, Michael, and Julian Reid. 2000. Global Governance, Liberal Peace, and Complex Emergency. *Alternatives* 25 (1): 117–45.
Dillon, Michael, and Julian Reid. 2001. Global Liberal Governance: Biopolitics, Security, and War. *Millennium* 30 (1): 41–66.
Dillon, Michael, and Julian Reid. 2009. *The Liberal Way of War: Killing to Make Life Live*. London: Routledge.
Dixon-Mueller, Ruth. 1993. *Population Policy and Women's Rights: Transforming Reproductive Choice*. London: Praeger.
Dixon-Mueller, Ruth, and Adrienne Germain. 1992. Stalking the Elusive "Unmet Need" for Family Planning. *Studies in Family Planning* 23 (5): 330–35.
Donzelot, Jacques. 1991. *Face à l'exclusion*. Paris: Editions Esprit.
Donzelot, Jacques. 1993. The Promotion of the Social. Trans. Graham Burchell. In *Foucault's New Domains*, edited by Mike Gane and Terry Johnson. London: Routledge.
Doty, Roxanne Lynn. 1996. *Imperial Encounters*. Minneapolis: University of Minnesota Press.
Dreyfus, Hubert L., and Paul Rabinow. 1984. *Michel Foucault: Beyond Structuralism and Hermeneutics*. 2nd ed. Chicago: University of Chicago Press.
Drezner, Daniel. 2007. *All Politics Is Global*. Princeton: Princeton University Press.
Dubber, Markus D., and Mariana Valverde, eds. 2006. *The New Police Science: The Police Power in Domestic and International Governance*. Stanford: Stanford University Press.
Dukes, Paul. 1990. *The Making of Russian Absolutism, 1613–1801*. London: Longman.
Durkheim, Emile. [1950] 1991. *Physik der Sitten und des Rechts. Vorlesungen zur Soziologie der Moral*. Frankfurt am Main: Suhrkamp.
Durkheim, Emile. [1950] 1992. *Professional Ethics and Civic Morals*. London: Routledge.
Elias, Norbert. 1982. *The Civilizing Process: State Formation and Civilization*. Oxford: Basil Blackwell.
Ezrahi, Yaron. 1990. *The Descent of Icarus: Science and the Transformation of Contemporary Democracy*. Cambridge: Harvard University Press.
Farquhar, Judith, and Quicheng Zhang. 2005. Biopolitical Beijing: Pleasure, Sovereignty, and Self-Cultivation in China's Capital. *Cultural Anthropology* 20 (3): 303–27.
Fearon, James, and Alexander Wendt. 2002. Rationalism v. Constructivism: A Sceptical View. In *Handbook of International Relations*, edited by Walter Carlsnaes, Thomas Risse, and Beth Simmons. London: Sage.
Feldbæk, Ole. 2000. Vækst og reformer—dansk forvaltning 1720–1814 [Growth and Reforms—Danish Government 1720–1814]. In *Dansk forvaltningshistorie I. Stat, forvaltning og samfund. Fra middelalderen til 1901* [*Danish History of Government, vol. I: State, Government, and Society from the Middle Ages to 1901*], edited by Leon E. Jespersen, E. Ladewig Petersen, and Ditlev Tamm. Copenhagen: Jurist-og økonomforbundets forlag.

Ferguson, James. 1990. *The Anti-Politics Machine: "Development," Depoliticization, and Bureaucratic Power in Lesotho.* Cambridge: Cambridge University Press.
Ferguson, James, and Akhil Gupta. 2002. Spatializing States: Toward an Ethnography of Neoliberal Governmentality. *American Ethnologist* 29 (4): 981–1002.
Ferguson, Yale H., and Richard W. Mansbach. 1996. *Polities: Authority, Identities, and Change.* Columbia: University of South Carolina Press.
Finnemore, Martha. 1996. *National Interests in International Society.* Ithaca: Cornell University Press.
Finnemore, Martha, and Kathryn Sikkink. 1998. International Norm Dynamics and Political Change. *International Organization* 52 (4): 887–917.
Florini, Ann M., ed. 2000. *The Third Force: The Rise of Transnational Civil Society.* Washington, DC: Carnegie Endowment for International Peace.
Foucault, Michel. [1975] 1977. *Discipline and Punish: The Birth of the Prison.* Harmondsworth: Penguin.
Foucault, Michel. 1979. *Michel Foucault: Power/Truth/Strategy.* Ed. Meaghan Morris and Paul Patton. Sydney: Feral.
Foucault, Michel. 1980. Two Lectures. In *Power/Knowledge: Selected Interviews and Other Writings, 1972–1977,* ed. Colin Gordon. Brighton: Harvester.
Foucault, Michel. 1984. *The History of Sexuality.* Harmondsworth: Penguin.
Foucault, Michel. [1982] 1989. An Ethics of Pleasure. In *Foucault Live (Interviews 1966–84),* edited by Sylvestre Lotringer, 257–77. New York: Semiotext(e).
Foucault, Michel. 1992. *The History of Sexuality.* Vol. 2: *The Use of Pleasure.* London: Penguin.
Foucault, Michel. 1994a. L'éthique du souci de soi comme pratique de la liberté. In *Dits et écrits (1954–1988),* 708–29. Paris: Gallimard.
Foucault, Michel. [1980] 1994b. Le philosophe masqué. In *Dits et écrits, IV (1954–1988),* 104–10. Paris: Gallimard.
Foucault, Michel. 1994c. Qu'est-ce que les Lumières? In *Dits et écrits, IV (1980–1988),* 679–88. Paris: Gallimard.
Foucault, Michel. 1994d. The Subject and Power. In *Essential Works of Foucault, 1954–1984,* edited by James D. Faubion, vol. 3: *Power,* 326–48. London: Penguin.
Foucault, Michel. [1980] 1994e. Table ronde du 20 mai 1978. In *Dits et écrits, IV (1980–1988),* 20–34. Paris: Gallimard.
Foucault, Michel. 1996. The Concern for Truth. In *Foucault Live: Collected Interviews, 1961–1984,* edited by Sylvère Lotringer, 455–64. New York: Semiotext(e).
Foucault, Michel. [1978] 2000a. Governmentality. In *Power: Essential Works of Foucault, 1954–1984,* edited by James D. Faubion, 201–22. Harmondsworth: Penguin.
Foucault, Michel. [1980] 2000b. Omnes et Singulatim: Toward a Critique of Political Reason. In *Power: Essential Works of Foucault, 1954–1984,* edited by James D. Faubion, 298–325. Harmondsworth: Penguin.
Foucault, Michel. [1982] 2000c. The Subject and Power. In *Power: Essential Works of Foucault, 1954–1984,* edited by James D. Faubion, 326–48. London: Penguin.
Foucault, Michel. [1976] 2003. *"Society Must Be Defended": Lectures Given at the Collège de France, 1975–1976.* New York: Picador Press.
Foucault, Michel. 2008. *The Birth of Biopolitics: Lectures at the Collège de France, 1978–1979.* London: Palgrave.

Fougner, Tore. 2008. Neoliberal Governance of States: The Role of Competitiveness Indexing and Country Benchmarking. *Millennium* 37 (2): 303–26.
Fox, Jonathan A., and David L. Brown, eds. 1998. *The Struggle for Accountability: The World Bank, NGOs, and Grassroots Movements.* Cambridge: MIT Press.
Geyer, Dietrich. 1987. *Russian Imperialism: The Interaction of Domestic and Foreign Policy, 1860–1914.* Oxford: Berg.
Gilpin, Robert. 1981. *War and Change in World Politics.* Cambridge: Cambridge University Press.
Goddard, Stacie E., and Daniel H. Nexon. 2005. Paradigm Lost? Reassessing Theory of International Politics. *European Journal of International Relations* 11 (1): 9–61.
Goldstein, Judith, and Lisa Martin. 2000. Legalization, Trade Liberalization, and Domestic Politics: A Cautionary Note. *International Organization* 54 (3): 603–32.
Gordon, Colin. 1991. Governmental Rationality: An Introduction. In *The Foucault Effect: Studies in Governmentality,* edited by Graham Burchell, Colin Gordon, and Peter Miller, 1–52. Chicago: University of Chicago Press.
Green, Jessica F., and Colleen Thouez. 2005. Global Governance for Migration and the Environment: What Can We Learn from Each Other? Global Migration Perspectives no. 46. Geneva: Global Commission on International Migration.
Grimsted, Patricia Kennedy. 1969. *The Foreign Ministers of Alexander I: Political Attitudes and the Conduct of Russian Diplomacy, 1801–1825.* Berkeley: University of California Press.
Guilhot, Nicolas. 2008. Limiting Sovereignty or Producing Governmentality? Two Human Rights Regimes in U.S. Political Discourse. *Constellations* 15 (4): 502–15.
Gurowitz, Amy. 1999. Mobilizing International Norms: Domestic Actors, Immigrants, and the Japanese State. *World Politics* 51 (3): 413–45.
Guzzini, Stefano. 1998. *Realism in International Relations and International Political Economy: The Continuing Story of a Death Foretold.* London: Routledge.
Guzzini, Stefano. 2005. The Concept of Power: A Conceptual Analysis. *Millennium* 33 (3): 495–522.
Hacking, Ian. 1999. *The Social Construction of What?* Cambridge: Harvard University Press.
Hall, Martin, and Patrick Thaddeus Jackson. 2007. *Civilizational Identity: The Production and Reproduction of "Civilizations" in International Relations.* London: Palgrave.
Hall, Ronald B., and Thomas J. Biersteker, eds. 2002. *The Emergence of Private Authority in Global Governance.* Cambridge: Cambridge University Press.
Halperin, C[harles] J. 1985. *Russia and the Golden Horde: The Mongol Impact on Medieval Russian History.* Bloomington: Indiana University Press.
Hamilton, Keith, and Richard Langhorne. 1995. *The Practice of Diplomacy: Its Evolution, Theory, and Administration.* London: Routledge.
Hansen, Lene. 1995. NATO's New Discourse. In *European Security 2000,* edited by Birthe Hansen, 117–34. Copenhagen: Copenhagen Political Studies Press.
Harkavy, Oscar. 1995. *Curbing Population Growth: An Insider's Perspective on the Population Movement.* New York: Plenum.
Hartley, Janet. 2001. Changing Perceptions: British Views of Russia from the Grand Embassy to the Peace of Nystad. In *Peter the Great and the West: New Perspectives,* edited by L. Hughes, 53–70. Basingstoke: Macmillan.
Hauser, Phillip. 1954. Research Needs and Suggested Projects. In *Proceedings of Round-*

table at Annual Conference. *The Interrelations of Demographic, Economic, and Social Problems in Selected Underdeveloped Areas,* 187–91. New York: Milbank Memorial Fund.

Held, David, and Mathias Koenig-Archibugi. 2004. Introduction. *Government and Opposition* 39 (2): 125–31.

Held, David, and Anthony McGrew. 2000. The Great Globalization Debate: An Introduction. In *The Global Transformation Reader,* edited by David Held and Anthony McGrew, 1–46. Cambridge: Polity Press.

Held, David, and Anthony McGrew. 2002. *Governing Globalization: Power, Authority, and Global Governance.* London: Polity Press.

Helliwell, Christine, and Barry Hindess. 2002. The Empire of Uniformity and the Government of Subject Peoples. *Cultural Values* 6 (1): 137–52.

Hellmann, Manfred. 1978. Die Friedensschlüsse von Nystad (1721) und Teschen (1779) als Etappen des Vordringen Russland nach Europa. In *Historisches Jahrbuch,* 270–88. Munich-Freiburg: Görres.

Hennis, Wilhelm. 1988. *Max Weber: Essays in Reconstruction.* London: Allen and Unwin.

Higgott, Richard, and Morten Ougaard. 2002. Introduction: Beyond System and Society—Towards a Global Polity. In *Towards a Global Polity,* edited by Morten Ougaard and Richard Higgott, 1–19. London: Routledge.

Higgott, Richard A., Geoffrey Underhill, and Andreas Bieler, eds. 2000. *Non-State Actors and Authority in the Global System.* London: Routledge.

Higher, Amy. 1996. Transnational Movements and World Politics: The International Women's Health Movement and Population Policy. PhD Dissertation, Brandeis University.

Hindess, Barry. 1996. Liberalism, Socialism, and Democracy: Variations on a Governmental Theme. In *Foucault and Political Reason: Liberalism, Neo-Liberalism, and Rationalities of Government,* edited by Andrew Barry, Thomas Osborne, and Nikolas Rose, 65–80. London: UCL Press.

Hindess, Barry. 1997. *Discourses on Power.* Oxford: Blackwell.

Hindess, Barry. 2000. Citizenship in the International Management of Populations. *American Behavioural Scientist* 43 (9): 1486–97.

Hindess, Barry. 2002. Neo-Liberal Citizenship. *Citizenship Studies* 6 (2): 127–43.

Hindess, Barry. 2005. Politics as Government: Michel Foucault's Analysis of Political Reason. *Alternatives* 30:389–413.

Hirschman, Albert O. 1977. *The Passions and the Interests: Political Arguments for Capitalism before Its Triumph.* Princeton: Princeton University Press.

Hirst, Paul Q., and Grahame Thompson. 1996. *Globalization in Question: The International Economy and the Possibilities of Governance.* Cambridge, MA: Blackwell.

Hobson, John M., and Leonard Seabrook. 2001. Reimagining Weber: Constructing International Society and the Social Balance of Power. *European Journal of International Relations* 7 (2): 239–74.

Hobson, John M., and Jason C. Sharman. 2005. The Enduring Place of Hierarchy in World Politics: Tracing the Social Logics of Hierarchy and Political Change. *European Journal of International Relations* 11:63–98.

Hodgson, Dennis. 1988. Orthodoxy and Revisionism in American Demography. *Population and Development Review* 14 (4): 541–69.

Hodgson, Dennis. 1991. The Ideological Origins of the Population Association of America. *Population and Development Review* 17 (1): 1–34.

Hodgson, Dennis, and Susan C. Watkins. 1997. Feminists and Neo-Malthusians: Past and Present Alliances. *Population and Development Review* 23 (3): 469–523.

Holsti, Kal J. 1992. Governance without Government: Polyarchy in Nineteenth Century European International Politics. In *Governance without Government: Order and Change in World Politics*, edited by James Rosenau and Ernst-Otto Czempiel. Cambridge: Cambridge University Press.

Horn, D. B. 1945. *British Public Opinion and the First Partition of Poland*. Edinburgh: Oliver and Boyd.

Hosking, Geoffrey. 2002. *Russia and the Russians: From Earliest Times to 2001*. London: Penguin.

Hoy, David Couzens. 2004. *Critical Resistance: From Poststructuralism to Post-critique*. Cambridge: MIT Press.

Hurd, Ian. 1999. Legitimacy and Authority in International Politics. *International Organization* 52 (2): 379–408.

Hurrell, Andrew. 1996. Vattel: Pluralism and Its Limits. In *Classical Theories of International Relations*, edited by Ian Clark and Iver B. Neumann, 233–55. Houndmills: Macmillan.

Huysmans, Jeff. 2006. *The Politics of Insecurity: Fear, Migration, and Asylum in the EU*. London: Routledge.

International Women's Health Coalition (IWHC). 1994a. Reproductive Health and Justice—International Women's Health Conference for Cairo "94." January 24–28, 1994. Rio de Janeiro: IWHC/New York and Citizens, Studies, Information, Action (CEPIA).

International Women's Health Coalition (IWHC). 1994b. Women's Voices "94"—A Declaration on Population Policies. *Population and Development Review* 20 (4): 637–40.

Jackson, Patrick Thaddeus. 2006. *Civilizing the West: German Reconstruction and the Invention of the West*. Ann Arbor: University of Michigan Press.

Jackson, Patrick Thaddeus. 2010a. *The Conduct of Inquiry in International Relations: Philosophy of Science and Its Implications for the Study of World Politics*. London: Routledge.

Jackson, Patrick Thaddeus. 2010b. Foregrounding Ontology: Dualism, Monism, and IR Theory. *Review of International Studies* 34 (1): 129–53.

Jaeger, Hans Martin. 2007. "Global Civil Society" and the Political Depoliticization of Global Governance. *International Political Sociology* 1 (3): 257–77.

Jaeger, Hans Martin. 2008. "World Opinion" and the Founding of the UN: Governmentalizing International Politics. *European Journal of International Relations* 14 (4): 589–618.

Jepperson, Ronald, Alexander Wendt, and Peter Katzenstein. 1996. Norms, Identity, and Culture in National Security. In *The Culture of National Security: Norms and Identity in World Politics*, edited by Peter Katzenstein, 33–75. New York: Columbia University Press.

Jespersen, Leon E. 2000. Tiden 1596–1660: Mellem personlig kongemagt og bureaukrati. In *Dansk forvaltningshistorie I. Stat, forvaltning og samfund. Fra middelalderen til*

1901, edited by Leon E. Jespersen, Ladewig Petersen, and Ditlev Tamm, 95–158. Copenhagen: Jurist-og økonomforbundets forlag.

Kalm, Sara. 2008. Governing Global Migration. Lund Political Studies 153. Lund: Department of Political Science, Lund University.

Kanbur, Ravi. 2005. Reforming the Formula: A Modest Proposal for Introducing Development Outcomes in IDA Allocation Procedures. In *Discussion Paper no. 4071, March*. London: Centre for Economic Policy Research.

Kantorowicz, Ernst H. 1957. *The King's Two Bodies: A Study in Mediaeval Political Theology*. Princeton: Princeton University Press.

Karamzin, Nikolai Mikhailovich. [1818–1824] 1998. *Istoriya gosudarstva Rossiiskogo*. Vol. 6. Moscow: Izd-vo "Nauka."

Katzenstein, Peter J., ed. 1996. *The Culture of National Security: Norms and Identity in World Politics*. New York: Columbia University Press.

Kaufmann, Daniel. 2006. *Measuring Governance: Possibilities and Pitfalls*. Transcript of meeting hosted by the Center for Global Development, Washington, DC, December 1, 2006. Washington, DC: Center for Global Development.

Keck, Margaret E., and Kathryn Sikkink. 1998. *Activists Beyond Borders: Advocacy Networks in International Politics*. Ithaca: Cornell University Press.

Kennedy, Paul. 1987. *The Rise and Fall of Great Powers: Economic Change and Military Conflict from 1500 to 2000*. New York: Random House.

Keohane, Robert O. 1984. *After Hegemony: Cooperation and Discord in the World Political Economy*. Princeton: Princeton University Press.

Keohane, Robert O., and H. Milner, eds. 1996. *Internationalization and Domestic Politics*. New York: Cambridge University Press.

Keohane, Robert O., and Joseph S. Nye Jr., eds. 1972. *Transnational Relations and World Politics*. Cambridge: Harvard University Press.

Khagram, Sanjeev, James V. Rider, and Kathryn Sikkink, eds. 2002. *Restructuring World Politics: Transnational Social Movements, Networks, and Norms*. Minneapolis: University of Minnesota Press.

Kiersey, Nicholas J. 2009. Political Economy, Security, and Scale: Debating the Biopolitics of the Global War on Terror. *New Political Science* 31:1.

Kingsbury, Benedict, Nico Krisch, and Richard B. Stewart. 2005. The Emergence of Global Administrative Law. *Law and Contemporary Problems* 68 (3): 15–61.

Kissinger, Henry. 1957. *A World Restored: Metternich, Castlereagh, and the Problems of Peace, 1812–22*. Boston: Houghton Mifflin.

Knutsen, Torbjørn. 2002. Krig som sosial praksis. In *Global politikk: Krig, diplomati, handel og kommunikasjon som praksiser*, edited by Iver B. Neumann. Oslo: Cappelen Akademiske.

Koenig-Archibugi, Mathias. 2002. Mapping Global Governance. In *Governing Globalization*, edited by David Held and Andrew McGrew, 46–69. Cambridge: Policy Press.

Koskenniemi, Martti. 1990. The Politics of International Law. *European Journal of International Law* 1 (2): 4–32.

Koskenniemi, Martti. 2004. *The Gentle Civilizer of Nations: The Rise and Fall of International Law, 1870–1960*. Cambridge: Cambridge University Press.

Kozyrev, Andrei V. 1994. Russia and NATO: A Partnership for a United and Peaceful Europe. *NATO Review* (August): 3–6.

Krasner, Stephen. 1982. Regimes and the Limits of Realism: Regimes as Autonomous Variables. *International Organization* 36 (2): 497–510.
Krasner, Stephen, ed. 1983. *International Regimes*. Ithaca: Cornell University Press.
Kratochwil, Friedrich V. 1989. *Rules, Norms, and Decisions: On the Conditions of Practical and Legal Reasoning in International Relations and Domestic Affairs*. Cambridge: Cambridge University Press.
Krisch, Nico, and Benedict Kingsbury. 2006. Introduction: Global Governance and Global Administrative Law in the International Legal Order. *European Journal of International Law* 17 (1): 1–13.
Kuper, Adam. 1999. *Culture: The Anthropologists' Account*. Cambridge: Harvard University Press.
Laffey, Mark, and Jutta Weldes. 2005. Policing and Global Governance. In *Power in Global Governance*, edited by Michael Barnett and Raymond Duvall, 59–79. Cambridge: Cambridge University Press.
Langslet, Lars Roar. 1997. *Christian IV. Konge av Danmark og Norge*. Oslo: Cappelen.
Larner, Wendy, and Richard Le Heron. 2004. Global Benchmarking: Participating "At a Distance" in the Globalizing Economy. In *Global Governmentality: Governing International Spaces*, edited by Wendy Larner and William Walters, 212–32. London: Routledge.
Latham, Michael. 2000. *Modernization as Ideology: American Social Science and "Nation-Building" in the Kennedy Era*. Chapel Hill: University of North Carolina Press.
Latham, Robert. 1999. Politics in a Floating World: Toward a Critique of Global Governance. In *Approaches to Global Governance Theory*, edited by Martin Hewson and Timothy J. Sinclair, 23–53. Albany: State University of New York Press.
Leira, Halvard. 2008. Justus Lipsius, Political Humanism, and the Disciplining of 17th Century Statecraft. In *Review of International Studies* 34 (3): 669–92.
Lenin, Vladimir Il'ich. [1917] 1953. *Imperialism, the Highest Stage of Capitalism: A Popular Outline*. Moscow: Foreign Languages Publishing House.
Lewin, Moshe. 1989. *The Gorbachev Phenomenon: A Historical Interpretation*. London: Radius.
Lincoln, W. Bruce. 1982. *In the Vanguard of Reform: Russia's Enlightened Bureaucrats, 1825–1861*. De Kalb: Northern Illinois University Press.
Lind, Gunnar. 2000. Den heroiske tid? Administrationen under den tidlige enevælde 1660–1720. In *Dansk forvaltningshistorie I. Stat, forvaltning og samfund. Fra middelalderen til 1901*, edited by Leon E. Jespersen, Ladewig Petersen, and Ditlev Tamm, 159–225. Copenhagen: Jurist- og økonomforbundets forlag.
Linklater, Andrew, and Hidemi Suganami. 2006. *The English School of International Relations*. Cambridge: Cambridge University Press.
Lipschutz, Ronnie, with James K. Rowe. 2005a. *Globalization, Governmentality, and Global Politics: Regulation for the Rest of Us?* London: Routledge.
Lipschutz, Ronnie. 2005b. Global Civil Society and Global Governmentality: Or, the Search for Politics and the State amidst the Capillaries of Social Power. In *Power in Global Governance*, edited by Michael Barnett and Raymond Duvall, 229–48. Cambridge: Cambridge University Press.
Litfin, Karen. 1994. *Ozone Discourses: Science and Politics in Global Environmental Cooperation*. New York: Columbia University Press.

Löwenheim, Oded. 2008. Examining the State: A Foucauldian Perspective on International "Governance Indicators." *Third World Quarterly* 29 (2): 255–74.
Lund, Joachim, ed. 2003. *Partier under pres—Demokratiet under besættelsen København.* Copenhagen: Gyldendal.
Malia, Martin. 1999. *Russia Under Western Eyes: From the Bronze Horseman to the Lenin Mausoleum.* Cambridge: Harvard University Press.
Mattern, Janice Bially. 2005. *Ordering International Politics: Identity, Crisis, and Representational Force.* Basingstoke: Palgrave.
Matthews, Jessica T. 1997. Power Shift. *Foreign Affairs* 76 (1): 50–66.
McCalla, Robert B. 1996. NATO's Persistence after the Cold War. *International Organization* 50:445–75.
Medushevskii, Andres. 2001. Administrative Reforms in the Russian Empire: Western Models and Russian Implementation. *Peter the Great and the West,* ed. Lindsay Hughes, 39–50. London: Palgrave.
Meissner, Boris. 1956. Die zaristische diplomatie, A. Der Gesandtschafts-Prikaz (Posolskij Prikaz). In *Jahrbucher für Geschichte Osteuropas, Neue Folge.* Munich: Osteuropa-Institutes München.
Merlingen, Michael. 2003. Governmentality: Towards a Foucauldian Framework for the Study of IGOs. *Cooperation and Conflict* 38 (4): 361–84.
Meyer, John W. 2009. *World Society: The Writings of John W. Meyer.* Edited by Georg Krücken and Gili Drori. Oxford: Oxford University Press.
Meyer, John W., and Ronald Jepperson. 2000. The "Actors" of Modern Society: The Cultural Construction of Social Agency. *Sociological Theory* 18 (1): 100–120.
Miller, Toby. 1993. *The Well-Tempered Self: Citizenship, Culture, and the Postmodern Subject.* London: Johns Hopkins University Press.
Mitrany, David. 1943. *A Working Peace System: An Argument for the Functional Development of International Organization.* London: Royal Institute of International Affairs.
Moravcsik, Andrew. 1999. A New Statecraft? Supranational Entrepreneurs and International Cooperation. *International Organization* 53 (2): 267–306.
Morgenthau, Hans J. 1940. Positivism, Functionalism, and International Law. *American Journal of International Law* 34 (2): 260–84.
Morgenthau, Hans J. 1948. *Politics Among Nations.* New York: Knopf.
Morgenthau, Hans J. 1967. *Politics Among Nations.* 4th ed. New York: Knopf.
Morton, Stephen, and Stephen Bygrave, eds. 2008. *Foucault in an Age of Terror: Essays on Biopolitics and the Defence of Society.* New York: Palgrave.
Mosse, W. E. 1996. *An Economic History of Russia, 1856–1914.* London: I. B. Tauris.
Muppidi, Himadeep. 2005. Colonial and Postcolonial Global Governance. In *Power in Global Governance,* edited by Michael Barnett and Raymond Duvall, 273–93. Cambridge: Cambridge University Press.
Muse, Kenneth R. [1981] 1991. Edmund Husserl's Impact on Max Weber. In *Max Weber: Critical Assessments,* edited by Peter Hamilton, 254–63. London: Routledge.
Nanz, Patricia, and Jens Steffek. 2004. Global Governance, Participation, and the Public Sphere. *Government and Opposition* 39 (2): 314–35.
NATO. 1990. North Atlantic Council Ministerial Communiqué, December. Document M-2 (90) 76.
NATO. 1991. The Alliance's Strategic Concept, Rome, November 7–8.

Nekrasov, G. A. 1972. Mezhdunarodnoe priznanie rossiyskogo velikoderzhaviya v XVIII veke. In *Feodal'naya Rossiya vo vsemirno-istoricheskom protsesse*, edited by V. T. Pashuto, B. N. Florya, and A. L. Horoshkevich. Moscow: Izdatel'stvo Nauka.

Neumann, Iver B. 1999. Norsk sørpolitikk: Den disaggregerte stats diplomati. *Internasjonal Politikk* 57 (2): 181–98.

Neumann, Iver B. 2001. *Norge—en kritikk. Begrepsmakt i Europa-debatten.* Oslo: Pax.

Neumann, Iver B. 2002a. Harnessing Social Power: State Diplomacy and the Land-Mines Issue. In *Enhancing Global Governance: Towards a New Diplomacy*, edited by Andrew F. Cooper, John English, and Ramesh Thakur, 106–32. Tokyo: United Nations University Press.

Neumann, Iver B. 2002b. Returning Practice to the Linguistic Turn: The Case of Diplomacy. *Millennium* 31 (3): 627–51.

Neumann, Iver B. 2004a. *Ispol'zovanie "Drugogo": Obrazy Vostoka v formirovanii evropeyskikh identichnostey.* Moscow: Novoe izdatel'stvo.

Neumann, Iver B. 2004b. Beware of Organicism: The Narrative Self of the State. *Review of International Studies* 30 (2): 259–67.

Neumann, Iver B. 2005. Russia as a Great Power. In *Russia as a Great Power: Dimensions of Security under Putin*, edited by Jakob Hedenskog, Vilhelm Konnander, Bertil Nygren, Ingmar Oldberg, and Christer Pursiainen, 13–28. London: Routledge.

Notestein, Frank W. 1961. Letter from Frank Notestein to Dana Creel, The Rockefeller Brothers Fund, Sept. 22. Rockefeller Archives Center (RAC) RAC, IV3B4.2 Box 4, "Demographic Division 1957–1966," Folder 41.

Notestein, Frank W. 1968. The Population Council and the Demographic Crisis of the Less Developed World. *Demography* 5 (2): 553–60.

Oestreich, Gerhard. 1982. *Neostoicism and the Early Modern State.* Cambridge: Cambridge University Press.

O'Hagan, Jacinta. 2002. *Conceptualizing the West in International Relations: From Spengler to Said.* London: Palgrave.

Oikonomides, N. 1992. Byzantine Diplomacy, A.D. 1204–1453: Means and Ends. In *Byzantine Diplomacy. Papers from the Twenty-fourth Spring Symposium of Byzantine Studies, Cambridge, March 1990*, edited by Jonathan Shepard and Simon Franklin, 73–88. Aldershot: Variorum.

Okonjo-Iweala, Ngozi. 2006. *Measuring Governance: Possibilities and Pitfalls.* Transcript of meeting hosted by the Center for Global Development, Washington, DC, December 1, 2006. Washington, DC: Center for Global Development.

Olesen, Jens E. 2000. Middelalderen til 1536: Fra rejsekongedømme til administrationscentrum. In *Dansk forvaltningshistorie I. Stat, forvaltning og samfund. Fra middelalderen til 1901*, edited by Leon E. Jespersen, Ladewig Petersen, and Ditlev Tamm. Copenhagen: Jurist- og økonomforbundets forlag.

Onuf, Nicholas G. 1989. *World of Our Making: Rules and Rule in Social Theory and International Relations.* Columbia: University of South Carolina Press.

Onuf, Nicholas G. 1998. *The Republican Legacy in International Thought.* Cambridge: Cambridge University Press.

Ottaway, Marina. 2001. Corporatism Goes Global: International Organizations, Nongovernmental Organization Networks, and Transnational Business. *Global Governance* 7 (3): 265–92.

Owen, David. 1997. *Maturity and Modernity. Nietzsche, Weber, Foucault, and the Ambivalence of Reason.* London: Routledge.
Paris, Roland. 2002. Peacekeeping and the Constraints of Global Culture. *European Journal of International Relations* 9 (3): 441–73.
Park, Susan. 2006. Norms and International Relations Theorizing Norm Diffusion within International Organizations. *International Politics* 43:342–61.
Petersen, Ladewig. 2000. Reformationstiden 1536–96: Modernisering—justering. In *Dansk forvaltningshistorie I. Stat, forvaltning og samfund. Fra middelalderen til 1901*, edited by Leon E. Jespersen, Ladewig Petersen, and Ditlev Tamm. Copenhagen: Jurist- og økonomforbundets forlag.
Petersen, Nikolai. 1997. *The H. C. Hansen Papers and Nuclear Weapons in Greenland.* Copenhagen: Danish Institute of International Affairs.
Peterson, Claes. 1979. *Peter the Great's Administrative and Judicial Reforms: Swedish Antecedents and the Process of Reception.* Stockholm: A.-B. nordiska bokhandeln.
Pierre, John, and B. Guy Peters. 2000. *Governance, Politics, and the State.* London: Macmillan.
Podberezkin, Aleksey. 1996b. Vyzovy bezopasnosti Rossii. Rasshirenie NATO. *Svobodnaya mysl'* no. 12: 63–69.
Poe, Marshall T. 2000. *"A People Born to Slavery": Russia in Early European Ethnography, 1476–1748.* Ithaca: Cornell University Press.
Poggi, Gianfranco. 1978. *The Development of the Modern State: A Sociological Introduction.* London: Hutchinson.
Population Council. 1958. Present Activities and Future Needs of the Demographic Division. Five Year Program of the Population Council. 1. Rockefeller Archives Center: Record Group 5, Series 1, OMR Files, Box 81, Folder 679.
Population Council. 1965. Minutes, meeting at the Population Council October 5–7, 1965. 1. Rockefeller Archives Center: Folder 2364, Box 128, IVB4.6 "Population Subject File."
Porter, Theodore. 1996. *Trust in Numbers: The Pursuit of Objectivity in Science and Public Life.* Princeton: Princeton University Press.
Pouliot, Vincent. 2010. *International Security in Practice: The Politics of NATO Russia Diplomacy.* Cambridge: Cambridge University Press.
Powell, Jeff. 2004. *The World Bank Scorecard: A New Conditionality?* Update 43, 22 November. http://www.brettonwoodsproject.org/article.shtml?cmd%5B126%5D=x-126-84455.
Powers, Michael. 1999. *The Audit Society: Rituals of Verification.* Oxford: Oxford University Press.
Price, Richard. 1998. Reversing the Gun Sights: Transnational Civil Society Targets Land Mines. *International Organization* 52 (3): 613–44.
Price, Richard. 2003. Transnational Civil Society and Advocacy in World Politics. *World Politics* 55 (4): 579–606.
Prozorov, Sergei. 2006. *Understanding Conflict between Russia and the EU: The Limits of Integration.* Basingstoke: Palgrave.
Raeff, Mark. 1983. *The Well-Ordered Police State: Social and Institutional Change through Law in the Germanies and Russia, 1600–1800.* New Haven: Yale University Press.

Ranke, Leopold von. [1833] 1950. The Great Powers. In *Ranke, the Formative Years,* edited by T. H. von Laue. Princeton: Princeton University Press.

Ransom, John S. 1997. *Foucault's Discipline: The Politics of Subjectivity.* Durham: Duke University Press.

Raz, Joseph, ed. 1990. *Authority.* New York: New York University Press.

Reus-Smit, Christian. 1997. The Constitutional Structure of International Society and the Nature of Fundamental Institutions. *International Organization* 51 (4): 555–89.

Reus-Smit, Christian. 1999. *The Moral Purpose of the State: Culture, Social Identity, and Institutional Rationality in International Relations.* Princeton: Princeton University Press.

Reus-Smit, Christian. 2004. *The Politics of International Law.* Cambridge: Cambridge University Press.

Rhodes, R. A. W. 1996. The New Governance: Governing without Government. *Political Studies* 44:652–57.

Rieker, Pernille. 2006. *Europeanization of National Security Identity: The EU and the Changing Security Identities of the Nordic States.* London: Routledge.

Ringer, Fritz. 1997. *Max Weber's Methodology: The Unification of the Cultural and Social Sciences.* Cambridge: Harvard University Press.

Risse, Thomas. 2000. "Let's Argue!" Communicative Action in World Politics. *International Organization* 54 (1): 1–39.

Risse, Thomas. 2002. Transnational Actors and World Politics. In *Handbook of International Relations,* edited by Walter Carlsnaes, Thomas Risse, and Beth Simmons, 255–74. London: Sage.

Risse, Thomas, Stephen C. Ropp, and Kathryn Sikkink, eds. 1999. *The Power of Human Rights: International Norms and Domestic Change.* Cambridge: Cambridge University Press.

Rose, Nikolas. 1990. *Governing the Soul: The Shaping of the Private Self.* London: Routledge.

Rose, Nikolas. 1999. *Powers of Freedom—Reframing Political Thought.* Cambridge: Cambridge University Press.

Rose, Nikolas. 2000. Governing Liberty. In *Governing Modern Societies,* edited by Richard Ericsson and Nico Stehr, 141–76. Toronto: University of Toronto Press.

Rose, Nikolas, and Peter Miller. 1992. Political Power Beyond the State: Problematics of Government. *British Journal of Sociology* 43 (2): 173–205.

Rosenau, James N. 1999. Toward an Ontology for Global Governance. In *Approaches to Global Governance Theory,* edited by Martin Hewson and Timothy Sinclair, 287–301. New York: State University of New York Press.

Rosenau, James N. 2000. Change, Complexity, and Governance in Globalizing Space. In *Debating Governance: Authority, Steering, and Democracy,* edited by John Pierre, 167–200. Oxford: Oxford University Press.

Rosenau, James N. 2002. Governance in a New Global Order. In *Governing Globalization: Power, Authority, and Global Governance,* edited by David Held and Anthony McGrew, 70–86. Cambridge, UK: Polity Press.

Rosenau, James N. 2004. Governing the Ungovernable: The Challenge of Global Disaggregation of Authority. Paper presented at the International Society for New Institutional Economics. Tucson, AZ, Sept. 30–Oct. 2.

Rosenau, James N., and Ernst-Otto Czempiel, eds. 1992. *Governance without Government: Order and Change in World Politics.* Cambridge: Cambridge University Press.

Ruggie, John G. 1983. Continuity and Transformation in the World Polity: Toward a Neo-Realist Synthesis. *World Politics* 35 (2): 261–85.

Ruggie, John G. 1998. *Constructing the World Polity: Essays on International Institutionalization.* London: Routledge.

Ruggie, John G. 2004. Reconstituting the Global Public Domain—Issues, Actors, and Practices. *European Journal of International Relations* 10 (4): 499–531.

Ruggie, John G., and Friedrich Kratochwil. 1986. International Organization: A State of the Art on the Art of the State. *International Organization* 40 (4): 753–75.

Salter, Mark B. 2002. *Barbarians and Civilization in International Relations.* London: Pluto Press.

Samuelsson, Kurt. 1968. *From Great Power to Welfare State: 300 Years of Swedish Development.* London: Allen and Unwin.

Sandholtz, Wayne. 1999. Globalization and the Evolution of Rules. In *Globalization and Governance,* edited by Aseem Prakash and Jeffrey A. Hart, 77–102. London: Routledge.

Sassen, Saskia. 2006. *Territory, Authority, Rights: From Medieval to Global Assemblages.* Princeton: Princeton University Press.

Schatzki, Theodore R., Karin Knorr Cetina, and Eike von Savigny, eds. 2001. *The Practice Turn in Contemporary Theory.* London: Routledge.

Schimmelfennig, Frank. 2001. The Community Trap: Liberal Norms, Rhetorical Action, and the Eastern Enlargement of the European Union. *International Organization* 55 (1): 47–80.

Schmidt, Brian C. 1998. *The Political Discourse of Anarchy: A Disciplinary History of International Relations.* Albany: State University of New York Press.

Schmitt, Carl. [1932] 1995. *The Concept of the Political.* Chicago: University of Chicago Press.

Scholte, Jan Aart. 2002. Civil Society and Democracy in Global Governance. *Global Governance* 8 (3): 281–304.

Schroeder, Paul W. 1986. The 19th-Century International System: Changes in the Structure. *World Politics* 34 (1): 1–26.

Schytte, Andreas. 1773–76. *Staternes indvortes Regiering.* Copenhagen: Gyldendal.

Scott, James C. 1998. *Seeing Like a State: How Certain Schemes to Improve the Human Condition Have Failed.* New Haven: Yale University Press.

Seabrooke, Leonard. 2007. Legitimacy Gaps in the World Economy: Explaining the Sources of the IMF's Legitimacy Crisis. *International Politics* 44 (2–3): 250–68.

Sending, Ole Jacob. 2003. How Does Knowledge Matter? The Formation, Content, and Change of International Population Policy. Bergen: University of Bergen, Norway.

Sending, Ole Jacob, and Iver B. Neumann. 2006. Governance to Governmentality: Analyzing NGOs, States, and Power. *International Studies Quarterly* 50 (3): 651–72.

Senellart, Michel. 2007. Course Context. In Michel Foucault, *Security, Territory, Population: Lectures at the Collège de France, 1977–1978,* edited by Michel Senellart, 369–401. London: Palgrave.

Sewell, William. 1992. A Theory of Structure: Duality, Agency, and Transformation. *American Journal of Sociology* 98 (1): 1–29.

Shafirov, Peter P. 1973. *A Discourse Concerning the Just Causes of the War between Sweden and Russia, 1700–1721.* Dobbs Ferry, NY: Oceana.

Sharman, Jason C. 2008. Power and Discourse in Policy Diffusion: Anti-Money Laundering in Developing States. *International Studies Quarterly* 52 (3): 635–56.

Shepsle, Kenneth A., and Mark S. Bonchek. 1997. *Analyzing Politics: Rationality, Behavior, and Institutions.* New York: W. W. Norton.

Sigley, Gary. 2006. Chinese Governmentalities: Government, Governance, and the Socialist Market Economy. *Economy and Society* 35 (4): 487–508.

Simmons, Beth A., Frank Dobbin, and Geoffrey Garrett, eds. 2008. *The Global Diffusion of Markets and Democracy.* Cambridge: Cambridge University Press.

Singh, Jyoti S. 1998. *Creating a New Consensus on Population Policy.* London: Earthscan Publications.

Spidsboel-Hansen, Flemming. 2002. Past and Future Meet: Aleksandr Gorchakov and Russian Foreign Policy. *Europe-Asia Studies* 54 (3): 377–96.

Sterling-Folker, Jennifer. 2000. Competing Paradigms of a Feather? Constructivism and Neoliberal Institutionalism Compared. *International Studies Quarterly* 44 (2): 97–119.

Swidler, Ann. 2001. What Anchors Cultural Practices. In *The Practice Turn in Contemporary Theory,* edited by Theodore R. Schatzki, Karin Knorr Cetina, and Eike von Savigny, 74–92. London: Routledge.

Szakolczai, Arpad. 1998. *Max Weber and Michel Foucault: Parallel Lifeworks.* London: Routledge.

Thakur, Ramesh, and William Maley. 1999. The Ottawa Convention on Landmines: A Landmark Humanitarian Treaty in Arms Control? *Global Governance* 5 (2): 273–302.

Thomas, George M., John W. Meyer, Francisco O. Ramirez, and John Boli, eds. 1987. *Institutional Structure: Constituting the State, Society, and the Individual.* Newbury Park, CA: Sage.

Thomson, Janice E. 1995. State Sovereignty in International Relations: Bridging the Gap between Theory and Empirical Research. *International Studies Quarterly* 39 (2): 213–33.

Trinborg, Kim J. 2007. Performing Participation. Stakeholders, Translations, and Power in the World Bank Participation Sourcebook. Master's thesis, University of Oslo, Department of Social Anthropology.

Tvedt, Terje. 1998. *Angels of Mercy, or Development Diplomats? NGOs and Foreign Aid.* London: James Curry.

Tvedt, Terje. 2003. *Utviklingshjelp, utenrikspolitikk og makt.* Oslo: Gyldendal Akademisk.

United Nations. 2005a. *In Larger Freedom: Towards Development, Security and Human Rights for All.* Report of the Secretary General. A/59/2005. New York: United Nations.

United Nations. 2005b. *2005 World Summit Outcome. Resolution Adopted by the General Assembly.* A/Res/60/1. New York: United Nations.

Utenriksdepartementet. 1991–92. Om utviklingstrekk i Nord-Sør forholdet og Norges samarbeid med utviklingslandene. Stortingsmelding nr. 51 (1991–92). Oslo: Norwegian Ministry of Foreign Affairs.

Valverde, Mariana. 2003. Police Science, British Style: Pub Licensing and Knowledges of Urban Disorder. *Economy and Society* 32 (2): 234–52.

Valverde, Mariana. 2007. Genealogies of European States: Foucauldian Reflections. *Economy and Society* 36 (1): 159–78.
Walker, R. B. J. 1993. *Inside/Outside: International Relations as Political Theory.* Cambridge: Cambridge University Press.
Waltz, Kenneth. 1967. *Foreign Policy and Democratic Politics.* Boston: Little, Brown.
Waltz, Kenneth. 1979. *Theory of International Politics.* New York: Random House.
Wapner, Paul. 1995. Politics Beyond the State: Environmental Activism and World Civic Politics. *World Politics* 47 (3): 311–40.
Watson, Adam. 1985. Russia and the European States System. In *The Expansion of International Society,* edited by Hedley Bull and Adam Watson, 61–74. Oxford: Clarendon.
Weaver, Catherine. 2008. *Hypocrisy Trap: The World Bank and the Poverty of Reform.* Princeton: Princeton University Press.
Weber, Cynthia. 1995. *Simulating Sovereignty: Intervention, the State, and Symbolic Exchange.* Cambridge: Cambridge University Press.
Weber, Max. [1904] 1949. "Objectivity" in Social Science and Social Policy. In *The Methodology of the Social Sciences,* edited by Edward A. Shils. Glencoe, IL: Free Press.
Weber, Max. [1922] 1968. *Economy and Society.* 2 vols. Edited by Günther Roth and Claus Wittich. Berkeley: University of California Press.
Weber, Max. 1976. *Wirtschaft und Gesellschaft: Grundriss der verstehen Soziologie.* 5th ed. Tübingen: Mohr.
Weber, Max. [1904–5] 1976. *The Protestant Ethic and the Spirit of Capitalism.* London: Allen and Unwin.
Weiss, Thomas G., and Leon Gordenker. 1996. Pluralizing Global Governance: Analytical Approaches and Dimensions. In *NGOs, the UN, and Global Governance,* edited by Thomas G. Weiss and Leon Gordenker, 17–50. London: Lynne Rienner.
Wendt, Alexander. 1999. *Social Theory of International Politics.* Cambridge: Cambridge University Press.
Wendt, Alexander, and Raymond Duvall. 2008. Sovereignty and the UFO. *Political Theory* 36 (4): 607–33.
Westlake, John. 1914. *The Collected Papers of John Westlake on Public International Law.* Ed. Lassa Oppenheim. Cambridge: Cambridge University Press.
Wight, Martin. 1977. *System of States.* Leicester: Leicester University Press.
Williams, Michael C. 2004. Why Ideas Matter in International Relations: Hans Morgenthau, Classical Realism, and the Moral Construction of Power Politics. *International Organization* 58 (3): 633–65.
Williams, Michael C., and Iver B. Neumann. 2000. From Alliance to Security Community: NATO, Russia, and the Power of Identity. *Millennium* 29 (2): 357–87.
Wohlforth, William C. 1987. The Perception of Power: Russia in the Pre–1914 Balance. *World Politics* 34 (3): 353–81.
Wohlforth, William C. 1999. The Stability of a Unipolar World. *International Security* 24 (1): 5–41.
Woods, Ngaire. 2002. Global Governance and The Role of Institutions. In *Governing Globalization,* edited by David Held and Andrew McGrew. London: Polity Press.
World Bank. 1960. World Bank Press Release no. 621, February 7. Washington, DC: World Bank.

World Bank. 1998. *Assessing Aid: What Works, What Doesn't, and Why.* New York: Oxford University Press.
World Bank. 2004a. CPIA Process and Methodology. Washington, DC: World Bank.
World Bank. 2004b. Determining the Weights for the CPIA Index. Washington, DC: World Bank.
World Bank. 2005. Country Policy and Institutional Assessments. 2005 Assessment Questionnaire. Washington, DC: World Bank.
World Bank. 2008. *Doing Business 2009.* Washington, DC: World Bank.
World Health Organization (WHO). 1990. Research in Human Reproduction. Biennial Report 1988–1989. Edited by Development and Research Training in Human Reproduction Special Programme of Research. Geneva: WHO.
Wörner, Manfred. 1989a. Opening Address to the North Atlantic Council Meeting at the Level of Heads of State and Government, May 29. *NATO Review* 3:21.
Wörner, Manfred. 1989b. A Time of Accelerating Change. *NATO Review* 6:1–5.
Yeltsin, Boris. 1992. Statement. *International Affairs* (Moscow) 39 (11): inside cover.
Young, Oran R. 1994. *International Governance: Protecting the Environment in a Stateless Society.* Ithaca: Cornell University Press.
Zanotti, Lara. 2005. Governmentalizing the Post–Cold War International Regime: The UN Debate on Democratization and Good Governance. *Alternatives* 30 (4): 461–87.
Zorin, V. A., A. A. Gromyko, and I. N. Zemskov, eds. 1959. *Istoriya diplomatii.* 2nd ed. Moscow: Gospolitizdat.
Zuckerman, Frederic S. 1996. *The Tsarist Secret Police in Russian Society, 1880–1917.* London: Macmillan.
Zürn, Michael, and Jeffrey Checkel. 2005. Getting Socialized to Build Bridges: Constructivism and Rationalism, Europe and the Nation-State. *International Organization* 59 (4):1045–79.

Index

balance of power, 99, 109. *See also* equilibrium
Barnett, Michael, 7, 8, 11, 12, 55, 61, 132–33, 135–37, 140, 148, 173
Bartelson, Jens, viii, 67, 115, 167, 170, 171
biopolitics, 8, 41, 168, 180. *See also* biopower
biopower, 14, 24, 28, 138. *See also* biopolitics

civil society, 2, 5–6, 17, 19, 44, 67, 112–46, 150, 161, 165, 167, 170, 175

Dean, Mitchell, 9, 10, 12, 18, 34, 37, 41, 61, 114, 138, 158
development, 69, 118, 120–28, 141–54, 173
discipline, 9, 10, 14, 19–22, 24, 27–28, 30–33, 35, 39, 60, 155, 165, 172, 179

equilibrium, 70, 87, 155–56. *See also* balance of power

Foucault, Michel. *See chapter 1* (18–45 passim)
fragile states. *See* state building

global governance. *See chapter 4* (110–31 passim)

governmentality. *See chapter 1* (18–45 passim)

Hindess, Barry, 11, 12, 14, 22, 37, 42, 60, 65, 70, 116, 144, 150–51, 155, 156, 176

international, as a concept. *See chapter 2* (46–69 passim)
international organizations. *See chapter 5* (132–56 passim)

land mines, 123–30
Lipsius, Justus, 30, 32, 84

Morgenthau, Hans, *chapter 2* (esp. 49–51), 62, 157–62, 169–73

nongovernmental organizations. *See chapter 4*

Oestreich, Gerhard, 28, 30–33, 35, 67, 84, 89–90

pastoral power, 36–37, 39–41, 138
police, 3, 11, 14–17, 28–37, *chapter 5* (46–69 passim), 59, 67, 70–71, 78, 90–92, 97–98, 108, 177, 181
polity, 13, 29, 158, 160–61, 165, 170–78

population, 14, 29, 33, 35, 40–41, 43, 65, 75, 80, 96, 115–23, 129, 138, 147, 151, 153–56, 166, 168, 174, 177, 179

sovereignty: as a mode of power (*see chapter 1 and conclusion*); as a status (*see conclusion*)
state building, 134, 145–49, 152–53, 156, 175, 181
states system, *chapter 3* (70–109 passim), 161, 163, 169, 171

transnational actors, increased importance of, 112
transnational corporations, and governance, 131
transnational criminal networks, 176, 178
transnational movement to ban land mines, 124–25, 128
transnational relations, described as increasingly dense, 57
transnational social movements, studies of, 110
transnational women's health movement, 120

Waltz, Kenneth, 72, 73, 76, 134, 157, 163–68
Weak states. *See* state building
Weber, Max, *chapter 2* (46–69 passim), 157–59, 161–63, 178
Wendt, Alexander, 2, 6, 54–55, 161, 166, 168–69
World Bank, 17, *chapter 5* (132–56 passim), 173